RESTLESS FOR MOROCCO

RESTLESS FOR MOROCCO

P B Rogers

The Book Guild Ltd
Sussex, England

First published in Great Britain in 2001 by
The Book Guild Ltd
25 High Street,
Lewes, Sussex
BN7 2LU

Second Revised Edition 2001

Typesetting in Times by
Keyboard Services, Luton, Bedfordshire

Printed in Great Britain by
Bookcraft (Bath) Ltd, Avon

A catalogue record for this book is
available from the British Library

ISBN 1 85776 536 2

CHAPTERS

v

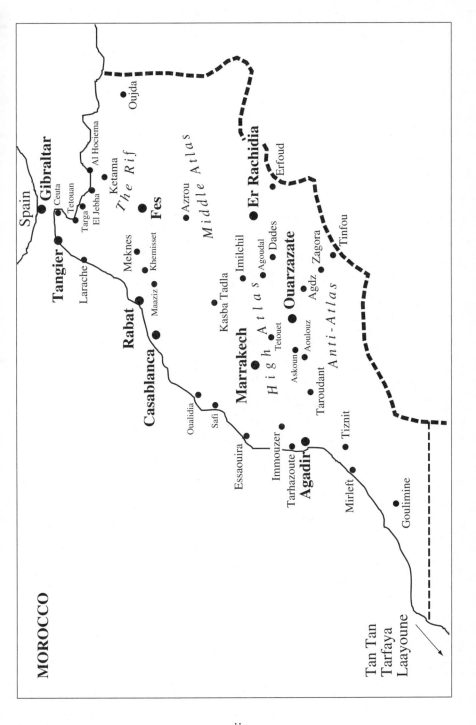

A MAGIC CARPET

We travel not for trafficking alone:
By hotter winds our fiery hearts are fanned:

James Elroy Flecker

One of the Sunday papers recently ran an article on the male menopause. 'How often,' it began, 'does a man nearing fifty suddenly realise that he has never slept out under the Sahara stars?'

As an officer in the British Army, nearer 50 than 40, I had just been posted to a UN Mission to the south of Morocco. Conditions were tough, so we worked 30 days straight for seven days' leave. Those who were married went home. I spent my free time exploring Morocco, a country 8 miles from Europe about which I knew nothing.

Here was the opportunity to both sleep under the Sahara stars, and also experience other adventures which might so easily have been only pipe-dreams. My travels revealed a country of stark landscapes and a beguiling people.

At work, I lived in a four-star hotel, but wandering Morocco I opted for a less predictable lifestyle. With minimum luggage and no firm itinerary, I was unsure at the start of each day where I would next lay my head. Trusting in desert hospitality and the Will of Allah, I was seldom disappointed.

Guidebooks to Morocco abound. I have tried here to paint a picture of the country and everyday life and to indicate the kind of experiences awaiting those who wish to venture beyond the tourist trail. I hope that for them my enthusiasm will be infectious, and that for those who have missed the Sahara stars these pages will act as something of a magic carpet. Everyone described in these pages exists, although in some places I have changed names to obscure identity. I regret that even in the time it has taken to write the book, most of the prices quoted will have become sadly out of date!

This reprint has undergone minor revision from the first edition.

1

Setting the Stage

The wind is in from Africa,
Last night I could not sleep.

Joni Mitchel

The pulse of Morocco beats fast and strong. From the moment of first arrival the heat, colours, noise and bustle demand attention. A potent cocktail of old and new, rich and poor, beauty and squalor – you know straight away you will either love it or hate it. Adrenalin which may have lain unstirred for months will start to flow as soon as the familiarity of the airport slips from view. But more gradually a different aspect emerges. Beneath the fever of life runs an under-current of strangeness born as much from embroidered stories of a wild past as from the closed doors of Islam today. The visual appeal is enhanced by an insidious air of mystery.

I had worked previously with the Zimbabwe Army and travelled extensively in southern Africa. But from the moment of first arrival in Morocco, I realised here was somewhere completely different. Indeed it is hard to even think of Morocco as African, so strong are the Islamic, Arab and European influences. King Mohammed's dynasty dates from the time of King Charles II. His forebears were Sultans when most of black Africa was in the Stone Age. Morocco has a feeling of antiquity and civilisation which simply does not exist south of the Sahara. By civilised I do not mean modern. The way of life, by European standards, is still medieval in much of the mountains and desert. But even there it is clear that recognisable communities exist with a social structure, an independence and a regulated way of life. They have gone about their business, much like their cousins in Arabia, for hundreds, even thousands of years.

Slightly smaller than Spain, Morocco is greener than I had ever imagined. Naturally the extent of this greenness depends on the time

1

of year. Acres of wheatfields which look rich and lush in May will turn to red-brown dust by September. But driving inland from Tangier in the spring is like crossing the Lowlands of Scotland, the landscape a patchwork of fields, rich pastures of grass and clover, swathes of wild flowers on every fold of rough ground. Streams run with water, clouds hang over the distant mountains, the land flows with milk and honey.

Even in the Atlas the snow provides enough water to irrigate tiny fields wherever soil has found a foothold. Peering from sunbaked heights, it is almost always possible to see, miles below, patches of the darkest green foliage – these and the roofs of houses giving evidence of water.

But huge areas exist where the supply of water is uncertain or even non-existent. On the edge of the Sahara permanent habitation is restricted to certain water-courses and oases. In these parts even the winter sun scorches without mercy, keeping the country parched by day, while a drop in temperature at sunset can chill the very bones. For days on end these extremes can be accompanied by a ferocious wind that whips up sand, making European dress painfully inadequate. Any moisture that might have survived in some tiny north-facing crevice is soon dried up or smothered in gusts of sand that know no barrier.

There is no current history of Morocco in English, but most guidebooks contain an historical section. As a start I strongly recommend Walter Harris's *Morocco That Was*. This romanticised account written a century ago shows how Morocco's history has been shaped by an exotic mix of races and characters. Cruelty, avarice and savagery lie side by side with tolerance, culture and nobility; a country where skill at arms and horsemanship was no more important than poetry and study of the natural sciences. By any standards Walter gives a colourful account, made more so by the harsh backdrop of mountains and desert against which it unfolds.

For those who must forgo Walter Harris and who wish to skip the detail, I have added as an appendix at the back of this book a simplified history covering the main trends in the evolution of 'Morocco That Is'. I commend this before starting the narrative.

To me the most fascinating aspect of Morocco is the people, although it would be wrong to think of them as a single entity. Without even contemplating the various tribes, the population consists of three quite different groups. Very roughly there are Arabs in most parts, Berbers in the mountains and Saharawis in the desert in the south. For the outsider it is difficult to recognise one from another and it is only some knowledge of their dress that may

2

enable a guess to be made. However, I do not think this matters so I will speak of 'Moroccans' as anyone and everyone.

It is difficult for Europeans to make an objective judgement on the extent to which religion influences our lives. Although our culture is based on Christian ethics, its evolution has been gradually obscured. But while today in Europe the imprint of Christianity is hard to discern, in Morocco the influence of Islam cannot go unnoticed; not only the physical manifestations, which are everywhere, but also in law, family relations, attitudes to wealth, the giving of alms. The thread of Islam weaves unmistakably through every aspect of daily life.

An attractive facet to me is the relatively liberal attitude taken towards religion at this end of the Arab world. Of course the traditional customs of prayer, dress, diet, circumcision etc. are strictly adhered to, but others appear to be followed less slavishly. Morocco historically possessed a large Jewish population living in special parts of towns. During the Second World War the Sultan protected Moroccan Jews from deportation by the Vichy French. The number has declined since the foundation of the state of Israel, but Jews today are treated no differently to anyone else.

Morocco grows excellent wine and also possesses a number of breweries. Alcohol is hard to find away from the main towns, but I know of no constraints on its sale. Overall it seems these matters are left to the individual conscience.

Moroccan women lead what by our standards are unbelievably restricted lives. Segregated during adolescence, they are heavily chaperoned. Both before and after marriage they stay in the home, keeping house and preparing for the return of their menfolk. Outside, faces are covered and they mix only with other women, the majority still wearing traditional dress.

Much of this is changing in the main cities, where it is normal to see girls in jeans talking to boys in the street. But in the country, particularly the mountains, the old ways persist. You will never, for example, see a husband and wife shopping together. Even in Casablanca or Tangier, if you walk down-town of an evening you will see hundreds of men sitting out at street cafés, but it is exceptional to see a woman amongst them.

Like Europeans, Moroccans may have two or three wives although theirs can be concurrent rather than consecutive! Recently, financial penalties have been introduced to discourage extra wives, and the written agreement of the first is necessary before a second can be taken on. Arranged marriages are still quite common but so too is divorce.

3

In other words Moroccan society is strongly male oriented. Certainly the number of women I met on my travels could be counted on one hand and were all Europeanised city girls. In the country I would expect no contact.

One of the first things I noticed about the men was their elegance. Most Moroccans are slender, with athletic bodies and small bones. Hair is invariably short and tidy. Skin colour varies from a white indistinguishable from southern Europeans, to pitch-black, most frequently found among the Saharawis. Features range from pure Caucasian to pure Negro, with every permutation in between.

The Berbers were the original inhabitants of this part of the world, followed by Arabs from the East, Moors and Jews expelled from Spain, and Negroes brought as slaves from West Africa. The majority of Moroccans have good bone structure and neat features, indeed it would take a dull eye not to be struck by the long limbs and clearcut features of the tribesmen and women in the Atlas. Some are quite stunning, their looks beautifully offset by kohled eyes and the bright colours of clothes and turbans.

They seem to be born with something which most Europeans lack, namely a sense of style. Despite the rich dyes of cottons and silks worn by women, the colours never clash, always complement. Similarly, men in European dress stick to plain colours and, by some natural sense of what is right, are able to look elegant in the simplest of clothes. Most garments are anyway faded by sun so that even if they did clash the result would not be disastrous. The shell-suit and baseball cap have sadly arrived but are seldom seen away from the towns. In the country even the young still wear the djellaba or kaftan with a turban wrapped round the head.

When I say that Moroccans are elegant, this is not only in physical appearance and dress but also their gestures and movement. I have to caution myself though because as a result of a population explosion, the average age of people in a normal gathering is very young – probably under 20. To someone nearing middle age, part of the appeal of these people must be their very youth itself. From this point of view it may be unfair to compare them with Europeans, where I believe a decline in the birth rate is producing exactly the opposite phenomenon.

I have not written much about the cities of Morocco simply because I preferred the countryside and small villages for my wanderings. Certainly the 'royal' cities are worth visiting, but I tended to do so quickly and move on. Although to the expert each city has a history and character all of its own, to the passing traveller they seem much the same. It would take a long time for a European to

4

get beneath the surface, particularly in Fez, which has an almost tangible air of mystery. One of the most enduring legacies of Marshal Lyautey, the French Administrator during the First World War, is the concept of 'new' towns built outside the old city walls. Thanks to this the hearts of the great cities remain remarkably intact.

Morocco has no equivalent to the National Trust. Religious buildings with few exceptions are closed to the infidel (non-believer), which is understandable but unfortunate since they constitute the lion's share of buildings of architectural importance. The breathtaking city walls, kasbahs (castles), medinas (old towns) and souks (markets) are fascinating in themselves but remarkably similar. City dwellers too, being more exposed to foreigners, display a commercial hardness which can be offputting.

For such an ancient civilisation, buildings of great merit are fewer than might be expected due to the practice of building in clay and straw, or *pise*. All over the country, particularly in the south, castles and even complete villages stand empty, their mud walls crumbling, floors and roofs collapsed.

Outside the cities it is unusual to find anyone who can speak English except perhaps near Agadir or Marrakech, where they see most British tourists. All my conversations were conducted in French, and although far from fluent, it never caused a problem. One of the reasons, I suspect, was that since French is the second language for both Moroccans and myself, our vocabulary was of a similar size, consisting of basic French rather than idiom or slang. Strangers always started by asking if I was German, then French and finally, well, what was I? It was nice to see the surprise and pleasure which greeted the announcement that I was British even if, on reflection, it was more from the fact that I was neither of the others!

Invariably I would ask the younger ones if they spoke English, to which the reply would be a shy 'a leedle' followed by the discovery that it was either surprisingly good or non-existent. Those who can speak some English do so in an attractive way hard to describe. Voices which in Arabic can be unpleasantly harsh seem to soften, and great pains are taken to pronounce every syllable so that even simple words have an individual charm.

Berbers speak Berber at home but it is not taught in school, a bone of political contention. Arabic is universal and has to be mastered before starting on French. In some parts of Morocco, notably the Rif Mountains and right down in the south, French gives way to Spanish, to add to the confusion. Generally, though, Moroccans are exceptional linguists.

On the whole I do not find Maghrebi Arabic an attractive language to listen to. It often has a tone of urgency and dispute which grates on the British ear, making casual conversation sound like serious argument. Most words come rather forcibly from the throat, so heaven knows what they make of us when we speak only with our lips and the forward part of *la bouche*. The Arabic of Iraq and Syria has a much more gentle sound.

In such a romantic setting there were many times when I longed for female company. However, as I have already mentioned, the segregation of the sexes is such that contact with local women was almost inconceivable, and those I met holidaying in Morocco were always accompanied. It was therefore inevitable that I spent much of my time in the company of young men – themselves constrained in a similar way. I am not so naive as to imagine they saw in me anything more than a possible source of revenue in the first instance. For someone of my age to be travelling alone must anyway have sent the wrong signal. However, after the preliminary battle of wits, they invariably became open and friendly. As the reader will see, I often spent hours in the most odd circumstances, talking about everything under the sun, finding myself both interested and entertained. The fact that I was sometimes 30 years older than my companions never seemed to create the slightest barrier.

I found them to be bright and astute, completely uninfluenced by differences of age, colour, social status and all the other pigeonholes of Western civilisation. Living largely on their wits, they can sometimes appear aggressive. But further acquaintance usually reveals warm, outgoing characters whose unsophisticated sense of fun is often allied to a tactile and persuasive manner some might call flirtatious. In my view great charm is underscored by a natural sensuality difficult to overlook. Perhaps most of all they are completely unselfconscious in a way hard to imagine in the British. I concluded that in addition to constantly searching for ready sources of income, Moroccans are a gregarious people with a genuine interest in foreigners.

Visitors to Morocco often complain of the unwelcome attention of hustlers in the larger towns. That nice British woman who walked the length of Africa a couple of years ago singled out Morocco as the country of greatest harassment. While not yet in the league of India or Egypt, there is no doubt that the eternal '*Monsieur, Monsieur*', can try the patience of even the most sanguine of visitors.

However, the subject must be seen in context. Firstly, most Europeans are rich beyond the dreams of unemployed Moroccans. Secondly, visitors sometimes show a painful disregard for Islamic custom, displaying enough naked flesh to lose all respect. Thirdly, in my experience, Moroccans have a marvellous approach to life and sense of humour. Hustlers treated in the right way can often become part of the experience, to be humoured and enjoyed rather than confronted. If they con you out of a few pence, so what? Approached sensibly, the problem can be minimised, although I do concede it has not done Moroccan tourism any favours.

Asked if I ever felt afraid on my wanderings, the answer is that despite many occasions when both I and my possessions were completely unprotected, anxious moments were few, certainly fewer than would have been the case in Britain. Admittedly I was mainly in the country, but I never experienced theft or any real harassment. One should remember too that scarcity of alcohol away from the towns has thankfully kept European lager-louts away.

I have briefly mentioned the country and said something about the people. Perhaps what is so appealing overall is the way the two combine. Looked at as if through the lens of a camera, there is something to delight the eye at every turn. It may be a gathering of laughing women in bright tribal dress doing the family washing in a stream, or a group of donkeys grazing while their owners sit talking in the shade. It may be the casual wave of a shepherd-boy silhouetted in the evening sun, or an old fortress, unused and decaying, with goats picking their way through the outer rooms. It may be nothing more than a simple country scene whose normal aspect is enhanced by a desultory palm tree sited by chance in precisely the right place.

In her marvellous book *In Morocco*, Edith Wharton says: 'To visit Morocco is like turning the pages of some illuminated Persian manuscript all embroidered with bright shapes and subtle lines.' In the modern idiom the whole country might be described as a film-set awaiting the cue for action.

And how did my relationship with Morocco begin? It started when, as a professional soldier, I was posted to a small United Nations Mission in the Sahara. Some 350 Observers are stationed across the desert, monitoring a cease-fire between the Royal Moroccan Army and the Frente Polisario, the military wing of the Saharawi nation. The dispute concerns sovereignty of what was formerly Spanish Sahara.

On the wall of my office was a map of the Maghreb (North West Africa) to which my eye was frequently drawn. As the fan circled the ceiling and the noonday sun baked the wasteland outside, my mind would stray north across the desert border into Morocco. It was a country about which I knew nothing but whose very name conjured up images of mountains and tribesmen, horses and harems; vague but romantic notions from childhood reading and snatched conversation. The land of a 'thousand and one nights' or, as they say, *'mille et une nuits'*.

My first leave was spent in a luxury hotel in Agadir, giving me enough of a glimpse of the country to want to see more. After that I divided my map into areas and passed much time at work planning my next trip. In the end I spent virtually all my spare time and several subsequent leaves wandering footloose round each area, enjoying the encounters recorded in this book.

Finally, these words would be incomplete without mention of Barnaby Rogerson's *Guide to Morocco*, published by Cadogan. This book gave me more pleasure than I can say, both in content and more particularly in the style and wit of his writing. History, fact and advice is well balanced with thoughtful views on some of the more quaint or annoying Moroccan customs. So much did I enjoy it that on many occasions when alone, I read about places I had no chance of visiting, just for the pleasure of his prose.

If this introduction has hinted at the romance of Morocco, I hope the following pages of personal experiences will bring out the flavour of the country and its people. What may also become apparent is possibly the most compelling aspect of all, namely that against such a rich and exotic patina the single wanderer can never be entirely certain what is going to happen next.

2

A Room with a View

Charm'd magic casements, opening on the foam
Of perilous seas, in faery lands forlorn.

John Keats

It is last light. I am standing at the back of a bus hurtling along the
coast road north of Agadir. I am looking for somewhere to spend
the night.

Inside, four figures sit between me and where the conductor
sways by the driver. The seats between us are low and basic, the
interior almost dark. Open windows suck in warm air, which
brushes my face and causes litter to dance across the floor.

Outside to our left, the sun which seemed such a permanent fix-
ture all afternoon has slipped suddenly into the sea leaving just a
reflection on the darkening water. On the right the foothills of the
Atlas Mountains rise sharply into gloom. Ahead our headlights follow the road as it climbs and drops, picking out bare earth and scrub
and the occasional eucalyptus.

My predicament is self-inflicted. This is my second leave from
work in the Sahara, having decided after the first that smart hotels
are a bore. What I want to find is the real Morocco not a cocoon of
European comfort. Somewhere ahead is the village of Tarhazoute,
where I intend to try my luck.

🌴   🌴   🌴

With a hissing of brakes the bus stops abruptly on the edge of a
village square. At one end robed figures stand round brightly lit
stalls of fish and vegetables, while in the centre kids play football in
the half-light. As I step down, the haunting cry of the muezzin

9

echoes across the rooftops from the minaret of a nearby mosque. I head towards the crowd.

'*Oui Monsieur?*' A stall-holder has seen me and comes forward. I ask if he knows of anywhere I can spend the night.

'You can stay here with us if you like,' he says, indicating two young boys who presumably make up the 'us'. Sleeping behind a stall with three strangers is not at all what I had in mind, but his smile is welcoming and the experience will certainly be novel.

He must have noticed my hesitation. 'Or you may find a room down by the beach.' A room by the beach sounds more in line so, memorising instructions, I thank him and set off.

The village consists of houses of one or two storeys ranged round a small bay. Nothing smart or modern, just peasant dwellings cling-ing together on rock. Electricity clearly exists in the square but beyond that no proper lighting. Only here and there a solitary lamp illuminates corners or casts long shadows down cobbled steps and secret walkways. Just enough for someone who knows where he is going, but of no real help to a stranger.

Bag over shoulder, I take a narrow passage heading down to the sea, passing on the way children playing by dimly lit doorways. When I reach the beach the sands lie dark and silent, people and lights now left behind. I set off in the direction of the house he has described.

The door is locked, closed windows staring blank and dead. The battered stone front of the house shows no sign of life but the sound of spent waves washing up the beach is one of such serenity that I become all the more anxious to stay. A noise draws my attention to where a woman is throwing out rubbish. When she tells me the owner is away, I realise I must try elsewhere.

I retrace my steps to a small café with the menu displayed in French. I am peering inside when the proprietor comes out to see if he can help. Amazingly he speaks English and after the usual pleas-antries asks me in. I explain that I have just arrived and am in search of a bed; the best I have come up with so far is the floor of someone's stall – can he suggest anything better? As we talk my attention is diverted by someone with the dress and movements of a youth but the delicate face of a girl who passes en route to the kitchen. Introduced later as Aziz, he is referred to thereafter as the 'maid' or 'waitress'. Whether this is a joke or muddle is hard to decide but in the circumstances it is not inappropriate.

I soon discover that the man, Hassan, is a prosperous Moroccan who has fallen on hard times. Fine-looking and about my own age, he has lived in both London and New York. Now his wife has left him and he runs this restaurant. He tells me I am welcome to sleep in the next room if I do not mind sharing with him and Aziz. He also offers me supper as guests are due at any minute and all is ready. Deciding that this looks more salubrious than the stall, I accept both.

Hassan starts setting the table. Eager to have a look at the accommodation, I excuse myself and wander next door. The room is being redecorated, with piles of pictures leaning against the walls and furniture stacked in the middle. Just as I am puzzling at the absence of beds, the maid appears. He does not speak French but smiles and mumbles something friendly. To my surprise he then starts to take off his clothes.

Hello! What's he up to? Aziz's striking looks have already caused me to ponder the relationship with his employer, but this is most unexpected.

Unconcerned by my presence the boy replaces his tee-shirt and jeans with a loose fitting smock and baggy white pantalons. Over both he hangs an ornamental dagger on a sling of silver cord, completing this picture of elegance with a red fez on his head. So that's it. The maid is simply dressing to serve dinner!

Shortly afterwards the other guests arrive: a delightful young French couple and a middle-aged Swede of strange appearance. His wife too has gone and he has chosen a summer in Morocco to recover. The unfortunate gentleman turns out to be nice enough except for an annoying giggle which accompanies everything he says and must surely have hastened his wife's departure. Luckily he does not say much as he has no French and is only starting on English.

Aziz turns out to be a good cook. Soon we are enjoying excellent fresh fish and salad, as well as a pleasant evening of conversation on matters Moroccan. Aziz understands just enough French to join in from his cooking and as the evening wears on his ready smile and lively manner make him the centre of attention. Everyone seems more than ready to humour him.

Eventually dinner finishes and the guests leave. The maid does the washing-up and then he and Hassan make up camp-beds next door. In the absence of running water I ladle some from a large jug to clean my teeth. By the time I have done so the bedroom is ready, with Hassan and me at one end, and the boy on the floor at the entrance.

It is at this stage that Hassan informs me that the house has no WC and we must use the beach. This does not worry me now, though it is not hard to think of times when it might. Once again I find my way in the dark down the narrow alley which leads to the

11

sea, uncertain where to head for, but reassured by cover of darkness. Robed figures pass in the gloom, their sandals clacking on the stone steps. By the time I get back all is set for the night, so I undress and climb under a blanket. The others visit the beach, as presumably does all the rest of the village, and then return and lie fully clothed on their beds.

Despite the heat and novel surroundings I sleep soundly until woken next morning by noise outside. The sun is already streaming through skylights in the top of the wall. Hassan is kneeling over Aziz, trying, I assume, to rouse him. A few minutes later they prepare me breakfast on a table in the street – excellent coffee, delicious fresh orange juice, and two doughnuts still warm from the oven. I sit in the sunlight eating and watching people going about their business until hot water appears. Then, with the maid holding the mirror and studying every move, I am able to wash and shave.

I pay Hassan about £12 for dinner and breakfast and for allowing me to stay the night – not much but probably more than he expects. I discover later that his standard dinner costs £3, so he should be happy, but I am not sorry to leave. My host is nice enough but rather too anxious to unburden himself of his misfortunes. Also, as he is teaching Aziz to cook, every conversation is interrupted by a flow of Berber instructions over his shoulder.

The maid himself has been an interesting source of entertainment though somewhat inhibited by his master's close attention. A few days later when I see him in the street he is very friendly, bidding me a warm welcome despite being unable to communicate. Anyway, they have proved a useful port in a storm.

Liking the look of the village, I determine to find better accommodation. Hassan directs me to a kiosk whose proprietor rents rooms. He turns out to be a tall, spare man of about 40, wearing a dark brown burnous, the traditional thick outer coat with hood, similar to the robes of monks in this country. To my surprise he too speaks some English and soon understands what I am after, namely a room, or *chambre*, to sleep in – preferably alone!

He takes me back down my route of the previous night, now bright with sun reflecting off the sides of houses. Near the beach, he unlocks a door and ushers me into a square courtyard off which lead four pale-blue doors. The second opens into a small white-washed room with rush matting floor, solitary table, and piled in one corner an assortment of foam mattresses and blankets.

The window is closed and shuttered. When he pushes it open the brightness of the sun dazzles for a second, then I see the beach immediately below. Although the tide is out the sound of breaking waves rushes in and I can tell at a glance that the view is superb. Straight ahead, lines of surf race up the beach. Round to the right, 50 or more small fishing boats lie drawn up on sand the colour of butter which spreads right up to the foot of the building. A perfect spot.

Apart from the sleeping facilities, it is just what I want so I take it for a week for £40, a sum I later discover to be wildly inflated. The compound has electric light but no water, with just a squat WC in a tiny room off the courtyard. Water has to be drawn from a nearby well by means of a bucket and rope.

Examining the mattresses, I choose a couple to sleep on and then shake out blankets, trying not to imagine who has used them before or, worse still, when they were last washed. Hygiene is clearly going to be an early casualty of my new lifestyle.

Soon I meet my next-door neighbours, two friendly young German males who have been coming here for years. Whenever I appear they are always at home, but I never discover how they pass the time. I conclude that their main pre-occupation is the smoking of hash.

I later find that the roof of my room supports a terrace from which it is possible to overlook the fishing fleet coming and going as well as locals playing on the beach. On several evenings I sit out with a book and a bottle of whisky, watching the goings-on while the sun slips gently into the sea. A most pleasant experience even on one's own.

As I get to know Tarhazoute I develop an ambivalent feeling towards it. Although scruffy, its site on the coast, perched around the crescent of brilliant sand, is perfect. The fishing fleet and all that it entails makes a picturesque backdrop to every other activity. My room is basic but adequate and it has that lovely view out to sea. These are all major plus points.

However, there is another aspect which dawns more slowly. Rogerson describes entertainingly the way the village became a centre for hippies during the sixties and goes on to tell us that 'an

13

obstinate rearguard of the acid revolution remains'.

This mirrors my own observations. Apart from my neighbours, I come across a number of other strange-looking Europeans wandering around with several weeks' growth of beard and a dreamy look in their eyes. They are seldom to be seen during daylight, their pale skin indicating a nocturnal lifestyle, but they provide the *raison d'être* for a criminal element and the consequent attention of the law. For an innocent abroad, the 'atmosphere of mild degeneracy' is coupled to a sinister feeling of being a potential target for both pushers and police.

In fact it is while staying here that I first become aware of the tightrope to be trodden by anyone wishing to travel outside the tourist ambit in Morocco. For example, although it is not available in villages, locals can buy alcohol quite easily in the main towns. However, for a tourist to give alcohol to a Moroccan is frowned upon, even if he has rendered you a service and asks for it, which they frequently do, usually for no reason at all. Similarly, while it appears that a blind eye is sensibly turned to locals smoking dope, the same would not be the case if a tourist was involved. Buying drugs is, of course, a criminal offence and one gets the feeling a Moroccan jail would not be an edifying experience.

A third area of difficulty stems from the fact that due to a population explosion, 70 per cent of Moroccans are aged less than 20, with nowhere near enough jobs to go round. As a result single tourists are fair game and, when it comes to earning money, anything goes. Natural friendliness can be taken further than most Europeans expect, persistence being allied to considerable charm. As the reader will see, it is not difficult to sometimes find oneself heading into what for most of us are uncharted waters.

South of the village is a camping site run by a redoubtable Irish lady who has lived there many years. I spot her buying vegetables and find out who she is from my landlord. In the evening I walk to her café on the beach and we sit for ages discussing the subject. A friendly soul, she knows more or less everything about the village. She tells me the three cardinal sins for tourists centre round drugs, alcohol and sex, warning me that the police employ informers along this part of the coast. She says that anyone travelling alone will be a suspect on all three counts. At best erring will incur a fine; at worst a stretch of porridge in some benighted Moroccan lock-up.

My dilemma is that I have come in search of the real Morocco beyond the tourist trail. I can only do this by mixing with locals, and on leave from the desert I am inevitably alone.

14

It is early days in my travels away from civilisation. Negotiating my way back in the dark across the sands, I wonder if, over the next few months, I will achieve my aim of getting under the skin of the country. I am well aware of the need to respect local sensibilities, but at the same time do not want to be restricted in my wanderings. My conversation with the Irish woman leaves a bitter-sweet taste in the mouth.

When I finally get back to the *chambre* a light is showing under my German neighbours' door and the courtyard smells of hash. Once inside I go straight to open the window as the air is hot and stuffy from the afternoon sun. The sound and smell of sea pour in, freshening the room in an instant. Without turning on the light I stand for some time looking out. In the darkness ahead I can sense waves washing gently up the beach. Peering round towards land the silhouette of mosque and houses can just be detected against the night sky. A marvellous feeling of calm pervades.

The village goes to bed early by European standards. By ten not many lights are showing. Few people are still abroad, and the streets and passageways become the province of dogs whose anguished cries punctuate the stillness of the night.

3

Village People

The night has made a nosegay of the stars
Bound with a straying fragrance from the south.

Sybil Grant

'*Monsieur, Monsieur*, you want something? What is it you are looking for?

It is dark. I am sitting at a table outside a café, dissecting a pomegranate and whistling to myself 'The Laughing Policeman', an old favourite. Not aware that I am looking for anything, I turn to find the figure of the speaker half hidden in shadow at the corner of the building.

'You want something to smoke?'

His insistence makes it sound like a fact not a question. It is only my third day in Tarhazoute, but already I have been on the receiving end of several such invitations. They come as no real surprise as the smell of recreational drugs mixes perceptibly with other less easily identified aromas around the village.

'No thanks, I don't smoke.'

It is no secret that kif, the pot or marijuana of North Africa, is smoked extensively throughout the Maghreb, Tarhazoute being a well-established centre. Rolled from leaves of hemp (cannabis), kif is cheaper and more available than hashish which comes from resin of the same plant. Those with access to hash normally sell it on to tourists and satisfy their own needs with greater quantities of kif.

Although keen to try most things once, drugs have never interested me. I soon realise, though, what an enigma I must be to the locals, who cannot imagine a European coming there on his own for any other good reason. They seem to have some difficulty with the word 'no'.

I come to like the café where I am sitting for two reasons. The first is that the proprietor, Hussein, has a particularly charming manner and is one of the few Moroccan shopkeepers I ever meet who is not constantly trying to extract money. The second is that he has an excellent collection of taped Berber music. Once he knows I approve, he plays it whenever I appear, instead of Western music, which seems so inappropriate.

I am not a fan of Arab music with masses of groaning string and wind instruments and eternal repetition. To one raised on pop it grates most terribly. But Berber music is different even though it too can be repetitive. Played largely on banjo and guitar and other unrecognised instruments, it is usually accompanied by tom-toms and drums of varying sizes.

Berber music is not totally unlike that of Irish folk bands, the singing, performed with great intensity, being high-pitched, with a certain mystic quality. To me it seems to have within it something of the wildness and melancholy of the Atlas Mountains.

Staying in the *chambre*, routine soon becomes established. I wake early, not out of inclination, but because of noises outside my window. The rasping sound of fishermen's outboards being tested out of the water stirs my slumbers before dawn. Then come the crowing of cocks kept on roof-tops or wandering the streets. After that the shouts of people on their way to work, and soon the general hubbub of everyday life.

Once up, I stroll down to the café and sit outside, watching the beach and fishing boats not going out that day. An unfortunate donkey is always to be seen tied to one of the boats. I do not know his purpose as I never see him working, but he seems condemned to spend his whole life in the sun, pacing up and down his tiny domain, now and then giving vent to a bray that sounds more like a sob at his misfortune.

Hussein's boy, Jammal, brings me a glass of *café au lait*, and another of a shake made of milk and bananas. I then sit in the fresh, early-morning sun watching the goings-on among the boats, or *barques* as they are rather charmingly called, while he boils shaving water. Then back to my *chambre* with the water in an old fruit tin, prop a mirror against the window, and shave as best I can. After that I pack a bag with my camera and book and head up the passageway to buy lunch.

Moroccan bread is generally excellent as well as incredibly cheap by British standards. It comes either as a round flat loaf or as a baguette, both in several sizes. The round loaves are ideal for sandwiches being easily split and hollowed, and the bread invariably has a delicious crusty outside, often still being hot from the communal oven.

For fillings there is a wide choice. I sometimes buy processed cheese, and then add sliced tomato; otherwise freshly cooked sardines, hard-boiled eggs, which can be purchased individually at most grocers', or hard cheese. The fruit and vegetables in Morocco are quite outstanding, the country being blessed with a climate that caters for everything from cotton and tobacco, through bananas and citrus fruits, to every conceivable vegetable. In the larger towns the grocers' displays are as impressive as I have seen anywhere.

Two items deserve special mention; despite skins like tractor tyres, Moroccan oranges, from October to spring, are the sweetest and cheapest I have ever tasted. Tomatoes, too, are not the sort that would grace Mr Sainsbury's shelves, having no uniformity of size, shape or even colour. Most of the skins are split but the flavour is so good that it is easy to overlook their appearance. They taste home-grown, with no sign of artificial additives or genetic engineering. Quite superb, although I always give them a good wash first, either in mineral water or the sea.

In fact one of my only concessions to health concerns water. I reckon it would be madness to drink from the wells, so I always stick to bottled mineral water, which we anyway drink at work. Moroccans are great ones for sharing. If they open a bottle they always offer it round and, by the same token, if I get out my water I do likewise. This of course means that the supply runs out faster than planned, which can be annoying miles from anywhere. I am also a little worried by the fact that many of the young have herpes sores on their lips. Anxious to avoid these, I adopt the rather sorry tactic of carrying two bottles, only one of which is for public consumption.

Overall, the simple diet of my travels makes me realise what an absurd amount of food most of us eat in Europe. An EC hygiene inspector might get an attack of the vapours at the way food is handled in Morocco, but it never does me any harm. Indeed, I can only imagine a rest from riboflavin and monosodium glutamate does nothing but good. The dry heat at most times of the year is also most invigorating. A feeling of physical well-being is matched, throughout my time in the Maghreb, by mental alertness stemming from an absence of television and newspapers. For once the brain is allowed to carry out its function uncluttered by the complexities of cyberspace, Mad Cow disease or the strengths and weaknesses of the European Union!

Fishing along this part of the coast is entirely for squid. The port of Agadir has a large fleet of ocean-going boats that catch what has been missed by the Spanish sardine fleet, but the small inshore ones concentrate on squid, sold on the shore and exported to Europe. The prime time for catching squid is at dawn and dusk, so the little fleet leaves the village at half past four in the morning and gets back by ten, or at four in the afternoon, getting back at last light. Fifty or sixty wooden *barques* live on the beach, of which perhaps twenty-five go out at any one time. Propelled by either an outboard or rough wooden oars, the normal crew seems to be three, from old men to young boys.

In order to get the boats to the water a rope is attached to each end with a wooden bar on it. This is shouldered by one man on each side so that a total of four heave the boat down the beach while another fetches the outboard. When all is ready they push it into the waves, climb aboard and crash through the surf until the outboard can be lowered. The return is much the same in reverse and is picturesque when the evening fleet comes in. Being a west-facing shore, the sun does not dip behind the mountains but slides slowly into the sea. As it does so, its dying rays shimmer in the sheen of wet sand above the tide. The fleet is in silhouette as it draws ashore. With the loss of light all colour fades. The boats look black. Figures walking back up the beach become faceless forms recognised only by the familiarity of their gait.

At the top of the beach two groups gather in the half-light to watch the buyers, well-fed individuals wearing striped burnouses against the evening breeze. In front of each is a set of scales and a gas lamp. A crowd of hangers-on collect around them to view the day's catch and what it will fetch. The *patron* of the boat carries the squid up in wooden boxes and then stands patiently awaiting his turn until he can lift out handfuls and transfer them onto the scales. Well-prepared *calamar*i may be a great delicacy, but raw live squid must be one of the most ugly fish in the business. A glance into the bowl shows eyes, tentacles and bodies jumbled in an unholy mass. Real nightmare material.

As the *patron* works, several beggars pester for scraps, waving arms and entreating with agitated voices. For the most part he pays no attention, but every so often he throws something out, sending them scuttling off like jealous seagulls that have won a morsel and do not intend to share it.

19

After the weighing comes arguing over the price. I imagine this will go on forever but in fact it does not. With a going rate of about £5 a kilo, there is little to discuss.

🌴 🌴 🌴

If Moroccans have a national sport more popular than pursuing tourists, it has to be football. Even the smallest group of houses seems able to find enough bodies to make up a team, and a village as large as this has several. From about four every evening the beach is divided into pitches drawn out in the sand, the players being graded by age and size. From then until dark, and indeed after dark sometimes, games continue, the whole area becoming a mass of figures chasing, tackling, following up. With no apparent supervision, the games progress without mishap although every now and then a foul causes a scuffle. The game stops while everyone gathers round to jeer and encourage. All very sportsman-like, with the protagonists left to fight it out on their own and no harm done.

The standard of football appears to my inexpert eye to be good – perhaps not surprising in view of the amount of practice they get and the natural athleticism of most of the young men. The Chleuh tribes around Agadir are tough wiry people, renowned for their gymnastic ability. Since the first traders penetrated the Maghreb centuries ago, young Chleuh acrobats were taken by caravan to spend their lives in the travelling circuses of Europe.

Nowadays it is common in restaurants as far away as Casablanca or Tangier to have your dinner interrupted by a troupe of performers who somersault between tables and throw each other into spins of giddying daring. Usually these are family affairs, and the star will be a boy of ten or twelve, devoid of all fear, his body immune to the stress of eye-watering contortions. The act over, he will saunter among the diners, acknowledging applause and collecting money in a flirtatious manner few can resist.

🌴 🌴 🌴

My first full day in the village is a Sunday. I decide to walk out of town to look at the neighbouring beaches and am soon on the coast road, with the sun burning into my arms and neck. Moroccans adore the beach but Sundays are the only occasion out of season when they can get there, so traffic is heavy with other groups coming by taxi or bicycle or simply walking like me.

Suddenly, the unaccustomed noise of Western music! A car drives

20

slowly by, radio blaring, three girls sprawled inside. Their gazes linger in my direction at the same moment as I notice the driver holding a can of beer to her lips. Most unusual! They drive on by, the girl in the back watching from the rear window until the car reaches a corner.

Where I work in Laayoune a sight like this would be unthinkable, so I spend some time contemplating it. About half an hour later I am about to climb down from the road for a swim, when I see the same car coming back. Again the loud music, but this time to my complete surprise it draws up beside me.

'*Bonjour*. Where are you going? You French?' The buxom driver speaks while the others smile out at me.

'No, English.'

'Oh, English. Hello. How are you? I am very well.' I wonder if her repertoire goes any further. It does.

'You want a ride?'

'Sure.'

I go to the rear door, assessing in a second that the girl in the back is the prettiest. Amazed at my good fortune, I climb in. The driver turns in her seat and introduces me to her companions. Her name is Fatima.

'You alone? Why?'

'I'm on holiday on my own.'

'Oh.' She tuts surprise. As we talk I steal a look at my companion on the rear seat and notice that her shorts are undone at the front, brown skin showing quite clearly across her stomach. Although she returns my smile it is soon clear she cannot speak French. The driver offers me a beer, which I take, and then starts the car and drives slowly off in the direction from which I have just come. At the outskirts of the village she parks overlooking a small bay.

We sit talking, getting immediately on to the fact that she is married, the others single. This leads on to a discussion as to whether I find Moroccan women attractive, do I have a girl-friend, will I come into Agadir, which is where they live? The whole thing is completely natural, spoilt only by the fact that the others can do nothing more than stare at me and comment to each other in Arabic. My companion must have realised about her shorts. By shifting position she has buttoned up unnoticed.

As we chat I try to decide what possibilities lie ahead, bearing in mind that because of my job in the Sahara, I have had no contact of this sort for ages. On the face of it I have fallen on my feet. But weighing up the pros and cons, I reluctantly decide that the mechanics of furthering any relationship will be complicated and will almost certainly use up the rest of my holiday, not to mention most of my money. They are fun girls, very friendly, and the one next to me is certainly pretty. But I know that moving back into Agadir is not what I have come for. Neither, with my halting French, is there likely to be any great meeting of minds.

When Fatima decides it is time to go we say a fond farewell, making all sorts of promises about next week.

This is early days as far as my trips to Morocco are concerned. I might have played things differently had I known it to be one of the only times I will have contact with Moroccan women the whole time I am here. Strangely enough it is not until my return to England that I have anything more than the most casual relationship.

In fact, even that nearly ends in disaster. I am flying home wearing an old pair of trainers. Made of synthetic material, they have slowly developed a most unpleasant smell as a result of much use and many soakings in the sea. My intention is to ditch them when I get home. I am too embarrassed to give them away.

It is a relief to find the Royal Air Maroc aircraft at Casablanca only half full. As soon as I sit down the smell from the trainers begins to percolate upwards, enveloping the empty seats around me. At this point a late arrival boards the aircraft and advances up the aisle. With a mixture of pleasure and horror I watch as an extremely pretty Moroccan girl pauses beside me and then sits in my row. After take-off we are soon in conversation, particularly when I find she speaks perfect English and is coming to London on a university exchange. I feel conscious of having discovered little, during my time in Morocco, about life 'behind the veil' and suddenly here is the opportunity to do that and hopefully more.

It all depends on the trainers. Should I reveal the source of the smell which now hovers enticingly between us? Smartly dressed and fastidiously turned out, she may not be quite ready for such a topic. I keep quiet, but make sure that on our subsequent meetings in London I always arrive well scrubbed and awash with delicious fragrance.

My week in the village ends too quickly, but I fly back to Laayoune well pleased with my first attempt at life away from tourist centres. Having enjoyed this part of the coast so much I resolve to return to the same area on my next leave, but this time to explore the more remote beaches a few kilometres further north.

4

Sleeping Rough

So many adventures couldn't happen today,
  So many songs we forgot to play
So many dreams swinging out of the blue
  We'll let them come true.

Alphaville

As soon as I reach Agadir at the start of my next leave, I catch a bus up the coast to see what goes on further north. An hour later, when it stops at a group of huts, I jump down, finding myself among a small fishing community. Several *barques* lie on the sand beyond, although the full extent of the beach is hidden by palm trees.

Having waited for the bus for some time in the sun, I decide to buy a drink at one of the kiosks before going down to the sea. As I approach, faces watch me while pretending to go about their business. The arrival of a single European must be a novelty. I buy a Coke – not cold, of course, because villages like this have no electricity, and therefore no fridges – and stand outside drinking it.

'*Allemagne?*' I look round and find the owner of the voice, a youth of about 20.

'*Non, Anglais,*' I reply. This brings a smile of pleasure to his face and a conversation quickly develops. His name is Mustafa and he points to the house a short way along the beach where he lives with his parents and brothers. He is open and friendly and we talk for several minutes before I say that I must be getting along. He bids me goodbye and I head for the beach.

This particular one is a spectacular size. About 4 kilometres of golden sand stretch to a rocky headland in the distance. A few houses follow the line of the road, but out by the sea's edge they do not intrude. I walk some way and then stop for a swim. I am the only human there, my companions being large seagulls standing in

23

lines along the tidemark. They seem to be queuing for a special event – possibly the sight of a European bathing?

The beach is relatively shallow so waves are breaking far out and then re-forming before finally spending themselves over the hot sand. How strange that in the space of perhaps a minute such a powerful force of water has no more lasting epitaph than Rupert Brooke's 'little dulling edge of foam'. It is a good beach for swimming, the sand firm, the water warm, with the waves further out large enough to stir the adrenalin. The view back towards land – wide beach merging into empty scrub-covered hills and beyond them mountains – adds to the sense of solitude. To me it is a sort of paradise in as much as I can think of nowhere I would rather be.

Carrying my clothes in a bag, I walk on to the headland. In order to see what lies round the next corner I follow a small path worn into the rock and soon reach, of course, another huge beach. Here I choose a place to settle among the rocks, and then set about my usual occupations of reading, swimming and generally beachcombing for shells and pools. Experience has taught me to always wear long-sleeved shirts but I also look for boulders or cover of some sort in order to avoid the midday sun. Despite several months of exposure I still find its direct rays overpowering.

As always, the time passes too quickly. At about four I start the slow journey back over the headland with the intention of walking the length of the first beach before rejoining the road. Round the point I come across a group of figures playing football along the edge of the tide. I soon recognise my friend of that morning, Mustafa, amongst them. He calls out a greeting and the game stops for me to be introduced to all of them. Every introduction of this type involves a handshake, after which Moslems invariably kiss their fingers or cross their hand over their heart. Being such outgoing people, introductions to everyone are quite normal and most charming.

Suddenly I am confused. Am I imagining it or are all these kids called Mohammed? It certainly seems so. Later I learn that it is usual for the eldest son to be named after the Prophet, which is why there are so many about. It is also hard to distinguish between names from the same derivation. For example, spoken quickly, Mohammed, Hamid and Ahmed all sound like 'Hmed'; similarly Hassan, Hussein and Lahcen (phonetically La Hassen) are hard to separate. These introductions alert me to the need to pay attention in the first instance to avoid embarrassment later.

After a short chat Mustafa asks if I would like to go to his home for tea. Interested to see how he lives, I thank him and accept. We

24

leave the others still playing and walk across the sand, passing on our way a small herd of camels picturesquely drinking at a well. As we approach the house it looks old with plenty of character. One storey only, it sits just back from the sand with palms, bent over by the wind, providing shade. The white-washed outside has no windows so as to maximise protection from sun and wind. We push open a door, cross a small courtyard, and stop outside one of the rooms.

Following Mustafa's example, I shake off my shoes. After such strong sunlight I am momentarily blinded by the darkness inside, but gradually make out a small room with no furniture, just rugs on the floor. At the far end someone sleeps, his head hidden under a blanket.

Before going for tea, Mustafa wakes the slumbering figure, who turns out to be his eldest brother. I later learn that the family consists of six boys and two girls. For the rest of the afternoon new faces – male only – keep appearing, being introduced, sitting and watching me for a bit, and then disappearing when the French becomes too much of an effort. Mustafa's brother has little French, so to fill lengthening gaps in our conversation he produces a guitar, which he plays most beautifully. Not only is he an expert musician, but he also gives every indication of a wonderfully placid temperament, which appeals to me.

Eventually Mustafa comes in with the tea, consisting of a pewter teapot shaped much like a European coffee pot, and several glasses. The tea is already brewing, the pot having also been filled with sprigs of mint. Mustafa adds sugar. Sugar is bought by the poor in Morocco in rough slabs from which the required amount is broken off.

Glasses are set up in a line and he pours tea into two of them. These are then picked up and the contents decanted into other empty ones. Instead of passing these round, the tea is then poured back into the pot and the whole process starts again. On other occasions I have sat for hours watching this excruciating ritual, which has no more sinister purpose than to mix the sugar into the tea. It can go on interminably, the more so when you are in a hurry.

Mustafa also produces a loaf and a plate containing a dip of olive oil. I had always been told that Moslems never handle food with their left hands, but this is instantly disproved when he holds the loaf in his left hand while tearing off pieces for each of us with his right. He then passes round the glasses of tea.

'Whisky Berber,' he smiles; then, 'Eat, eat.'

We sit talking and eating. Mustafa, a great extrovert, tells me that

25

his brother and a friend are members of a band specialising in Berber music. He too plays the guitar, a fact which he proves by picking it up and strumming. He also plays tom-toms. We talk for a long time in a most relaxed way while his brother plucks and strums from his corner.

Suddenly I realise it is half past six and I have probably missed the last bus back to my *chambre* in Tarhazoute. I tell Mustafa but he seems not at all concerned.

'Don't worry, you can spend the night here.'

I am not keen to be separated from my belongings in the village, nor, after years of military training, do I like being without my washing and shaving kit. At the same time it offers the chance of a new experience so I am inclined to accept, although I am not certain where he is offering me space. I ask and he explains that the four older boys, ranging from 22 to 14, sleep in one room, the two younger boys in another, the two girls in a third and his parents in a fourth. I can sleep with the older boys. There is only one problem. He rolls up his sleeve to reveal a mass of bites up his arm. *Les moustiques.*

Mindful of stories I have heard earlier about malaria in West Africa, I decide that this is not a good idea. I tell him that I prefer to wander out onto the road and see if I can pick up a passing taxi. Mustafa quite understands, so, promising to look in the next day, I put on my shoes, say goodbye and walk to the road.

By now the sun is low in the sky and not quite as hot as before – my favourite time of day. Whenever I am able to savour such moments I think of that evocative passage in the Bible 'And they heard the voice of the Lord God walking in the garden in the cool of the day.' I sit at the side of the road in the cool of the day to await a taxi. No one is about. Grey leaves of nearby eucalyptus catch the sun as they flicker in a slight breeze coming off the sea. On the other side of the road a long valley of rough fields and argan trees climbs into the Atlas. It looks incredibly peaceful, with not a human habitation in sight. I promise myself a trip there sometime in the future.

After several minutes lost in thought, I notice two men walking along the road from the well. When near, one calls out *'Bonjour'*, and I recognise them from playing football with Mustafa earlier that afternoon.

'Qu'est ce que tu fais?' he asks. 'What are you doing?' When I

26

explain that I have missed the last bus and am hoping for a taxi back to the village, he tells me I will never get one now.

'Why don't you come back with us? We've got a room where you can stay the night.' If a taxi is unlikely then this probably is the answer, so, feeling slightly like the subject of a game of 'pass the parcel', I agree to go with them, the mosquito problem somehow forgotten.

My new friends are another Mohammed, 19, a fisherman, and Ahmed, a year younger, whose uncle is the *patron* of a *barque*. Mohammed is tall, about my height, and as usual, incredibly thin. Clean-shaven with dark olive skin, he has high cheekbones and eyes which slant interestingly beneath a green baseball cap. Ahmed is shorter, with a young face and ready smile. As the sun lowers itself into the sea we walk once more across the beach to the houses I spotted near the headland. With wind in our faces and surf roaring in our ears, we pass the deserted fleet of *barques* pulled up on the sand. We then thread our way up a steep set of steps between two smart houses whose windows are shuttered and barred.

At this stage I have absolutely no idea what to expect. This small clutch of houses is obviously a rather select group of Moroccan holiday homes. Is it possible the two boys live in one of them? It seems hardly likely. At the top of the steps we take a narrow passage between stone walls and suddenly stop at a rough wooden door. Mohammed produces a key and soon I am standing in a room about half the size of the one in which I had tea with Mustafa earlier this afternoon! I discover later that a number of *pêcheurs'* huts are sandwiched between the grander holiday homes on this part of the coast.

It is now virtually dark. Mohammed lights a candle and the tiny room comes to life. Again no furniture, not even mattresses, just a few old rugs and cushions up one end. At the other is a large water-container, a gas cylinder with cooking ring, and one or two pots and pans plus boxes for storage. White-wash peels from the walls, while exposed wooden beams covered in baked mud form the ceiling. If I have entertained any idea of a room to myself I see my mistake the moment the candle illuminates the hut. Clearly we will all sleep together on the floor.

I take off my shoes and light a cigarette, settling at one end of the room to see what will happen next. The first thing is a quick inventory of available food, accompanied by a commentary in Berber from Mohammed. I do not know the conclusion until I see him going through his pockets for money. Ahmed is about to be dispatched to the *magasin*, so I give him a pound, which should do.

Ahmed leaves and Mohammed busies himself assembling various utensils. The gas cylinder with its ring-burner is pulled out and lit, and a pan of water placed on it. Another candle is placed in an empty bottle, which we balance on the rug near me. He then washes his hands in a tiny amount of cold water, throwing the slops out of the door into the darkened passageway.

When Ahmed returns, further conversation in Berber ensues. He has bought *des legumes*, vegetables. Mohammed squats down with a bowl in front of him and scrapes carrots, potatoes, etc. in a most expert manner. Ahmed also squats and watches, humming to himself and occasionally lifting the lid of the water to see if it has boiled. Mohammed adds cooking oil to the boiling water. As the steam rises he drops in *les legumes* and covers them with a lid. He is quite clearly well organised and a proficient cook even if it is not exactly haute cuisine.

As I get to know them better, I start to observe their relationship. Mohammed is the natural leader who makes all decisions. He is very capable both as a cook and at organising the limited resources of food and water in the hut. Ahmed, on the other hand, seems willing to be bossed around. Although 18 and displaying the beginnings of a moustache, his voice is unexpectedly high. This, combined with a less confident manner and easy smile, makes him appear very young and somehow rather endearing. They have worked out a modus vivendi which suits them both. They are clearly good friends.

Once the vegetables are cooked to his satisfaction, Mohammed drains them and cracks two eggs into the pot, mixing the whole into something resembling a Spanish omelette. He then replaces the water-pot on the gas ring and brings it back to the boil. A minute or two later everything is ready at once. A piece of flat wood appears as our table and we sit cross-legged around it, while both candles are placed nearby. Tea is poured, the plate of food set in the middle, and Mohammed breaks each of us a large piece of bread.

'Bismilla,' he says.

'Bismilla,' replies Ahmed, and we set to at the communal plate, using our hands and scooping up food with the bread. *Bismilla* is the rough Islamic equivalent of 'for what we are about to receive...'

Sitting there in that tiny room, with candlelight flickering shadows against the wall, the sound of the running sea in the background, and the faces of my new friends concentrating on their food but

28

always ready to smile and nod, the concoction Mohammed has made far exceeds my expectations. We eat mainly in silence with a few words every now and then between mouthfuls.

This occasion makes me aware of what is to prove a perennial problem – namely, how to get comfortable on the floor. Having practised from birth, Moroccans tend to squat and can do so for hours. But being a novice I find anything more than a few minutes decidedly painful. Kneeling is difficult for long periods and sitting too can be awkward without a backrest, particularly when I know from 'Arabian Sands' that to point your feet towards others is bad manners. My unsatisfactory solution is to alternate between all three, resigned to the fact that I will never be totally comfortable and never quite measure up to the high standards of Wilfred Thesiger.

The food soon disappears. When it has gone the house-proud Mohammed gathers up the dish and glasses and puts on water for washing up. I discover later that all water has to be fetched from the well about a kilometre away. What impresses me is the orderly routine the two boys have established to economise on its use. Only one container can be dipped into the main plastic reservoir. Certain water can be used twice, the rest has to be used and then poured into the waste container before being thrown out of the door. I wonder why the passageway outside has not become fouled by so much jettisoned material. My conclusion is that the sun is so hot during the day that everything which might go bad simply shrivels up or evaporates.

Much less appealing is a later discovery that all solid rubbish like tins, bones etc. is carried up and dumped in a ditch by the road, where it can do nothing but deteriorate into a running health hazard. The scrub above the road is also the loo for anyone who cannot be bothered to go to the beach. An area of last resort as far as I am concerned!

Over the days I find myself studying the way they live. They always wash their hands before eating, and also face and hands when they get up in the morning, but I never see either of them shave. Indeed I notice how the faces of most Moroccans remain remarkably smooth well after puberty. But it is impressive how clean they keep themselves in adverse circumstances. Though they never appear to sweat like Europeans, these boys wash frequently in the sea, using sand as soap. Both here and in other parts of the country I have seen men spend hours in the water meticulously preening themselves in this way. It clearly works well.

Most young Moroccans have thick black hair, curly or straight and invariably short, although I am not sure who cuts it. Probably each other. When these two wash their hair they go to *le puits*, the well, and wash it in cold fresh water drawn up in a bucket, the one rinsing the other's head. This is another area that interests me – not the head, but the well. It is used by the whole village both as a water supply for their houses, for washing themselves and their clothes in situ, and for watering flocks of goats and herds of camels. Yet when I walk over to it I can find no evidence of any of these activities, not even an old soap wrapper or two. It seems that here at last is somewhere kept consciously clean and tidy. Although I try to avoid drinking the water, I wash in it on many occasions.

I ask them how they clean their teeth. Ahmed rather delightfully just says 'Signal'. Mohammed agrees and also produces from his pocket a piece of shaped wood which he uses as a toothpick. I would be very surprised if either of them has ever visited a dentist but their teeth and mouths are a picture of health. In fact, despite the lack of fresh water, they both look after themselves well so that wandering around their room with bare feet and sharing blankets and even towels never gives any qualms. Their clothes too are never noticeably dirty, thanks to washing powder and weekly trips to *le puits*. Remarkable considering the shortage of ready cash.

I had realised the moment we arrived at the hut that there would be no bathroom. While Mohammed finishes the washing-up and Ahmed smokes a cigarette, I wander out and down the darkened steps to the beach. By the time I return they have laid three makeshift pillows and blankets in a row on the floor and the room is ready for the night. While they go outside I light another cigarette and enjoy a moment's contemplation on the strange turn my life has taken.

On returning they remove their day clothes and put on old trousers and tee-shirts to sleep in. I notice Mohammed secure the door from the inside with a breeze block. Perhaps because there has been no hint of anything shady I have forgotten about the warning I was given a few days earlier by the Irish woman about mixing with locals. Now here I am about to sleep on the floor with these two young Moroccans. I ask Mohammed if the police are active on this part of the coast. He shrugs his shoulders and laughs.

'*Non. Ici c'est très calme.* Very calm,' he says. So why has he blocked the door? Although my conscience is clear I do see that my presence on the floor of this fishermen's hut might take some explaining.

30

Everyone finally settles. Mohammed puts himself in the middle, with me on one side and the faithful Ahmed on the other, each about half an arm's length apart. After we have blown out the candles I lie listening to the sound of the sea below.

Because no glass covers the tiny windows at the top of the wall, it is cold lying on rush matting with only one blanket. Unfortunately I have nothing else to put on so can only sleep in what I wear. The whole thing is such a far cry from the luxury of the hotel room where I work, and absurdly different from anything in England. I drop off eventually although the unfamiliarity of my surroundings and the proximity of the others keep me drowsing for ages.

Suddenly I am awake. People are moving outside the door. Who are they? It is early as no daylight shows at the windows. Footsteps shuffle in the passage just feet from me. I am gripped by a sudden fear remembering the warnings I had received earlier. Quickly I start trying to formulate an explanation in French as to what I am doing on the floor of this tiny hut.

Then a voice calls out, 'Ahmed, Ahmed.'

My friend groans but does not answer.

'Ahmed,' the voice calls again, and someone bangs our door. This time Ahmed's shrill voice shouts a reply.

'What's going on?' I whisper to Mohammed.

'They want Ahmed to crew one of the fishing boats.'

Ahmed gets up and stumbles to the other end of the hut, where he lights a candle. In its light I see it is four fifteen. As my pulse starts to settle I watch him dress, noticing he puts on two pairs of trousers. He washes his face and hands and then shoves bread and processed cheese into a plastic bag. With that in his hand and a lighted cigarette between his lips he disappears out into the gloom of early morning, leaving Mohammed and me to our slumbers on the floor.

5

Days and Nights Along the Coast

For I have learned
  To look on nature not as in the hour
Of thoughtless youth; but hearing oftentimes
  The still sad music of humanity

                              William Wordsworth

I am woken again at about half past seven by the sound of Mohammed lighting the cooker. I lie for some time watching him. He is enormously house-proud and busies himself tidying pots and pans and sweeping round the far end of the hut. Soon he has made tea, pouring it out in the usual way to mix the sugar. When he brings a glass across to me I push back the blanket and stand, bruised and stiff.

Mohammed offers cold water for washing, taking me outside into the passageway already bright in early sun. I notice straight away the contrast of deep blue sky with the green of sea below us, and the freshness of air after so many cigarettes in the confined space of the hut. He passes me a small packet of Tide which he calls 'Teed'. Presuming this is instead of soap, I shake some onto my hands while he pours water to wet them and in due course rinse them using the bare minimum each time. All water has to be carried, as I have said, from the well half a mile away.

I ask Mohammed if he has a mirror. The answer is no, but he will borrow one. He disappears off to another hut and comes back with a tiny round one in which he peers at himself. It suddenly strikes me that people like him never see a mirror in the normal course of events and therefore must hardly know what they themselves look like. What a glorious contrast to Europe!

My friend finds a stale loaf, which he breaks into pieces, handing one to me. We squat together round the teapot, eating the bread and sipping the glasses of tea as it cools. He tells me that Ahmed

32

usually goes fishing with the dawn fleet, and will probably get back at about ten o'clock. He hopes that he himself will go out that afternoon, not because he likes it, but because he needs the money.

While we are having tea, or rather breakfast, I decide to catch a bus back to my *chambre* to shave and check my belongings. I say goodbye to Mohammed and tip him for feeding me and allowing me to stay the night. I then take the steps down to the beach and set out to walk the length of it to the road.

It is about eight thirty. I have seldom been on a beach at such an early hour. I find myself uplifted by the feeling of freshness, clearness of atmosphere, sharpness of colours. Needless to say there is no one about except a couple of distant figures by the *barques* beyond the high-tide line. To my front a huge expanse of sand without a single footprint stretches as far as the eye can see. I take off my shoes and walk along the edge of the waves. The sea is cold at first, but after a few seconds I get used to it.

To start with, the sight of the beach and the intense freshness on this May morning gives me a sense of elation. But as I walk my mind starts turning and I am suddenly filled with deep depression. The cause of it is the two boys. This is probably the first time in my life I have come into such direct contact with real poverty. That in itself is not what upsets me. It is the cycle in which they are trapped that seems so hopeless.

Both are bright but neither has completed his education so they have no qualifications of any sort. Money from fishing just about keeps them alive while healthy, but there is nothing left to improve their lot. They tell me in detail about the lack of jobs and how any that come up in the rural areas always go to friends, or friends of friends. But they have no friends with jobs or influence to help them. I wonder where they will be in ten years' time.

What causes me the greatest sadness is the enthusiasm of Mohammed. Having watched him take such trouble inside the hut, I wonder what it is within him that makes him do so. With no prospects and nothing to look forward to, surely the temptation must be to let standards slip, and degenerate into little better than an animal governed by basic instincts of survival. Yet Mohammed's face and bright slanting eyes have an enthusiasm and keenness which is at once admirable and pitiable.

And what of their emotional lives? How strange in a way to find two boys, barely adolescent, who have left their homes in the

33

mountains and come to live together in this tiny hut, at the mercy of the *barque patrons*. I wonder how many British boys would manage to cope unguided with all domestic chores, and exist with no help whatever from family or state. I am sure many would rise to the occasion, but it is the very youth of these two that sparks my melancholy.

I wonder whether they miss their families, and whether they have ever received or given real affection. They clearly have no contact with women as none live in this fishing community. Their close relationship is touching, but what do their minds turn to in the quiet moments? What are their hopes for the future? Viewed from my perspective, it is hard to see their lives as anything more than hopeless, and that I find most depressing.

Eventually I reach the road. Out in the bay several *barques* cling together in a small group. Ahmed is probably in one of them. It must be almost time for the fishermen to head back to the beach. The ones that have outboards are all right but I sympathise with those that have to row all the way against a falling tide. I remember a *pêcheur* showing me the thick pads of skin across his palms, the result of years of rowing with rough oars. It also strikes me how cold it must be in those open boats before dawn, particularly if the legs have got wet during launching. No wonder Ahmed wears two pairs of trousers.

🌴🌴   🌴🌴   🌴🌴

Very little traffic shows on the road, but in the end a bus dips down the far side of the valley and makes its way towards me. Bus-stops as such do not exist. People who want a lift simply wave and the bus halts. I duly do so myself and am soon spinning along the coast road, dropping down to follow along the back of deserted beaches, then climbing the headlands between them.

I plan on a quick change-round at the village. An hour later, my spirits revived, I am coming back in the opposite direction, having shaved, checked my belongings and bought lunch. I head for another beach beyond the one of the previous day, unable to resist the temptation to see around just one more headland. It does not disappoint and I spend another good day in the solitude and heat.

In late afternoon, saturated by sun, I decide to walk back to Mohammed's hut for tea. I am in no hurry so wander along the edge of the sea, examining shells and even small fish washed up by the tide. Further south, I have sometimes found dead turtles on the beach – a sorry sight, particularly after the razor-sharp beaks of

34

seagulls have done their worst. Just occasionally on this beach I find large and most unattractive jellyfish of unknown type, stranded above the water-line. Horrible to meet out swimming. Certainly if looks are anything to go by, they must be lethal. On another beach I once saw one the size of a football, or *ballon*, as Moroccans say. To step on that would mean curtains for me just from the wobbly texture of its mass!

I meet Mohammed on the road by his hut. When he sees me his face lights up with genuine pleasure and he welcomes me with a kiss. I am touched and glad that I have returned. He invites me for tea, saying that Ahmed has been summoned back to his parents in the mountains, although quite how he has been summoned it is hard to imagine as no telephones exist in this rural community. I ask Mohammed if he has been fishing, and then get a big disappointment. No, he has not been fishing. With the money I gave him he has taken the bus into Agadir and bought hashish. I save comment until later so as not to spoil the moment.

On his way back from Agadir, Mohammed stopped off at Mustafa's. The brothers are apparently planning a musical session this evening, and are very happy for me to come along. He suggests supper at his place and then a walk across the beach to the rendezvous. It will be too late for me to get back to my *chambre* afterwards so I can spend the night in his hut again.

Despite bruised hips, I agree, although there is one slight problem. During my time back in Tarhazoute this morning I bumped into the 'maid' Aziz, who told me that Hassan is having a special dinner this evening and would I come? Against better judgement I tentatively agreed but now feel I must get back and cancel so as not to let them down. I also want to see my landlord to retain the *chambre* a couple of extra days. I explain this to Mohammed, saying I will leave now, hurry back to the village, sort things out, and then get the last bus back along the coast.

Realising the clock is against me, I finish tea and get up to leave. Mohammed asks if I will buy a few dirhams of meat to add to his menu, meat of course being a great luxury. 'Just buy ten dirhams' worth.' I ask what sort but he says it does not matter. I walk up onto the road and am soon on a bus back down this by-now familiar route.

Hassan is quickly squared. As Aziz has not yet donned his outfit and started preparing dinner, I am thanked for letting them know, with no hard feelings. Shaving things and pullover are soon packed, then I find the butcher, a rather unfriendly soul, asking him as I have been instructed. I might have known it is not a good way of doing business. The meat which is meant to be a treat for Mohammed

35

turns out to be quite disgusting to the extent that it is inedible as far as I am concerned. It would have been more sensible to ask a friendly local to buy it for me, but this is my first attempt at such an enterprise.

🌴🌴　　🌴🌴　　🌴🌴

I do not know the precise time of the last bus – no one does for sure – but I am a little apprehensive as I leave the butcher and start out of the village on the coast road. I decide to walk about a mile. If a bus or taxi has not come by then, it will be just about dark so I will turn back and call it a day.

The evening is beautiful although for some time I have noticed a stronger wind than usual blowing on-shore which is by now rustling in the scrub and singing in my ears when they face the sea. The sun hovers just above the horizon as if willing itself to stay aloft long enough to light me back along the coast. As I clear the village the evening prayer is called from the minaret of the mosque by the bus-stop. '*Allah Akabar, Allah Akabar*, God is Great.'

The road is single-lane tarmac, hewn out of rock with scrub and argans clinging either side against all odds. Soon I am alone and making good time despite no sign of a bus.

Turning a corner, I unexpectedly find a group of mules and donkeys walking towards me across the road. That in itself is not unusual, but what is special about this is that the three old men and four boys with them are wearing colourful traditional dress rather than working clothes, and someone is banging a drum. The donkeys, draped in bright saddle-blankets, carry musical instruments of various kinds. On one, sticking up from its saddle, is a pole flying a large ornamental flag of great age. Quite by chance I have stumbled into a travelling troupe of musicians and dancers! And what a picturesque sight with the golden setting sunlight on their clothes, and Atlantic rollers breaking against the coast behind them. Annoyingly I know the light is no good for a photo.

We greet each other and pause. They are, I think, as surprised to meet a single European on foot on this lonely road as I am to come across them, the successors to the wandering minstrels or troubadours of the Middle Ages. I learn later that the men play instruments while the boys dance or perform acrobatics. I ask if they are going to Tarhazoute as I am most anxious to see them. As far as I can make out, they will stay there several days, so I decide I can afford to miss their performance this time and catch it later.

When they move off, the old man beats a slow rhythm on the

36

drum. The others turn in their saddles and wave as I watch them disappear – strange ships that pass in the twilight.

By the time this dramatic but welcome interlude is over, the sun is crouching in the water and only ten minutes of light remain. I am in a dilemma. I have seen no sign of either bus or taxi, in fact virtually nothing has moved on the road at all, and Mohammed's hut is at least 14 kilometres along the coast.

An instinct for self-preservation tells me to return to the village and the safety of my *chambre*, but two other thoughts crowd my mind. The first is the memory of the undisguised pleasure of Mohammed when I reappeared at his house this afternoon. I do not want to let him down. The second is my maxim of living dangerously to stave off middle age. A walk along the coast road in the dark seems to offer greater possibilities than an early night in the village. My watch says eight o'clock. The decision made, I adjust my bag and set off at speed.

A few hundred metres ahead I know there to be a ruined building, sitting on its own on a small headland. I have seen it during the day and thought what a charming private house it would make. What I have also noticed are several wild dogs living in the derelict outbuildings, so it is with a degree of caution that I approach. Some light remains in the sky and I decide they will be less afraid if they can see what is coming.

I spot them from some way off so show myself and walk noisily down the middle of the road. In the gloom two of them raise their heads. Will they feel threatened? Worse still, might they have rabies? A few anxious moments as they stare in my direction and my chest tightens; then the ruse seems to work. I pass observed but unchallenged.

The first headland rises steeply. Again I know this because from the bus spectacularly high cliffs can be seen on the seaward side. As I climb, the wind becomes more insistent. Whether it has in fact increased, or whether a slight change in direction has made it more apparent, I cannot tell. I walk on, taking pleasure from the threads of silver which edge a single line of cloud high in the heavens. How strange it is that sky which has been such a hard blue all day can suddenly turn so thin and clear and totally infinite just before dark. I stop for a moment to remove my jacket. Even at night this walk will be hot and it will be worth having something warm to put on at the other end.

On reaching the headland the road winds down through rock to the next cove. This one too I know, having once bathed there early in the morning. About 2 kilometres of sand with no boats or fishermen, just a solitary house overlooking the road. By now the remaining light has almost gone. Up on the headland the force of wind drowns the sound of the sea, but as I sink towards the beach the remorseless rushing of surf is clearly audible. Indeed the whiteness of foam shows along the shore long after all else is lost in darkness.

Again a steep climb to get over the next headland. The road twists and turns between argan trees and rock. It is warm work but round the headland the wind strikes, quickly cooling the sweat on my body. Rather late in the day I start to wonder if I might not be foolish to be undertaking this walk without drinking-water as there must be every possibility of serious dehydration. The wind has definitely got up. By the time I reach the top the only sound is a drumming in my ears.

Suddenly a car swings round the corner behind me, its lights picking out the road and twisted scrub. As it draws level the glow of instruments inside reminds me how comfortable it would have been to have made this journey in such secure ease. But soon the lights are way down the hill, the sound of the engine long since swallowed by the wind. I am alone again high above the sea.

I push on, noting it is now nearly nine o'clock. I do not want to be too late in case Mohammed gives up waiting and cooks supper without me.

Back once more at sea-level, I become conscious of the lowering of noise. Protected from the wind, I can hear again the backdrop of waves and countless crickets calling in the verges. Overall it is a relief to get away from that constant battering.

Virtually no traffic has moved on the road all evening, perhaps half a dozen cars only. It is not until several days later that I hear of the danger of doing this sort of thing. When I tell some *pêcheurs* that I have walked along the coast at night, they say it is most unwise. One or two bad incidents have happened in the past. The danger stems, not from people lying in wait, but from a passing car with several passengers, probably high, noticing a lone traveller and deciding on an impulse to relieve him of his possessions. Maybe I am naïve, but as I have so far met with nothing but honesty and good-will I have never seriously considered danger of this sort.

Another bay, another dark headland, but as I reach the next rise I know there is not far to go. To my front some kilometres up the coast, the beam from a lighthouse comes into view, circling every few seconds and casting strange reflections into the warm sea air. I

38

turn to look behind towards the distant glow of Agadir. It gives me a huge sense of satisfaction to think that I could be sitting there in luxury in some smart hotel, drink in hand, surrounded by German and French tourists. But I have done all that before. As it is, I am alone with the night; the sea and solitary coast are my only companions; a salt wind off the Atlantic is buffeting my body and an unknown prospect lies ahead.

I smile to myself and hurry on.

6

A Little Night Music

Sweep thy faint strings, Musician,
  With thy long lean hand,
Downward the starry tapers burn,
  Sinks soft the waning sand...

Walter de la Mare

I decide to stay on the road for the final few kilometres and only cut across the sand at the last moment. The going will be better on tarmac. In the far distance lights from the holiday houses near Mohammed flicker but are then obscured by the headland. A deep thirst begins to gnaw at my stomach – not surprising as I must have lost a lot of liquid from sweat and the drying wind. At this speed I will have completed about 12 kilometres in an hour and a half, which is reasonable. It gives me a sense of satisfaction to know that despite difficulties I have not let Mohammed down.

The first group of fishermen's houses appears with a light blinking unexpectedly in one of the little shops. I head straight for it. A gas lamp hisses on the counter, circled by moths and other insects of various sizes, its light reflecting outwards to nearby palms swaying strange shadows in the wind. Looking half asleep, the proprietor peers blankly into the dark at my approach. I buy a large bottle of orange and drink most of it on the spot. When I tell him I have walked from the village, it is difficult to tell whether the look on his face is one of admiration or pity. At any rate I wish him '*bon soir*' and start off on the last lap of my journey.

After a kilometre I turn off the road near the well where Mohammed and Ahmed draw their water, and start across the beach towards their steps. Nearer the sea the wind grows stronger. I can hear and then see that the waves are now a lot bigger than this morning when I walked away from the hut. Twelve hours ago seems an age and there will now be no fishing tomorrow.

In the dark I find the bottom of the steps up to the hut. I start to climb, flicking my cigarette lighter a couple of times to find the way. Soon I am at the door and to my relief able to see light inside. I think Mohammed has given up waiting. He kisses me when I appear and is doubly delighted when I produce the meat, neither of us being at that stage aware of its quality.

While he cooks supper I rest my tired legs and take on more liquid. Sitting at one end of the hut, the sweat drying on my body, a cigarette going and the candlelight flickering on the walls, I am suddenly filled with a marvellous sense of contentment.

I mentioned the poor standard of the meat. I am sorry, not for myself but for Mohammed, who eats fish often but for whom decent meat would be a real treat. When the food is finished I prop myself against the wall while he washes up. Despite earlier advice I have brought a couple of tins of beer, which we enjoy while Mohammed gets out cigarette paper and rolls himself a joint. We sit in silence while he savours it.

I have no intention of interfering in the young man's life. I know anyway that my chances of influencing him are slim. I do, however, feel I must raise the subject once and then keep quiet, so I ask why he smokes. Naturally he says it is because he enjoys it. When I press him by pointing out all the more worthwhile things he could spend his money on, his reply is straightforward. He says without a trace of self-pity that he is a poor person who leads a hard but simple life. There are many luxuries in the world which he cannot even dream of because he knows he will never have them. If he gets money from time to time he allows himself hash as about the only pleasure he can afford. It does no harm. It has a calming effect. It keeps him out of trouble.

I tell him I understand that, but would he not get more long-lasting pleasure from, say, a radio? But the more we talk the more I can see that the sort of long-term planning and balancing of priorities that we do are not part of the thought processes of someone living a real hand-to-mouth existence. If the opportunity presents itself for temporary escape from a no-hope environment it has to be grabbed. There may not be others. There is little point in making an issue of it so I suggest we walk over to Mustafa.

🌴🌴   🌴🌴   🌴🌴

Coming out into the blustering darkness is unpleasant at first after our cosy little room. Also I feel tired from all the walking I have done not only this evening but during the day as well. One major compensation is the simply magnificent panoply of stars. An hour earlier I hardly noticed them, but now the sky is so full of little flickering dots that I ask Mohammed to stop while I wonder at them. I have seen stars in both hemispheres and in the tropics, but I really cannot remember seeing quite such a profusion before. And they are not just up in the heavens, dipping equally thickly to the horizon. Hardly a single space is left for more. As I gaze I find myself trying to recall who it was who said that stars are the diamonds of the poor. Memory fails me, but standing alone with Mohammed in this small corner of Africa it seems curiously apt.

Once I have absorbed them we walk across the sand, more or less back the way I have just come, towards Mustafa's house. Despite no moon, the ambient light makes navigation easy. Round the house, palms sway perilously, their leaves clattering as the wind tears through them. We knock on the door. After a pause, Mustafa welcomes us in. With a torch he leads us across a courtyard and into a large room. The silence and soft light inside make such a contrast to the stormy beach. Mustafa's elder brother, another man of negroid appearance, and one who looks remarkably like Great Train Robber Ronald Biggs, are squatting against the wall, the smell of kif hanging unmistakably in the air. A candle burns on a high stick in the centre of the room, throwing a diffused light which seems appropriate to the occasion. I sit down between Mohammed and Mustafa.

The black man gets up and goes to an old fertiliser sack, from which he produces a set of tom-toms for Mustafa and a tambourine for Mohammed. I have heard Mustafa play the tom-toms before, but he carries out a few preliminaries which make an amazing sound. Impressive what can be done with such an insignificant instrument. The black man plays a guitar and Mustafa's brother a banjo. The inevitable session of tuning the one to the other begins while Mustafa and Mohammed get out cigarette paper and roll joints. Then a pause while these are passed round at least a couple of times before everyone is ready.

I have mentioned before my liking for Berber music. These people are not beginners and have clearly played a lot together. As soon as they start I can see that Mustafa's brother is equally proficient with the banjo as he is with the guitar. Their friend is also very able, while the backing from the others produces a strong rhythm. Ronald Biggs has a faraway look in his eyes as he and Mustafa's brother lead the singing.

Apart from the tremendous rhythm of Berber music, it does have this strange, etherial sound – magical and mysterious. I long to

42

know the subjects of the songs. What are these high pitched, sad-sounding words about? During one of the frequent pauses for joints I ask Mustafa.

'What are they singing about? Is it the mountains, the sea, love, life? What?'

'No, no, these songs are about *les Palestiniens.*'

Oh dear. What a disappointment. It is not until now that I realise that the fate of the Palestinians, which I assume to be very much an eastern Mediterranean, Arabian problem, is equally keenly felt at this end of the Islamic world.

The brothers play for a couple of hours, the music interspersed with breaks for smokes. In some songs just two of them sing, while in others, clearly old favourites, they all join, Mohammed turning out to be as tuneful as the others. I have noticed before that next to football, singing and dancing seem to be the favourite pastimes of Moroccans, their natural lack of inhibition allowing them to take advantage of any excuse to do so. Although they know I do not understand the words, they make a point of including me with nods and smiles so that I never feel left out.

The evening wears on, the candle grows smaller, flickering in the centre of the room, the atmosphere thickens with heady smoke. I do not ask again the subjects of the songs. The rhythms become slower and more mournful, and I begin to feel drowsy. That mysterious haunting sound seems to get inside one's head and play with the imagination. I cannot understand the words. I do not want them to be about politics or the problems of this world. As far as I am concerned they carry within them the spirit of solitary mountains, arid valleys and a proud, independent people. The spirit of a world more noble than the one to which I am accustomed and from which for a few snatched days I have managed to escape.

One last song, one last joint; it is finally time to leave. We say goodbye and go out into the night where the wind is still rattling the palms around the house. The silhouette of mountains seems so close as to cut us off from the rest of the world. I stand for a moment looking out across the beach and up at the sky. Do the stars seem all the brighter? Does the sound of breaking waves carry in it the rhythms of the music? Perhaps.

Mohammed and I walk slowly home across the sands. It has been marvellous to hear the music and a great privilege to be for a short time almost one of these wonderful people.

7

L'Amour

There is a rapture on the lonely shore,
There is society, where none intrudes,
By the deep sea, and music in its roar:
I love not man the less, but Nature more...

George Gordon, Lord Byron

'You like six?' In a hired car I was on the coast road and against better judgement had stopped for a youth who had tried to thumb me down and then chased after the car when I passed. Mid-teens, tall and incredibly thin, his unusual brown hair was streaked blond by the sun. Despite meagre clothes and poor appearance he looked harmless, so I relented and pulled to the side of the road.

'Where are you going?' I asked as he appeared breathless at my window.

'I am going to Agadir please.' His French was not good.

I cleared the passenger seat and soon we were climbing a steep hill between one beach and the next.

'Six what?' I asked to his question.

'You like six?' he repeated. Not understanding, I mumbled something and drove on.

'You like six with me?' he asked again, reaching over and placing his hand on my thigh. I glanced across to see he was holding himself with the other, smiling shamelessly.

'No, I'm OK thanks.' Without taking my eyes off the road I pushed his hand away.

🌴 🌴 🌴

That incident had occurred on my first trip to Agadir, when I stayed in a smart hotel. I was subsequently joined by a girl-friend from

44

England, and together we drove north towards Essouira. Where the High Atlas dip into the Atlantic the road is forced to follow the coast, and once clear of the suburbs of Agadir passes a series of brilliant beaches. Apart from three villages, including Tarhazoute, these beaches are empty except for a few fishermen's huts and boats. Other than on Sundays, when many young Moroccans come out to swim and play on the sands, they are deserted.

During that first visit my girl-friend and I stopped at one beach where it was possible to park the car at the edge of a small cliff and lie on the sand within sight of it. I did this because the area was isolated and I wanted to keep an eye on the car. So private, though, was the beach that she was able to go topless, something generally unthinkable in an Islamic country.

On my fourth leave I head once more for Tarhazoute to rent the room with a view for a couple of nights before trying my luck elsewhere. I want to see if I can find the beach I discovered with my girl-friend even though now I am alone and without a car. In the village I catch a long-distance taxi of the type common throughout Africa which make up a random load of strangers all going in the same direction. By eleven I have found the beach and am lying on it with a book and food. I spend a solitary couple of hours swimming and reading and then sit in the sun to have lunch.

At some stage I happen to turn and notice two figures walking along the cliff. I carry on eating, keeping track of them out of the corner of my eye. From their loose-limbed movement I can tell they are kids. When level with me they drop down onto the sand and approach. They come up, say hello, and then sit unbidden on a nearby rock. It does not take long to get into conversation and for me to discover that one of them, Abdulla, cannot speak French. His 'brother' Mohammed does the talking, turning every now and then to give an update in Berber.

This is an early introduction to a figure of speech met frequently in the Islamic world – namely the use of the term brother. As often as not the 'brother' is not a real brother at all, but a close friend or distant relative. Similarly 'he is family' is a much used expression which designates something more vague than in our usage – possibly just from the same village or tribe rather than of the same blood.

Mohammed speaks good French and is intelligent. We discuss all the usual things about where I come from, where I am staying, where they live and what they do. This turns out to be not much, although it seems they play a great deal of football and also go out with the squid fishermen to earn a few dirham. After a while, Abdulla says he is leaving.

The roar of surf is making conversation difficult so Mohammed moves closer. I offer him a cigarette and we continue talking, touching on subjects as diverse as the fact that the *pêcheurs* dislike calm weather because it keeps the squid far out, to which British football team I support. He talks easily with an engaging manner.

Somewhere between adolescence and manhood, Mohammed claims to be 20 although his youthful complexion belies this. Shorter than me, he has neat features and thick dark eyebrows. He wears jeans and a patterned shirt open to the waist. When a pause finally comes he stands to my front, fixing me with a direct look.

'Monsieur, veux tu faire l'amour?'

What's that? Have I heard him right?

Despite the earlier experience with the hitch-hiker, his offer of sex comes right out of the blue and for a moment I am stunned. The most astonishing thing is the total lack of embarrassment as if he is suggesting nothing more than a walk down the beach or a quick game of football.

Perhaps I should simply say no, but curiosity overcomes me and I find myself asking where. He says up beyond the road in the mass of argan trees which grow between mountains and sea. There are many secret places he knows where no one ever goes.

Having established what I think is a good rapport, I am not certain how to proceed. I explain in faltering French that my activities in this field are restricted to women, but he is not put off.

'You told me you are *célibataire*, bachelor.' He speaks as if that excludes women from my life. It is clearly time I took the initiative.

'Is that the reason why you came over in the first place?' Yes it is.

'Does Abdulla do the same thing?' Yes, but he is young. He is just starting.

'How often does this happen?' Not much, apparently, during the week because of the fishing, but at weekends he cruises the beaches in search of tourists – German mainly and sometimes French. Still amazed because he looks so fresh, I ask what exactly he means by *'faire l'amour'*.

A shy smile betrays the first embarrassment.

'Ce que tu veux.' Whatever you want.

The tide is coming in. A larger wave than most throws itself amongst the rocks at our feet, chasing in and around in a flurry of foam until quickly spent.

'You make love with women too?'

'Yes.'

'Moroccan or tourists?'

'No, no, tourists.'

Of course, it would be unthinkable with local girls, or 'gazelles' as they are colloquially called. I ask if he expects money from those he seduces.

'*Bien sûr.*' He tells me he can earn the equivalent of a week's wage for half an hour of *plaisir*. Recently, he was with a French couple. After frolicking with both, the husband told him to continue with the wife so he could record it on video. Mohammed says he did so but only after negotiating a larger fee as he knew the man would sell the film back in France! Later this very evening he is going to Agadir to see a German 'friend'.

Oh dear!

I wonder if he has considered the danger of AIDS, or SIDA, as it is in French. He makes out that he is careful and always uses a *capot*, although his words are unconvincing. I get the feeling that were I in a position to pull a *capot* out of my pocket here and now, he would not even recognise it.

For some time we talk round the subject, me having never before met anyone in this line of business. It is soon obvious that he is not remotely gay in the European sense and in a few years from now he will be happily married. Right now though, *l'amour* provides the simple solution to his two biggest needs. I just hope that he will get a proper job before becoming addicted to this lifestyle – or anyway before catching SIDA. The problem is that jobs are hard to come by. For people of his age *l'amour* is the easy option.

Deciding the conversation has gone far enough, I go in for a swim. Mohammed lies watching like a cat watches a mouse before the kill. I am sure he still sees me as prey. In fact I can almost sense a current between us as if he is willing me to accept his offer. Eventually he too comes in, raising my hopes that the diversion and cold water will dampen his enthusiasm. But when I tell him I must return to the village he says he will come as my guide.

By now it is four o'clock; the sun is still hot but sinking, the white light of mid-day turning to rich gold of evening. To reach the road we must climb the cliff and then pass through a mass of argans. The trees are the size of olives but with branches spread wider, creating a pool of dappled shade on the earth beneath.

Still in our swimming things, we set off, Mohammed balancing the bag of clothes on his shoulder. I watch as he starts up the cliff. Like most young Moroccans he is incredibly slender with not an ounce of spare flesh. But he is agile and strong, making light of a difficult climb despite the bag and bare feet. He waits for me at the top before we begin through the trees.

To our left, hills covered in scrub rise sharply into the Atlas. On our right, green sea heaves and dances in the sun, rollers cruising effortlessly towards the foot of the cliffs. Every now and then we come to a small dried-up stream, which means picking our way down the side and catching glimpses of the beach before climbing again through the trees. It is warm work although we are wearing very little.

After a while we stop beneath a large argan perched on the edge of the cliff. The place is like an eagle's nest looking along the coast both ways and down to where waves wash the sands below. We pause in the shade then sit on the bare earth for cigarettes. Apart from the buzzing of crickets and the whisper of the tide, the whole world hangs silent and motionless, brooding in late afternoon heat. We do not speak. Such magic needs no comment.

For a while Mohammed seems as entranced as I, but eventually the spell has to be broken. When we move on we soon reach another beach, behind which is a cluster of fishermen's shacks where I know the bus must pass. We say goodbye among the argans and I tip my guide for his help. Despite the unusual circumstances of our meeting, I have enjoyed his company.

I climb down onto the beach for another swim. It is late but there is no chance of a bath back in the village and I feel in need of one. The sea seems warmer in the cooling sun, the sand firm and coarse between my toes. I wash, in the way I have seen the locals, and then rinse in the surf. Before dressing I walk for some way along the shore to dry, but also to make the most of the solitude and freedom.

Fingers of shadow reach across the sand from outcrops of rock along the cliff. Ahead the beach stretches more than a mile with no sign of anything made by man. The roar of surf deafens, diffusing the turmoil of thoughts still crowding my mind as a result of the meeting with Mohammed. It has been one of those afternoons when England seems so very different and so very far away. When almost dry I reluctantly pull on jeans and a shirt and head for the road.

8

Wind, Sea and the Sound of Silence

With the wild fig for thy canopy, the marigolds thy quilt,
And, to serve thee for a lullaby, the thunder of the sea.

Laurence Hope

Where I work in Laayoune, on the seaboard edge of the Sahara, the wind blows for nine months of the year. During that time, still days sometimes occur, but so seldom that for Europeans anyway they are a talking point. Further north, around Agadir, the wind can also be persistent except in summer. In winter the prevailing wind blows from the North, but in summer it is replaced by a dry scirocco coming in off the desert.

The only effective headgear against this wind is the turban, wrapped round the crown of the head and then down over all exposed skin except the eyes. Most Moroccans have proper turbans made from a long length of cloth, although I see people wearing almost anything and everything on their heads for protection. The turban may be worn with traditional dress or equally well with jeans. Indeed, the sight of men on a building site dressed in working clothes but with black, blue or white turbans covering their heads, is picturesque.

It is not of course the wind itself that necessitates protection, but the grains of sand carried on it, which sting the skin and eyes. The wind can be very strong. When it is, the sand is not just an annoying inconvenience, it is extremely painful, making work outside impossible without cover. As far as the body is concerned, the seamless djellaba, as worn throughout Arabia under various names, is the ideal garment for keeping sand out of the folds and joins of Western clothes usually worn underneath nowadays.

Carried with such force, sand gets everywhere. Roads near sand dunes have to be cleared daily by bulldozer; pavements and patios

49

swept by hand; indoors needs constant dusting and sweeping even if windows have been kept shut; carpets must be hung up and beaten; cars accumulate sand inside and out. Fountains, should one be fortunate enough to find them, are quickly clogged.

On the frequent occasions when the wind blows hard for several days, sand gets drawn up into the sky, screening the sun and creating an eerie effect. Visibility drops to a few hundred metres or even less and it is impossible to tell the time of day. With the atmosphere smothered and the sun blocked out, a feeling of listlessness, almost foreboding, grips the countryside. Where colours are usually bright and sharp, they become matt. Shadows, essential for relief, are absent, giving an unfamiliar blandness to the landscape. Whether it is because of these factors, or simply the contrast from normal brightness, the scenery loses much of its appeal.

Before living in the Maghreb, I had not been aware of the persistence and force of the wind. I had always assumed that one of the pleasures of the desert must be the silence. The reality, particularly near the coast, is that since a wind is practically always blowing, complete silence is virtually impossible; always that drumming in the ears.

No doubt it is the wind that gives Moroccans such a negligent attitude to litter. If you know that no matter what precautions you take, the wind will eventually find a way to wrestle rubbish from any container, then probably the inclination to place it there in the first place dies within you. This attitude is inborn so that nobody makes the slightest effort to control litter. Usually it is dumped where it is used, or anywhere outside the house. As a result there are whole tracts of land on the leeward side of most villages festooned with every type of object that can be blown by wind. Worst offenders are small black polythene bags used by shop-keepers. These proliferate throughout the length and breadth of the country, hanging from trees, caught in the thorns of cacti and blown up against walls. Sometimes thermal currents will pick them up and whirl them so high they disappear from sight, only to swoop earthwards later like some sinister bird of prey.

On several occasions I have finished a packet of cigarettes and saved the carton to throw away later. Whoever is with me stares with disbelief as if I am quite mad not to drop it where I stand. It is pointless trying to explain. To a Moroccan it is beyond comprehension – a strange shortcoming in a people who take such trouble to create beautiful buildings and gardens.

I come to the conclusion that for sheer pleasure of contemplation perhaps the only sight more absorbing than the embers of a good log fire is the motion of the sea. During many days on the beach I have plenty of opportunity to study it.

One factor for which I can never account is the size of waves. I had imagined that a great wind meant more swell out to sea and therefore larger waves. However, this is not borne out by my observations. Some days when there is an imperceptible breeze and no sea-horses, the waves gather up far out and sweep majestically in towards the coast, starting their finale with a spectacular flourish some distance from shore. On other occasions when from the cliffs the conditions at sea look much the same, waves do not start to form until much closer, washing onto the beach with little impression. More often than not, the sea alternates between the two. Quiet and docile for many minutes, it suddenly undergoes a period of intense activity, quickly building up to a flurry of noise and fury which signifies nothing but is calculated, or so it seems, to attract the attention to anyone stirring along the shore.

Most of the beaches around Agadir are several kilometres long and relatively shallow. This means that waves approach on a wide front, gradually increasing in size and definition. Out in the bay they cue at a leisurely pace, but the speed of their advance increases as their destiny approaches. When it finally arrives they will break once far out and then re-form for a final gasp nearer shore. Usually, therefore, two or three lines of foam are advancing up the beach in series at any one moment.

The resulting sound of this is quite different from our shelving northern beaches. On them the sound of individual waves can be counted quite precisely as they crash onto the shingle, followed by a pause as the expended water draws back, sucking and grating pebbles in its undertow. Then quite distinctly the crash of the next wave eclipses that of its predecessor as the sequence is repeated.

On beaches in Morocco, the crash of the wave making its initial break far out is hidden by those of subsidiary breaks nearer the listener. Instead of a series of distinct individual sounds there is a constant roar of surf in various stages of exhaustion with no perceptible change in volume.

It is often hard to find shade on the beach in the middle of the day. When the sun becomes too hot I climb the cliff and lie under the argan tree where Mohammed led me, watching large waves developing from embryos out in the Atlantic. As each wave gathers I try to guess where the first surf will show. Just when I think I detect a pattern, a maverick glides in and breaks all the rules. I presume their actions must bear some relationship to the sea-bed, but it is hard to be certain. To the best of my knowledge the sand is remarkably even. In places where rocks lurk out to sea these can be detected from my perch on the cliffs by splashes of purple beneath the surface. In most cases the only rocks are around the headlands.

One of my favourite moments is on those odd occasions when a long pause in waves of any significance is followed by the arrival of a single much larger one. Generally a succession of small ones leads to an overall decrease in the level of noise. Unless an observer happens at that particular moment to be watching, the lowered decibels will cause him to momentarily forget that he is standing on the last land before South Carolina. Suddenly an audible crack. Startled, he looks up. Two hundred metres from shore is a low wall of green water, teetering on the verge of collapse. In just one place the crest has already fallen, crashing ahead of itself with an unforgettable sound – the crack that has just resounded along the beach. It is a sound I grew to love.

Perfect in mid-summer, the water of the Moroccan Atlantic is a pleasant temperature for swimming even on Christmas Day. However, the Canaries Current runs south from the Bay of Biscay to this part of the coast and can bring a nasty chill right inshore. Some days this makes the water noticeably colder than others but it is not something one can easily predict. Luckily the sun is generally hot enough to warm the top couple of metres and also to quickly revive anyone after swimming.

Along the coast a strong off-shore breeze has an impressive effect. On large rollers far out, a thin spray of water starts to stream back against the direction of the wave like snow blown from the top of a glacier. As the waves race for shore, this spray defies the mass beneath it and dances perversely across the surface. I spend ages watching surf from the tops of waves being lifted up and thrown back out to sea even as the mass of water beneath it hurtles up the beach. Swimming in these conditions is no fun.

The sea of the Atlantic coast is unexpectedly powerful; the waves really can knock a grown man over and, by the same token, enable someone who knows what he is doing to surf 50 metres or more without a board. Often a strong current pulls the swimmer sideways so that piles of clothes left on the sand soon turn to specks down the beach. Nothing too dramatic but worth a degree of caution, particularly when alone.

Not surprisingly, perhaps, for someone who has never lived near the coast, I begin to find the noise of the sea faintly intrusive. Whenever I spend the day on the beach I am subjected to it constantly; my *chambre* in the village is within a few metres of the high-water mark; the various huts of *pêcheurs* where I sleep along the coast are always near to where their *barques* are drawn up on the sand. In other words in this part of Morocco the whole business of my day and night is conducted against the blanket sound of running surf. One day I have a longing to escape and find real silence.

Opposite the little kiosk I sometimes visit when walking the coast road, I have noticed a wonderfully secluded valley running inland towards the mountains. Despite no sign of a village, a well-used track leads off the main road, indicating human habitation up there somewhere. Clearly defined fields hug the road though nothing grows there, possibly due to the time of year.

Scattered among these fields stand large argan trees, their branches providing oases of shade. The argan is a fascinating tree, being found in only one place in the world, namely the coastal belt of the Sous valley around Agadir. Similar in appearance to the olive, it is a slow grower so those with a girth of more than 4 metres may be over a hundred years old.

Although the foliage is protected by stiff thorns, the trees are the favourite haunt of marauding goats often seen grazing 5 or 6 metres up. The yellow fruit is the size of an olive, the kernel producing oil used in cooking. To me the argan has become a symbol for this part of Morocco.

The head of the secluded valley is high, though nothing like as high as the real Atlas further inland. Up the sides are other trees and scrub which I know well by sight but not name. Towards the top of the hills these trees and scrub thin, exposing summits of cracked pink rock. What attracts me to the valley is the appearance it gives of total solitude. Whenever I look at it I get a feeling of dry, brooding, silence. I want to go there.

My moment comes when a sudden scirocco strikes along the coast, making beach life intolerable. The sea is too dangerous for swimming or fishing, more particularly the wind is picking up loose sand and driving it back across the beach. When it does so, the edge of each receding wave becomes instantly dry as it is doused by flying particles. Sand is stinging my face and the noise of wind drowns even that of the sea. An excellent day for a walk inland.

As I set off towards the shop, I pass a line of eucalyptus bucking and sawing in the wind. Dead leaves and broken greenery join with paper and polythene rubbish to fly across the road, pausing for respite only if they can find somewhere to lodge. The aggravated surface of the sea sparkles so brightly it is impossible to watch without screwing up the eyes.

On reaching the shop, I am about to cross the road and start up the valley when I notice a group of half a dozen men praying, their djellabas flapping like washing on a line. Drinking a bottle of orange, I watch as they stand and kneel and bend forward and then kneel again. It is of course quite normal in Islamic countries to see people praying anywhere. Drivers, for example, may stop at the appropriate time of day and pray at the side of the road. I remember once taking lodgings somewhere and being welcomed by the Moroccan from the room next door. When I later went round to borrow a blanket, I walked through the opened door calling his name, only to find him on the floor in the middle of prayer – an embarrassing moment which taught me to give worshippers a wide berth.

As soon as these men have finished, I set off past them up the track. After a couple of hundred metres I look back and see them watching. Do I imagine it or are they shaking their heads in disbelief? The mad *Anglais* does it again. Where's he off to this time?

The track has a surface of baked red earth but no specific edge. Tyre marks indicate bicycles or scooters rather than cars, with donkey droppings, too, in evidence. Either side stand argans which, though growing in no particular order, look from their number to have been planted on purpose. Old trees now with trunks thick and gnarled.

As I climb further from the road, the wind seems to lose its constancy, finding its way up the valley in gusts and twisters. Every few minutes a cloud of dust and sand is picked up, rushed across open spaces and dashed into trees, rattling leaves and agitating shadows below. Other times it corkscrews up and circles over a particular spot, broadcasting dust into the air until spent.

It is by now five o'clock and the sun is dropping. The last bus back to my village is at six thirty, so only about half an hour remains before I must return to the road. Gradually the roar of surf recedes. The direction of the valley alters slightly and this seems to reduce the wind as well. Whether it is deflected or simply less strong further from the coast I am not sure. At any rate I am at last, after six days, finding a kind of silence. Just a little further and I will pause.

Of a sudden, two women appear round a bend in the track. In bright traditional clothes with faces uncovered, they talk loudly and I hear them before they come into sight. On seeing me, they giggle and then go silent. Berber women seldom cover their faces. They

54

may do so for protection from sun and sand but among men and strangers they show less of the modesty of their Arab cousins. These two are young and pretty, with olive skin and angular features. Had they been men it would be inconceivable to walk by without saying something, but I do not know what to expect from these two, who stare without embarrassment. White teeth and dark eyes flash in smiles but not a word is spoken as we draw level.

'*Bonjour*,' I try lamely. They are perhaps 15 or 16. Each mumbles something and giggles, then they are past. After a few seconds I turn. They are both looking back. One waves and I acknowledge her. It is not hard to imagine what they are saying, but I would love to know what excitements life has in store for them. I feel I have already learned a certain amount about the men of this part of the world, but with such strict segregation it seems unlikely I will ever find out about the women. Certainly in the country, girls of that age will never stop to talk to a stranger, even though flirtatious glances are not uncommon.

The moment I decide to stop coincides with a noticeable drop in the wind. As afternoon shadows lengthen, I find myself alone in something approaching silence. What a relief to have no intrusions – at long last I can savour the hills without distraction. Away from the seering sea winds the vegetation is noticeably greener, the argans now joined by wild figs and bushes of oleander. The oleander must be one of nature's gifts to desert regions, its pink or sometimes white flowers providing a striking profusion of colour all summer. Although favouring the dried-up beds of rivers or streams, it can survive almost anywhere, evergreen leaves providing abundant foliage throughout the year. Much of the oleander's pre-eminence stems from the fact that its leaves are poisonous and therefore almost unique in being immune to grazing by goats and sheep.

I am now beside a thicket of wild figs, their wide green leaves a tangle of lushness and shade. Finding a flat boulder to sit on, I light a cigarette.

For several minutes I sit lost in thought. I have always liked mountains. Although these hills are not the Atlas proper, they still have rocky peaks which stand solitary and silent in the baking sun; places where no one would ever go. Not even shepherds take flocks to such barren areas where scrub refuses to grow. I can see these peaks shimmering at midday. I can also picture them keeping silent vigil at night – timeless and solitary, known only to the Watchman of the Milky Way.

The Atlas Mountains take their name from the Titan of Greek mythology who, as punishment for his revolt against Zeus, was condemned forever to support the heavens on his head and shoulders. The task proving a trifle onerous, he begged Perseus to turn him to stone, and found himself transformed into a range of harsh and beautiful mountains. Presumably before this happened Atlas was married to Hesperis, who, for the ancient Greeks, personified the 'region of the west' or second paradise at the end of the known world. When exploration found this not to be the case, the location was presumed to have moved further towards the ocean which therefore took his name. Gerardus Mercator, who, at the end of the sixteenth century, made the first map of the world, used as a frontispiece a picture of the Titan, naming his work – an Atlas.

Amongst the trees where I am sitting the scene is quite domestic although even here the dryness of earth makes it far from benign. While I am contemplating the hills, my ear has begun to attune to the relatively unfamiliar sound of birdsong. Concentrating hard, I realise what marvellous noises are coming from the argans, full-throated calls bubbling from several trees. I peer into branches, trying to detect the singers. One looks remarkably like our own British blackbird with a similar call. Also a greenish yellow bird of sparrow dimensions in good voice nearby is not unlike a greenfinch in appearance, although I do not know the song. And more calls, new to me and therefore probably from distinctly African species.

As my ears probe the silence, I become aware of other sounds too which I had earlier missed. A flock of goats must be at large somewhere. Every so often I hear distant bleating as they scavenge among the trees. From the direction of the head of the valley, where I assume there to be a village, I catch the faint but familiar shouts of children at play. Annoying to get this far and not find the village, but I do not want to miss the last bus home. Somewhere back towards the coast a donkey brays, the unnatural noise forced and painful in such peaceful surroundings. It reminds me that I must start back. For a few more seconds I savour the solitude, then, throwing the bag over my shoulder, turn towards the coast.

Hardly have I done so when the peace is shattered by a deafening bang! Although clearly a shotgun, the closeness and suddenness take me completely by surprise and I am sure I jump! Not anxious to get shot but at the same time uncertain if I am trespassing, I hurry into an open space both to show myself and because no obvious target is to be seen there. A moment later a man appears in old clothes and turban, with a shotgun under his arm. In his hand he carries two dead partridge.

'*Bonjour, Monsieur,*' I call. He waves his gun in acknowledgement and soon I find myself in conversation, helped, no doubt, by the cigarette I offer him. For some time I admire the birds and then his gun and then ask about the strange variety of cartridges I can see poking out of a bandolier hanging loosely round his waist.

The largest, consisting of a single ball, are apparently for wild pig. I am aware that these live in the mountains but have never met one. He explains how dangerous they are, due to a pugnacious nature and vicious fangs, which I know to be true, having come across them in Zimbabwe. Interestingly, I hear later that mountain folk in Morocco usually eat the boar they shoot despite the fact that pork is not technically on the Moslem menu.

The next cartridge has three lead balls, used, he explains, for gazelle. Although I know these too exist in Morocco I have never seen one either and imagine they are very scarce. He assures me that he kills a few every year, although he agrees that their numbers are declining. Finally he pulls out a cartridge for jackal or foxes, both of which roam in large numbers all over North Africa, including the desert, where I have sometimes seen them.

The variety of wildlife to be encountered right down in the Sahara is in fact surprising. Apart from occasional snakes, we frequently see several varieties of lizard, some over half a metre long. Also rats and mice, rabbits and hares, foxes, jackal and even *inch'Allah*, butterflies. Also at large, but never seen by me, are hedgehogs and even the occasional ostrich!

Finally my new friend, by now on his, or rather my, third cigarette, pulls out the ordinary number six shot used for partridge. These delightful birds can be found throughout the foothills of the Atlas, normally in coveys of perhaps half a dozen. Similar but not identical to our English and French birds, I fancy they do not fly as well, although I have never seen them encouraged into the air Norfolk-style by a line of beaters and dogs.

By now I am beginning to worry about the bus. It has been an interesting interlude and I like the man even though his French is not easy to understand and frequently punctuated by a nasty cough and spit. He says he lives at the head of the valley and will I come home for tea? Sadly I feel compelled to thank him and decline, with the offer of a final cigarette, as the bus schedule is against me. When I set off, he takes my perch on the flat rock and sits contemplating the scene I have just enjoyed, my fourth cigarette between his lips.

It does not take me long to discover that the valley is indeed sheltered. As the track winds downhill, the gusts start once more, tops of trees swaying, long shadows gliding across the earth. I vaguely look out for the two Berber girls, assuming them to be tending goats somewhere among the trees. I never catch sight of them although I suspect they do see me.

Just where the track flattens, a donkey and rider come into sight – bulging panniers with the jockey perched between them, legs dangling down one side. As usual the animal is controlled by a long stick with which it is periodically beaten on either shoulder. I am always surprised at the ferocity of these beatings although I never see a donkey show any sign of complaint. This particular ensemble is approaching straight out of the sun so it is impossible to see more than the silhouette until they are very close. A few metres away the rider slips to the ground, a boy of about ten in an old djellaba with a tattered brown turban twisted round his head.

'*Bonjour, Monsieur.*' Soft olive skin and chalk-white teeth in an enchanting smile.

'*Bonjour. Ça va?*'

'*Oui Monsieur, ça va.*'

'Where are you going with that food?' The child goes on smiling but looks blank at my foolish question. He is probably like many of the poorer people who know certain stock phrases in French but cannot carry on a conversation. If I am right, then I also know what the next phrase will be, accompanied of course by a winsome look.

'*Monsieur, cinq dirham s'il vous plaît.* Five dirham please.'

For better or worse I am very weak-willed when it comes to such occasions. Whether it is the smile, the honest innocence of a direct question, even the whole magical scene of boy and donkey alone in the evening light, I cannot say. Indeed if I really think about it, I can probably come up with a much more prosaic explanation to do with a guilty conscience at the fortunate cards life has dealt me. I fish in my pocket for a suitable coin. Long dark lashes blink, wide eyes searching every movement. Even the donkey stands motionless with expectation. A 5-dirham coin comes fortuitously to hand and I hold it towards him. The boy walks carefully forward, watching intently lest at the last minute it should escape. He reaches out and picks it off my palm.

'*Merci, Monsieur,*' he smiles up at me. One unexpected step nearer and he offers his cheek. I kiss. He turns. In a second he has jumped back onto the donkey and struck a smart blow to its neck. I watch them move off and call goodbye when he turns to wave.

9

Tarfaya

Do you think there's a far border town somewhere
The desert's edge, last of the lands we know?

Rupert Brooke

On the coast some 500 kilometres south of Agadir, near the old border between Morocco and Spanish Sahara, sits the village of
Tarfaya. Apart from the Canary Islands just over the horizon, there
is nothing to the west for 5,000 kilometres except North Atlantic
Ocean. In the opposite direction, the Sahara Desert lies brooding
and empty for a similar distance.

On the map in my office my eye had frequently fallen on this
romantic-sounding village. It was reasonably close to where I
worked, so one day I decided to visit.

After an hour's drive through empty desert, I came to a crossroads and sign indicating the village. Turning left the road passed
between huge dunes of sand bleached white by sun. Quite suddenly
I topped a crest and the sea appeared to my front. A vast deserted
beach stretched for miles in both directions, great waves creating
line after line of surf as far as the eye could see. Through open windows the roar was deafening, but what immediately attracted my
attention was a number of large wrecked ships lying rusting along
the tideline. The whole picture was one of such grandeur that I
decided straight away that it deserved closer inspection – but I
would go to the village first.

Sitting as it does between desert and sea, Tarfaya gives the
impression of being perpetually under siege from sand. As I
approached, the road became less and less distinct. Smaller dunes
hovered along the edge, spilling onto the tarmac, the wind sending
their tops streaming across to join others piling up on the far side.
Driving on this sort of sand can be deceptive. Sometimes it is soft

59

and mobile, making bogging inevitable if the revs drop. On other occasions it somehow manages to pack itself hard and can give a nasty shock if hit at speed.

On an earlier occasion when I had tried to negotiate a rough track to a beach near Laayoune, my car had ground to a halt in a flurry of soft sand. After various single-handed and unsuccessful attempts to get out, I walked back to where I had noticed a tent and old Peugeot in the shade of scrub. The owner turned out to be a Saharawi with two wives and a marvellous sense of humour, but sadly no French. He walked back with me and shook with laughter at my predicament. Leaving me uncertainly by the car, he then disappeared, returning some minutes later in the Peugeot, accompanied by one of his wives. After a brief assessment of the problem, he reverses up to my bumper while his wife unravelled her head-covering, a long length of black cotton over half a metre wide.

On all fours she scooped away sand from around my axle while he smoked one of my cigarettes. She then rolled her scarf into a rope, and, disregarding my protestations, tied it to the two cars as a tow rope. A couple of sharp pulls and I was out, amid further rapturous laughter while the wife struggled to untie the tightened knots. I gave him what money I had and accepted his invitation to tea.

Their tent was not much more than an awning to keep out the sun. I was introduced to the second wife and a small, fly-blown child who nevertheless looked surprisingly well in such unpromising surroundings. As a fire was lit and the kettle filled, he produced a radio.

'BBC, BBC?' he questioned. 'World Service?' More laughs. A scan round the dials suddenly produced singing in English.

'Paul Young,' announced my extraordinary benefactor!

Because of the intrusion of sand it is not clear which road leads to the centre of Tarfaya. I take a guess, pass a small mosque, cross soft sand, and finally end up at a sea-wall slightly away from the main street. The first thing I notice is an attractive two-storey building of faded yellow stone, its handsome sash windows, the first I have seen for months, looking straight out to sea. An air of neglected elegance is reinforced by unkempt gardens and rusting wrought-iron work. I feel the building must be Portuguese. Beyond it in the distance stands another grand-looking old building of similar period and distinction.

Leaving the car, I climb over the sea-wall to find myself in dirty

60

dry sand above the high-water mark. Because of the perpetual desert winds the litter in some parts of Morocco, as I have already mentioned, has to be seen to be believed, and this corner of Tarfaya is no exception. On my right is a stone jetty which barely reaches the water as the tide is so low.

More interesting, though, is the sight straight ahead. Sitting majestically on its own, maybe 200 metres out in the sea, is a large rectangular stone building two storeys high, derelict, its windows gaping empty like the eye cavities of a skull. It is built on rock and even now at low tide I can see spray from waves breaking round its foundations on the seaward side. A causeway leading back towards land presumably gets covered when the tide comes in; indeed, it is hard to imagine how the building itself can survive a big sea. The stonework looks solid, though, having obviously withstood many years of pounding without undue harm.

The beach nearby is empty except for the inevitable boys playing football at the water's edge. Right over the other side is the unexpected sight of a modern breakwater of huge concrete tripods, dropped on top of each other and looking strangely out of place near the old building in the water to my front.

I cross the beach to the causeway. A channel of water a metre or so deep separates it from the beach, so I decide to take off my jeans and wade over in swimming trunks. Just as I go in I am joined by two teenagers, one of whom has a radio. The other indicates that where I am wading is too deep and that I should follow him. He is wearing a djellaba, which he proceeds to pull up, tucking the bottom rather elegantly into his belt. With bare legs he then wades confidently out, guiding me towards the causeway. After a couple of false starts he eventually climbs out onto the rocks and turns to offer a hand.

We walk to the side of the building. Although above the sea, it must have endured frequent soakings as patches of green seaweed cling to both the outside and inside walls. Everywhere has a slight sheen of dampness. Pools of water lie on the uneven ground.

No roof covers the inside, beams on the first floor having long since collapsed into piles of debris. Here and there a rusted, twisted girder points painfully to the sky, while the sound of the sea reverberates off the stone walls of the interior. Disturbed by our intrusion, a group of gulls takes leisurely wing, squawking disapproval as they depart.

'*Ici, Monsieur,*' says my anonymous guide, pointing at the outside wall. I walk across to where he is standing and look up. About 3 metres above us and covered in dried salt is a stone plaque which with some difficulty I manage to read. To my great surprise the inscription is in English. I cannot read the small letters, but the main heading says:

BRITISH NORTH WEST AFRICA COMPANY

Underneath is a date of 18 something, and below that the names of several people, presumably the principal shareholders – mostly Scottish names, I notice. Intrigued to find such a thing on a coastline famous for the attention of French, Spanish and Portuguese traders, I wonder what has become of these men whose names face the pounding Atlantic every day. Did they perish in Africa, or were their bones resting now in some gentle Scottish glen? And what of the company itself? Had it made people the fortunes it was expected to, or was this coastline and the country within too hostile to turn to profit? And what were they trading in anyway, slaves? Surely not camels and goats, the only other commodity which appears to be in plentiful supply.

My guide speaks little French, which is a shame as there is so much I want to ask. He has gone back inside the building, so I follow, finding him standing in the main room, roughly the size of a tennis court. He beckons me over and points to four holes in the floor about 60 centimetres wide. Inside them seawater moves gently, indicating underground contact with the sea. My friend makes a strange sight with his djellaba tucked up round his waist, long brown legs emerging from the bunched cloth like a doublet without any hose.

With a combination of gestures and broken French he tries to explain the purpose of the holes. If I understand him correctly, they were used as a torture or punishment for people – which people I do not know – who had fallen out of favour. They would be shackled in the holes at low tide, such as now, and would then be left as the sea came in, at the mercy of the cold and wet, not to mention crabs and other sea creatures which might swim in for easy pickings. The victims would not drown as such because their heads would remain above the water; nevertheless it all sounds most uncivilised.

Again I find myself wondering who these unfortunate people might have been, and why the company thought it necessary to go to the trouble of building out in the sea. What were they up to which needed such protection, or was the building perhaps some sort of prison?

We walk out on the rocks beyond the building for a while and then I suggest we return as the tide is on the make and I am not anxious for a swim. In fact we return without difficulty, I tip my guide and leave the two friends to their radio.

62

Walking back, I notice near the sea-wall a strange-looking object which I cannot identify. It turns out to be a memorial to the French writer and pioneer flyer Antoine de Saint-Exupéry, who passed this way en route to West Africa in the 1930s and was reputed to have landed on the beach. I do not like the memorial, which is modern and without charm, but at least someone has taken the trouble to commemorate him. His book *The Little Prince* is delightful, but so too is his autobiographical *Wind and Stars*, in the pages of which, as well as learning about this part of the world over 50 years ago, one can detect a man of remarkable character and sensitivity. Flying down this coast in the early days must have required huge courage. I am glad such a hero has been recognised for posterity.

I do not think many foreigners visit Tarfaya. Situated away from the normal tourist trails in Morocco, it is too far for a day trip and frankly not worth a special expedition. It is only passed by those heading south to the desert town of Laayoune, or on down to the border with Mauritania and eventually West Africa. As a result I get the impression I am being watched with curiosity as I drive slowly down the main street. I would not go so far as to say anyone is unfriendly, but there are none of the smiles and '*Monsieur, Monsieur,*' of the villages further north. There is anyway not much to see; just a few scruffy shops and several goats scavenging through rubbish. I decide to return to the wrecks along the beach.

In swimming trunks and with towel and camera in a bag, I pick my way from the road, across gravel and low dunes towards the sea. The sand below the high-tide mark is beautifully firm and clean with not a footprint on it. To the left the deserted beach extends far into the distance. Out to sea a never-ending belt of waves is building up, breaking then gradually collecting again to fling itself in final fury against the landmass of Africa.

To the right, about a kilometre away, a rather curious and unexpected sea-mist is blowing in, obscuring the distant view. Curious, because normally in England I would have associated such a mist with a cold dank feeling in the air. But in fact although nearly four o'clock, it is still marvellously warm, with the sky a deep blue and the sun hanging motionless in the heavens. From so close the noise of surf deafens. The whole beach has a feeling of vastness and solitude which I find most exhilarating.

Immediately ahead in the water the five rust-red wrecks lie like ancient gods reclining in the sun. Beached at a similar depth, two are still intact, both settled on the sand and facing inland as if their captains guided them there on purpose. Perhaps they did. I wonder if Lloyds' adjusters know of the beach! The other three have slid sideways with their backs broken. I can clearly see the main part of bridge and cabins in the sterns, but it is not easy to decide which of the rest is still attached. Lumps of twisted metal and smaller bits have broken adrift and are now scattered way down the beach.

As I study the wrecks I become aware of two figures approaching across the sand. Although only a few hundred metres away, it is impossible to see any detail due to the angle of the sun, but they are definitely coming towards me. For a second it crosses my mind that I am completely alone and defenceless in swimming trunks. If they have evil intent I am in trouble. However, as they get close I can see they are young boys and are smiling a friendly welcome.

I call to them in French. They must want to talk as they come straight up to me and shake hands. One of them has a typical Moroccan face with good features, hollow cheeks and dark penetrating eyes. His hair is wavy and skin olive rather than dark. The beginnings of a moustache make him look slightly older than his friend. This other one has a different look. His skin is much darker, almost black and tight curly hair above a rounder face gives more than a hint of Negro blood. What makes him instantly appealing is a ready smile showing beautifully white teeth. They are both on the tall side and as usual alarmingly thin, with rough shirts and trousers hanging loosely on tiny waists and bottoms.

After a few words in French I ask if either of them speaks English.

'I speak English – a leetle,' says the younger one in the husky sing-song of a voice in the process of breaking. He is laughing at his own audacity. It turns out that he is learning English at school and it soon becomes apparent that he is an intelligent child. But since his friend cannot speak English we stick to French.

We stand by the sea for nearly an hour talking and laughing in the most animated way about all sorts of things. We start by discussing the wrecks. They tell me when they think each one happened, writing the dates in the sand as they clearly have the same problem with French numbers as I do. The younger one surprises me by saying that this beach is a *cimetière des bateaux* – a cemetery for boats – a sophisticated notion in the circumstances.

They tell me they are Saharawis – from the nomadic desert tribes who have roamed this part of the world since the beginning of time. They try to steer me onto politics but I am not keen. The dispute between the Frente Polisario, the military wing of the Saharawi nation, and the Moroccans is the reason why I have been sent to this part of the world in the first place. But as an impartial employee of the UN I have no wish to be drawn into a political discussion. I simply say that I feel both nations should be able to live together. I go on to cite the way in Great Britain the English, Scottish and Welsh have learned to do so. Once more the younger one surprises me by saying, *'Mais les Irlandais?'*

We discuss England, its climate, which part I come from, etc. They both say they would like to visit but cannot afford to and that as Saharawis it would be difficult for them to get visas to travel abroad. When I ask what work they hope to do when they leave school, they both say 'anything', which is sensible but also rather sad.

We have been talking against the roar of waves breaking out to sea with surf swirling around the wrecks behind us and across the sand to our feet. The boys' voices are often drowned so we stand close together. One of the things I notice is how clean they are, both themselves and their clothes. Like so many others I have come across on my travels, people like this would live in huts with no electricity or running water. Considering this is a normal working day, I cannot help thinking how favourably they compare in these respects with their European counterparts despite vastly less privileged circumstances.

By now the sun is beginning to sink and warm sea is washing round our ankles. I am anxious to photograph the wrecks so I tell them I must make a move. Naturally I take pictures of them to record such a happy interlude. I then say that I am going down the beach to get a shot which will include all the wrecks as well as a translucent moon, which has put in an early appearance in the sky.

'*Très romantique,*' says my precocious little friend!

'Aren't you going to give me a surprise?' he asks as I turn to leave.

'How do you mean?'

'Haven't you got a surprise for me in that bag?' He is laughing and holding my arm. I realise rather late that he is playfully asking for a tip.

'I don't really have anything,' say I, 'but I will try to give you a copy of the photographs when I next come. Anyway, what have you given me?'

With a beguiling smile he extends his arm in a wave which encompasses in one the vast empty beach, the ocean, the deep blue sky and the sun.

'I have given you all of this,' says my young Saharawi friend, and in a way of course it is true.

10

A Night with Abraham and Absalom

Sad is the Evening: all the level sand
    Lies left and lonely, while the restless sea,
Tired of the green caresses of the land,
    Withdraws into its own infinity.

                Laurence Hope

Although the UN Mission in the desert normally worked Saturdays and Sundays, the Belgian General in command once offered me a weekend off. Before he could change his mind, I jumped on one of our Russian contract aircraft for the hour's flight up the deserted African coastline to Agadir.

On discovering that the owner of the room I had previously rented in Tarhazoute was away, I took the bus along the coast, eventually arriving at a group of houses I hardly knew. The almost immediate offer of a holiday home did not appeal and I was standing in the sun wondering where to look next when the inevitable stranger approached.

'What are you looking for?' he asked.

When I told him, he beckoned to follow, soon taking me down onto the beach. We headed for stairs leading from the sand up to a building where festoons of dark red bougainvillea smothered the roof and spilled down over the walls, obscuring windows and strangling the posts of a small patio. Beside the stairs a ramp led to double doors with a smaller entrance in one side. This he opened, revealing the most perfect room, which I would not otherwise have noticed. Clearly an old boathouse, the interior was white-washed, divided in two by a wooden screen. My surprise was complete when behind the screen I found a spotlessly clean shower, loo and sink. The perfect place.

'How much for a night?' I asked.

'Forty dirham. How long you want to stay?'

'Only two nights, I'm afraid.'

'Two nights too short. One hundred dirham.'

Puzzled by his logic, but not prepared to argue, I accepted. Eight pounds for the weekend still seemed a bargain.

As was so often the case, first impressions were deceptive; the electric light was kaput; the shower and loo likewise, due to lack of water. Other than that, though, it was fine, with the high-tide mark perhaps 20 metres across the beach from the door. As I took stock of the place my host appeared with blankets and pillows.

'There's no water,' I said, indicating the ablutions.

'No. Tomorrow *inch'Allah.*' He paused. '*Monsieur*, you have supper with us tonight?' He gestured towards the house above.

I did not want to have supper with him for two reasons. One was that I had specifically come here to be on my own; to enjoy the roar of waves across a deserted beach; to watch the dying sun sparkle on the water; to share solitary breezes with a glass of whisky. The other was that the man's manner hinted at something shifty. Nothing I could put my finger on, but just enough to cause hesitation. He was unshaven and must have been mid-thirties, with none of the carefree gaiety of the youths I had met so often on earlier trips.

'You come to supper. I have friends this evening. Very good.'

A prior engagement in this social desert was inconceivable nor could I ever explain my wish for solitude so, casting care aside I accepted. His name was Abselm, the Absalom of the Bible, the Old Testament being common, of course, to Islam as well as Christianity and Judaism.

Having bought the ingredients for a sandwich, I had a swim and then wandered off up the beach to spend a happy afternoon reading beneath a rock. Perhaps four people came by – youngsters I did not recognise and one old man who shuffled over to cadge a cigarette.

On the way back in the late afternoon I came across a man and boy working the tideline for octopus. Apparently pleased to have company, they did not object when I tagged along. Their technique was to walk through pools still filled by the tide, looking for tell-tale tentacles showing beneath rocks. As soon as an octopus was located, they would try to dislodge him by plunging their hand under the rock before he had caught on to their game. Usually, however the octopus sensed their arrival, withdrawing the offending tentacle before they managed to get a purchase. When this happened, the boy used a stick with a hook at one end, attempting to gaff the unfortunate victim.

This was not as easy as it sounds as the octopus has a remarkable will to live. Several times the hook would come out with bits of octopus attached although the main body survived to cling on beneath the rock. If and when the boy eventually succeeded the poor thing would appear torn and bloody, to be held aloft as a trophy before being bashed on the hard sand to remove the ink. While I was with them they caught three – a useful supper.

By the time I moved on it was practically dark. I bid goodnight and once more started back towards the houses, now some way down the coast. Where the beach narrowed a figure appeared in the gloom, bending about on the sand. Getting closer, I realised that it was Mhend, a youth I had known on earlier trips but not seen for several months. Extrovert and handsome, he was the mainstay of the football team which occupied so much of the time of my other *pêcheur* friends. Now, he was kneeling in a pool, washing.

Momentary surprise was followed by genuine pleasure. He embraced me warmly, then rinsed himself and pulled on jeans and a tee-shirt with German logo – no doubt the gift of a 'friend'.

'Where are you staying?' he asked.

'I've rented a *chambre* in the village.'

'Which one?'

'It belongs to a guy called Abselm.'

'No. Abselm a bad man. You should not stay there.'

'Why's he bad?' I asked.

'He's crazy. He smokes a lot. He will steal from your bag.'

We walked slowly along the darkening beach. Mhend told me that Abselm was a pusher who supplied most of this part of the coast with kif and cannabis. Nobody liked him but he provided an essential service.

'He's dangerous. Once he attacked a friend of mine with a brick. *Faites attention.*'

I thanked Mhend for his advice before changing the conversation onto lighter matters. His double ration of charm made the walk a pleasant occasion despite nagging doubts about supper with Abselm. When the lights of houses came into view, he stopped.

'I must return to my parents,' he said, '*Sois sage.*' A peck on the cheek and he disappeared into the night.

🌴 🌴　　🌴 🌴　　🌴 🌴

Back in my room, I light a candle and open a beer. It has been such a pleasant afternoon, rounded off by the chance meeting and walk down the beach with perhaps the most engaging of my former friends, that I would happily turn in. But having accepted supper there is little alternative but to put on a sweater and head up the steps to Abselm's front door.

The patio is dark. After greetings, he leads me by torchlight to a room where a single candle shows two other men sitting round a table. They are introduced as Hassan and Brahim, both in their thirties, the first short and slight but Brahim (Ibrahim, or Abraham) the opposite, with a reassuringly jolly look about his face. As my eyes grow accustomed to the light, I can make out bottles and glasses amongst various rubbish on the table. After the usual handshakes, I sit down.

'*Monsieur*, you like to drink something? Whisky, wine?'

'Thanks. Wine please.'

'Oh, the wine is finished,' says Abselm with surprise as he pours the dregs into my glass. '*Monsieur*, you have wine in your room?'

I might have guessed. In fact I do not grudge making a contribution, so return downstairs for a bottle. But his request alerts me to the fact that Abselm must have already searched my room.

Being older, these men do not speak French as easily as kids like Mhend, which leads me to conclude that the standard of education must have improved over the last decade. Neither are they so polite about including me in conversation, so there are long periods when I am forced to sit in silence, listening to their unintelligible Berber. They all smoke joints, usually rolling the next before the previous one is finished. It is clearly beyond their comprehension that I should decline, although one pull on my untipped Gitanes provides some sort of explanation.

Like most Moroccans, they are competent cooks. Having no idea what to expect in the way of food, I am slightly thrown when the first thing offered is a bowl of fruit. It is difficult to deduce their circumstances compared to the *pêcheurs*, so I am not certain whether this will be all or whether fruit is simply a prelude to a grander supper. Brahim is on whisky, frequently topping up his glass and draining it neat. The others make short work of my wine.

Fish follows the fruit, eaten in the fingers from a communal plate. Quite good, in fact. Then a pause before Abselm solemnly carries in a huge dish of cous-cous piled high with meat and vegetables, setting it by the candle on the table before us. This is standard fare for the better-off and confirms my growing impression that they are a cut above the fishermen. I later discover that Brahim works in Agadir, coming along the coast at weekends to stay with his friends. More interestingly, it transpires that Abselm does not own the house at all but is the *gardien* for a family who seldom use it. Sub-letting the boat-shed is a nice little earner about which the owner probably knows nothing.

We are eating camel. I have done so in the Sahara with local dignitaries but certainly never expected it here. Surprisingly the meat has an agreeable flavour with no hint of its origin. Not totally unlike beef in taste and consistency, in my experience it is pleasantly tender, although having seen the state of older camels working in the desert I suspect I may have been lucky.

Towards the end of supper Abselm turns on a radio, quickly tuning in to my least favourite Arab music. For a while the furious racket forms a backdrop to their chatter. Then Hassan stands and starts dancing, arms in the air, body bobbing and weaving, smoke from a joint waving in one hand.

His actions are at once absurd and elegant. Absurd because we are in the middle of supper, he has not moved from the table and the others are talking around him. Elegant because, like all Berbers, the movements of even this funny little man are rhythmic and fluid. At least it is easier than making conversation, conveniently filling the time before I feel able to leave.

Next morning I am lying in the sun after an early swim when the sinister Abselm appears. After pleasantries, I thank him for supper. He is looking at me in a way I find annoying.

'*Monsieur*, I have rented you the room, right?'

'Yes.'

'How much you give me for renting the room?'

'I've paid you one hundred dirham.'

'Yes, but that is for the *Patron*. How much for me?'

'We agreed one hundred dirham for the room and that is what I have given you. I am not paying anything more.'

Abselm has an evil look. I suspect he thinks he can frighten me into paying more – it has probably worked before. We are arguing round the subject when Brahim appears. Having formed a reasonable impression of him the night before, I grasp the bull by the horns and tell him of Abselm's demand. The large man shrugs. An exchange in Berber ensues before Abselm wanders off up the steps.

'Look, *Monsieur*,' says Brahim, 'Abselm is crazy, but he means no harm. Give him a few dirham, thirty or forty, and he will be happy.'

I explain that as far as I am concerned he should have added his tip to the asking price in the first place. It is too late now to start altering his terms. Brahim shrugs again and gets up. It is hard to tell if he is in league with Abselm or simply looking for a quiet life. He too heads back upstairs.

🌴🌴 🌴🌴 🌴🌴

Deciding to get away while things settle, I walk down the coast in the opposite direction, ending up in a small village at lunchtime. There is only one café so I go in and select a table overlooking the beach. Hardly have I done so when a huge motorbike roars into view on the main road, pauses and then cruises over to the same café. When he has climbed out of helmet and leathers, a European of about 30 comes to the table next to me, calling, as he does so, for coffee from the boy behind the counter.

It is not long before I find myself talking to Dieter, a German who turns out to be something of an expert on the Maghreb, having toured this part of the world for eight years – Algeria and Tunisia as well as Morocco. His English is faultless, so over lunch we spend a couple of hours comparing notes. I am impressed by the intrepidness of my new companion. Apparently he always travels alone, relying, like me, on locals for shelter. He also spends many nights sleeping out beside his bike. From his descriptions, it is clear he goes right off the beaten track, even now having just come down from the High Atlas.

I ask about Algeria. At the moment the only news is of mayhem caused by fundamentalists, so I am interested to hear how things are for travellers. He tells me that near the coast road-blocks and troops are in evidence, but that down towards the Sahara he has explored without any problems. He says that the whole vast area is incredibly unspoilt, due to lack of exposure to outside influences. He loves it.

In fact his best tale concerns Algeria. Apparently one evening he arrived at a village at dusk. After looking for lodgings he was taken in by a poor family whose home was a courtyard with lean-tos around the inside wall and a flock of goats in the centre. In one corner he fell gratefully asleep. Next morning while preparing to leave, he suddenly noticed a human of indeterminate age and sex, crouching among the goats. Barely clothed and filthy, the wretched creature was tethered by a rope. Indeed, so like an animal was it that he had to look carefully to make sure he was not mistaken.

'What did you do?'

He apparently made great play about photographing the family, using the light as an excuse to move them round until their retarded

71

relative appeared in the background. Sadly the evidence is now back in the Fatherland, but it is a macabre story I find hard to forget.

After lunch we part; he climbs back into his leathers and I head for the beach. This time I bypass Abselm, soon regaining the area where I walked with Mhend last evening. Without a book, I find instead a patch of shade for a siesta.

Sleeping on sand is not easy but the sun has started its downward path when I open my eyes. Two youths are kicking a football along the edge of the tide. I recognise Mhend as one of them so I walk over, getting a wave as I approach. Mhend's friend is Omar, another I have met on previous occasions but hardly know.

'How was your room?' asks Mhend.

I explain about supper and then how Abselm tried to get more money from me.

'Omar is a friend of Abselm,' says Mhend. 'He can go to the house with you. He will speak to Abselm.'

It sounds a reasonable idea so I agree before we wade in for a swim. Afterwards the three of us set off down the beach, Mhend turning back before we reach the houses.

'Will you be around tomorrow?'

'If it is the Will of Allah.'

Shorter than Mhend, Omar is one of the thinnest men I have ever met. In small swimming trunks I can see the outline of each individual rib, while his hip bones protrude from the flattest stomach it is possible to imagine. When I try to comment on his shape my French fails at the word thin but I am rescued when he smiles and says '*maigre*'. Meagre fills the bill nicely.

'How do you know Abselm?' I ask.

'Abselm sells kif. Very useful, Abselm.'

'You smoke a lot?'

'No. Not much.' A negative answer is accompanied by Arabs not with a shake of the head but by a horizontal waving of the index finger. An infinitely more authoritative gesture.

Outside my door, Omar squats and goes through the pockets of the jeans he is carrying. I notice the first item to appear is a nasty-looking knife, then a small paper packet.

'*Monsieur*, a cigarette please?' I hand him the Moroccan cigarettes I always carry for strangers. He breaks off the filter then slits down the length of the paper with his knife.

'Your lighter please.' From the packet he produces what turns out to be a cube of cannabis resin. This he holds above the flame, kneading it in his fingers until suitably pliable to be mixed into the tobacco. He then spreads the stuff along a new piece of paper and rolls the joint. After a couple of puffs he holds it towards me.

'No thanks, Omar, I'll stick to French cigarettes,' says our worthy cavalry officer.

Instead I fetch a couple of beers, which we drink while the sun sets. As the last bars of orange turn to haze along the horizon, I find myself studying my new companion. To him the sight of sun setting into sea is a daily occurrence which must surely be taken for granted. I am impressed, though, by the way he follows my lead of wordless contemplation, moving only to sip beer or draw on his joint. He appears as content and absorbed as I in the beauty of the scene before us. It is not until a light wind accompanies the arrival of darkness that we pull on clothes and go inside.

In the course of the next hour Omar smokes three or four joints. They have no noticeable effect except perhaps to exhaust his capacity for intelligent conversation. For long periods we sit in silence watching the candle-flame bending this way and that at the whim of a capricious breeze from under the door. I find my eyelids drooping but luckily come to just in time to remember the point of his being there.

'Omar, you are going to buy some dope from Abselm?'
'Yes.'

'Could you explain to him that you know me, and that I have paid him a fair price for this room. I am not going to pay him more, but I would prefer not to have a row about it. Perhaps you can help.' The gist of this message tests my French to the limit but Omar nods. I just hope his mind is clear enough to play the situation sensibly. Before going up the steps, he borrows my torch, spending some time collecting the filters and papers he has dropped in the sand.

'Don't worry, I'll tidy up,' say I, surprised by such untypical diligence.

'Be careful,' he says, 'If the *gendarmes* see these they will know someone has been smoking joints. I was once arrested in Agadir because I left filters on the floor of a café.'

When Omar disappears into the gloom, I stand on the sand looking up at Abselm's house. Sure enough a lamp comes to life on the patio. I watch for several minutes but as nothing happens, eventually go back inside to await his return.

Omar calls as he knocks on my door. I let him in and light a candle. He asks for a cigarette.

'Abselm very stupid man,' he says. 'Him very angry with you.'

'What, still?'

'He say you have not given him anything. He knows you have money but you have not given any.'

'I've paid him for the room. In fact I've paid for a room where neither the electricity nor the water works.'

'Best to give him money. Him dangerous man.' I remember what Mhend said about Abselm going for someone with a brick.

Omar the *maigre* looks gaunt in the candlelight but he manages a smile. There is something about him I like. He is probably only about 20 but his hollow face is already etched with the faint lines of hard living. Without the élan of Mhend, he nevertheless has a world-weary air I find appealing.

'Has Abselm been smoking?' I ask. Omar nods.

'He's drinking whisky too. Much whisky.' He tuts to himself.

It seems a shame to have found a perfect room but then have the pleasure of staying there spoilt by such a tiresome man. At the same time I am probably the only foreigner on this stretch of coast. A row with a man of his reputation who shows every likelihood of being both high and drunk could well end in tears, and there would be no one to turn to for help. The atmosphere is tense in the candlelight. I am tired but at the same time alert from a strong flow of adrenalin, my senses straining through the noise of sea and conversation to detect any movement on the steps outside.

'*Monsieur*, if you like you can stay with me.' An unexpected offer.

'That's very kind, Omar. Where do you live?'

'My *chambre* is about two kilometres along the beach.'

'What do you think?' I ask myself out loud. It is eleven o'clock. Is it really necessary to pack up everything and move?

'Whatever you wish.' I know that will be his reply. It does not help me with my decision, but there are two aspects to his offer speeding through my mind. The first is that if I stay here I will not get a decent night's sleep due to worrying about a visit from the drunken Abselm, who I know has a key to my door. The second is the mischievous thought of disappearing in the night, leaving Abselm empty-handed. I decide to play safe, although it is galling to do so having already paid for the room.

Omar helps bundle my belongings into the bag. As soon as we step outside I look up towards Abselm's patio but can see no sign of life. Leaving the key in the lock, we steal silently down the ramp onto the sand. Without pausing we set off along the beach.

The tide is half-way up. A large moon lights our way, shimmering down a path across the water and creating sinister shadows behind every rock. Despite the heat of day, the sand feels cold underfoot. I am suddenly glad to be about at such an hour.

Omar walks fast, keeping on hard sand near the water's edge. Several times I look over my shoulder to check no one is sneaking up under cover of the noise of the sea. Each time I do so the beach stretches empty and ghostlike into the gloom. Abselm's house is soon safely distant. Afterwards the whole episode will seem absurd, but now it has all the excitement of a major adventure.

Omar's *chambre* is similar to many others – one room only with minimum creature comforts. All the money for them goes up in smoke! I am sure he is as tired as me, but with typical courtesy he lights the gas ring for tea, laying out on the floor what he can find as bedding while the water boils. After tea my last tin of beer is shared while we both smoke a final cigarette.

When he changes into old shorts for sleeping, his emaciated body looks even more skeletal by candlelight. Knowing nothing of his lifestyle I find myself wondering if he could be seriously ill, SIDA even, but conclude he has probably always been that shape.

We lie side by side, the memory of Abselm soon obliterated by the roar of the tide. A happy conclusion to an eventful day but I will probably not go into details when I next see the General. I am sure he will assume I spent the weekend relaxing in a five-star hotel.

11

Calamar, Calamar

I am drawn nightward; I must turn again
   where, down below the low untrodden strand
There curves and glimmers outward to the unknown
   the old unquiet ocean.

Rupert Brooke

The fishing business begins to interest me. The more I watch the fleet leaving or returning to the village, and the more times I see small black shapes of *barques* bobbing out at sea, the more I start to wonder precisely what it all consists of. Not just the fishing, but what happens in the boats, how hard the work is, what the various duties of the crew might be. The only way to find out is to go out with them. I decide to make this a priority next time I have some leave.

A month or so later I am back in Tarhazoute, having set up shop again in the same room as before. My landlord is consulted about fishing. Needless to say, he produces a smiling friend who offers to take me out in his boat for about 40 pounds, which seems expensive even by the standards of the South Coast of England. It then dawns on me that it would be much more fun anyway to go out with the boys I know along the coast, so the next day when I meet up with them again I ask if it would be possible.

Seeing how pleased they are, I know I have made the right decision. In fact it causes some argument as several insist I come with them. But knowing the way their enthusiasm often overcomes the reality of what they are in a position to offer, I pick the brothers Ahmed and Lahcen with their friend Tahib to be my crew. I know from previous conversations that their uncle is the *patron* of a *barque*.

It seems that my old friend Mohammed with the slanting eyes,

76

who had previously lived with Ahmed, has moved south and found work on a larger boat. After his departure Ahmed moved in with the others.

Lahcen I have met several times on the beach. He speaks good French and seems to enjoy my company despite a permanent look of sadness on his face. Tahib is new to me. Slightly older, he has a reassuring air of competence. Over tea we make a plan.

They want to be on the beach and ready to go at four thirty in the morning. In the event of a rough sea, they will cancel as soon as one has stuck his head outside and seen the waves. In fact they can tell just from the sound of the sea whether it is too rough. I am told to come over next evening and spend the night with them so as to be sure to be ready on time in the morning.

Their hut is new to me. Still very basic, with no water or electricity, but, built round a small courtyard, it is marginally more luxurious than Mohammed's *chambre* and even has a wall-mirror!

Arriving after dark at the apparently deserted group of shacks necessitates the strange business of feeling my way along unfamiliar paths between the walls of houses and sensing with my feet the anticipated drop of steps. The moon is hidden, the air warm and salty. The sea can be heard but not seen below on the beach. Running my fingers along a wall, I eventually find the entrance I have been looking for. A knock. A call from inside and then a pause. Finally the door opens and Lahcen greets me, the candlelight from inside spilling out with the smell of cooking and a feeling of welcome.

A gas stove burns in the small courtyard, with a pot steaming away on top. Lahcen is cook for the night, Tahib is lying on the floor and there is no sign of Ahmed, whom I later discover to be playing cards with some old men under a nearby tree. A kiss for Lahcen and handshake for Tahib; leaving my shoes outside, I settle on the floor with a cigarette. Soon Ahmed is back and the four of us are sitting round a plate of unspecified food, dunking lumps of coarse bread and eating happily with our hands.

We chat for at least two hours. There are few moments of silence and never a second when I have to search for something to say. The times when the boys lapse into Berber are few, and even these are fun because it is a fascinating language to listen to, particularly when one can also study the expressions on faces – laughter and smiles, flashes of teeth, youthful brows knitted over dark intense eyes. For me the shadows cast by flickering candles accentuate the intimacy of the occasion. Somehow it feels wrong to speak out loud and our voices become whispers – part of a conspiracy to keep everything within that small room to ourselves.

I have developed a soft spot for Ahmed from the nights I spent with him and Mohammed on my previous visit. One particularly endearing quality is the way he speaks. Whenever he uses a French word he likes the sound of, he repeats it. His conversation is therefore sprinkled with *'Calamar, calamar'*, or *'Vitamin'*, which he pronounces *'Veetameen, veetameen'*. He tells me at length how terrified lobsters are of *'Poulpe, poulpe'* because the octopus is the only creature strong enough to prise open their claws. Sometimes if the fishermen catch both they place them together in a bucket and watch the ensuing battle.

Before sleep I am determined to go down to the beach to look at the stars. Ahmed volunteers to come with me. While the others clear supper I follow him down the steep steps onto the sand. The stars this time are nothing like as prolific as on my last visit but are there, nevertheless, watching silently over this little corner of Africa. The sea is half-way in, with strong waves that I hope will calm during the night.

For some time I stand absorbing both, while Ahmed waits nearby. Is it possible that he can understand why such commonplace sights to him should mean so much to me, an Englishman used to cloudy skies and cold grey sea? A cool breeze blows off the tide, bringing with it the salty smell of childhood memories, its freshness intoxicating. Not until I feel my senses can take no more do I turn and walk slowly back towards the steps. Ahmed takes my hand. After a moment's embarrassment it seems unimportant.

If I could list my five least favourite things, one without doubt would be the sound of alarm clocks. Sleeping on the floor is not comfortable, but when Tahib's alarm wakes the four of us, I pray for a second that the noise is nothing to do with me and that I can stay a few more hours under this dirty old blanket. The others must be feeling the same. For several minutes no one moves. I wonder – hope even – that they have decided from the sound of the sea that it is too rough to go. Then slowly my companions come to life. Tahib is first up and me last. He lights a candle and dresses. As before, they each wash face and hands while water is boiled for tea, then hard stale bread is handed out by Lahcen to go with the oversweet brew.

I put on all the clothes I can manage against the early morning chill. Curiously, it is less severe than I expect. Indeed, coming out from that little room into the night, I notice how balmy and sweet the air has become during the hours of darkness.

The sky holds no hint of dawn. We walk in silence along passage-ways and paths and down the steps to the beach. On arrival at the boats, I see three other crews mustering. Several men wear djellabas with hoods pulled over their heads, but it is still too dark to see faces. No one speaks. Everyone knows the drill. Conscious that I do not, I stand a few metres away, watching as they attach lifting ropes fore and aft, stow oars, load tackle. Within minutes they have carried the boats to the water and started fitting outboards.

The sea has thankfully died down, the waves washing steadily up the beach. Suddenly there is the hideous noise of one of the out-boards being tested with its propeller out of the water – screeching and grating to the ears but reassuring to those who will otherwise have to row. As soon as it fires, the motor is turned off and the boat pushed into the sea. Ours is next. Momentary worries as the out-board fails to respond, then comes that same intrusive scream. I am signalled to take off my shoes and chuck them onboard. Also that I will be sitting in the bows.

When I am ready, they face the boat into the waves and start pushing it out to sea. I walk beside, noting how much warmer the water is than I had expected. On a sign we jump in, until it is only poor old Ahmed who remains in the water, by now up to his thighs. His job is to keep the bow pointing seawards as Tahib wrestles with the outboard. Finally success, and Ahmed throws himself into the bottom of the boat as we hit the first proper wave.

Two other boats are with us and I never discover what happens to the third. Perhaps the outboard has let them down. Some anxiety as we crash through breaking waves and the boat rears and plunges, then suddenly we are beyond the surf, the water calms, the sound of waves gradually subsides. Either the first glimmer of dawn is in the sky, or my eyes have become accustomed to the dark. In any event I can now see the outline of horizon, beach and mountains behind, and the other two *barques* closing in on either side.

Soon we are line abreast, heading away from the coast, outboards purring, prows slicing into the dark waves with a sheen of spray. In a rather magical moment my crew start singing some wild Berber song, their voices swelling together above the sound of the engines.

The plan is to get clear of the shore and then turn north along the coast to where the squid might be feeding. As we move, the stars slowly fade and dawn creeps into the eastern sky. The sea turns from black to dark, dark green, while the details of trees and cliffs become discernible. No sand shows along the shoreline but every so often surf shoots into the air as waves hit rocks along the beach.

After half an hour we turn in a circle and Tahib cuts the motor. The three boats are left drifting perhaps a couple of hundred metres apart.

🌴🌴   🌴🌴   🌴🌴

Squid, or *calamar* as the *pêcheurs* call them, feed just above the sea-bed. They cruise along, usually in shoals, using their tentacles to ensnare whatever takes their fancy. Each squid has ten tentacles, which vary from almost non-existent to 20 centimetres long or even more on really big ones. The method used to catch them in this part of the world is to lower a weighted lure, similar to a Devon minnow but with a circle of bent nails around the tail. The lure is suspended just above the bottom and then jerked up and down by the fisherman to catch the attention of the wretched *calamar* as he sails innocently by. Once attracted, he naturally reaches out – only to find his tentacle irretrievably caught on the nails next time the lure is jerked.

Since each man operates two lines, neither of which is left unattended for more than a few seconds, constant and furious activity is needed with both hands all the time. The first line is jerked twice, then retrieved as fast as possible, hand over hand. Once in, the lure is checked and chucked out again, followed almost immediately by the retrieval of the second line from the opposite side of the boat.

One of the other boats is first to start fishing, but being unaware at that stage of the technique I am not sure what on earth is going on. From a distance it looks as if the boat is being dive-bombed by a swarm of particularly vicious wasps which the crew are doing their utmost to swat by hand. Moving from the sublime to the ridiculous, I then wonder if they have been watching a TV film of swinging London in the sixties. Sitting in that boat, or so it appears, is a demented crew dancing the hand-jive every bit as well as Cliff Richard. Finally I begin to wonder if what I am really watching is not a crew of Moroccan fishermen, but a pleasure boat full of tic-tac men on vacation from Epsom race course. All of these are what squid fishing calls to mind to someone seeing it from a distance for the first time.

Once the technique has been explained, I am given a line to operate and all four of us set to, with me copying Lahcen just to my front.

The first to catch a *calamar* is Tahib. Hearing a strange noise, I realise he has thrown one into the bucket at his feet. The wretched creature, about 30 centimetres long not including tentacles, is gasping quite audibly for air. I watch more carefully, interested to see the whole performance, and do not have to wait long as we have hit a shoal.

The gasping is bad enough. What is even less attractive is the fact that when each *calamar* breaks the surface it ejects its entire supply of black ink indiscriminately into the air with a hideous squelching sound. Perhaps a glassful of slimy black ejaculate shoots up about 2 metres, falling either back into the sea or, worse still, on top of all of us.

After our initial success the *calamar* get wise to our game and stop biting, if that is the right word. We move the boat several times, trying alternately nearer the shore and further out. Every now and then I hear a familiar squelch then splashes of falling ink followed by gasps as another lone squid kicks the bucket. By now there are only two stars still visible and the sky has turned from dark red to pale orange. The smell of earth and vegetation coming off the land is marvellous despite the fact that, apart from argans, this part of the coast is decidedly lacking in anything green.

When we move again, Tahib gives me an ordinary fishing line to catch something for lunch. Luckily the sea here teems with small fish and it takes no time to start lifting them in. In the absence of any other bait I am shown how to pull up one of the *calamar* tentacles from the bucket and break it off by squeezing between forefinger and thumb. This in itself is all right, I suppose, but I soon find that despite being dismembered, the tentacle remains alive, resisting my attempts to attach it to the hook by squirming and gripping my finger with all the little suckers along its broken-off underside. Not at all a pleasant feeling.

The bucket of *calamar* is by now half full. Apart from the rather human squelches and gasps, I cannot help finding their appearance a trifle unnerving. The *calamar* is transparent when alive, with a green-grey sheen to its exterior. Behind the clump of ten tentacles comes the long tapering body with two large air intakes at the front and transparent wings along the fuselage. Unfortunately, on its head are two disproportionately huge and heavily made-up eyes which gaze up balefully, even accusingly, from the bucket which is now at my feet. Poor old things. These eyes make squeezing off bits of tentacle even harder. A few minutes after dying, *calamar* turn a veiny blue-grey colour. By then the eyes seem to have lost their reproachful look – or any other look, come to that.

We fish on for about two hours after the sun has begun to burn our faces. The bucket is now full and I am ready for home. One of the other *barques*, also crewed by youngsters, comes over and pulls in against us to compare notes. With their permission I climb aboard to take a picture of my crew and then we spend an amusing few minutes changing boats and crews for various photo-calls while Ahmed strips off and dives overboard to cool down.

When we eventually head for home, Lahcen tells me they do not want me to be seen in the boat, and that he and I will therefore be dropped off at a deserted beach to walk back to the hut while the others return with the *barque*. This comes as something of a surprise, particularly as no explanation is offered. I do not ask for one now, hoping the reason will become apparent in due course but in fact it never does.

The most likely explanation is that they do not want the owner of the boat, the *patron*, to know that they have taken me out, since he will also know that I have paid them. As the provider of the wherewithal, and being a Berber, he will almost certainly demand the money for himself. Anyway, it does not matter and to say I am hurt would be an overstatement. But it does confirm what I have always thought, which is that one will never really be anything more than an outsider to these people.

Lahcen and I jump out in the shallows and wade ashore as Tahib and Ahmed crash back through the breaking waves. We walk along hot tarmac on the coast road towards the huts. Once home, I watch while he guts the fish, scraping the scales off the larger ones. We have not of course brought back any *calamar* as, being so valuable, they will be sold on for export to Spain or France.

For once it is a relief to be inside. On other occasions I have found the obsession with shade most frustrating. Spending much of one's life in an office it can be maddening always to be ushered from a sunny beach or garden into a dingy room, but the sun was hotter than usual on the water today and this time I have had enough.

Everything, plus various vegetables, is put into a large pot on the fire. It is by then about eleven o'clock. When the others get back, having sorted out the boat and sold the *calamar*, it is time to break the bread and eat in our fingers some of the freshest *fruits-de-mer* I can remember.

12

A Swim With a Sprite

Thy charms in their diversity
Half frighten and astonish me.

James Fenimore Cooper

After a surfeit of sea my interest switches to the mountains. One leave I decide to take a couple of days away from the beach to visit the famous waterfall at Immouzer des Ita Outane some 50 kilometres inland. I want to see the western end of the Atlas and am anyway intrigued by Rogerson's seductive description of the falls and valley.

In a hired car I am soon on a minor road climbing inland from the coastal belt. To start with it follows a *oued*, the dried-up course of a stream with no sign of recent water. Sparse greenery among bleached rock and alluvial sand. Even argan trees scattered across the valley look parched and dusty.

The sea is left behind as the road penetrates the Atlas proper. Not an interesting drive so it is with some relief that I reach a small summit and see in the next valley the dark smudge of palms and vegetation. After only a few kilometres of barren land this cultivation is welcome. The trees with their deep green canopy and elegantly curved trunks seem so lush and benevolent compared to the sun-scorched soil behind me.

I stop to savour the difference. The first sound is that of running water from a small stream meandering through the plantation. Above this the unfamiliar but exotic call of a bird from within the grove, deep and strong, gives proof of the life-giving property of water.

Looking in more detail I notice how dense palm fronds act like a ceiling to the secret world of dappled sunlight, cool shadows and mysterious pathways. It is clear that water from higher up reaches this far even if not enough gets through to fill the stream below.

Making a mental note to stop for longer on my return, I take the road through the palms, past a group of mud houses, to the beginning of a narrow gorge where water flows down from the mountains ahead.

In the course of a thousand years the stream has sliced into the rock, creating a deep gash whose floor is a series of pools. Road and stream share this same narrow defile so that in some places they run beside each other, while in others, where the defile is wider, their ways separate.

It is now after eleven and very hot in my little car. The more I see of these natural pools the more they entice me to swim. A few minutes later I spot what looks like a larger one than most, partly hidden by a vast boulder broken from the cliff above. I find a space to park and with a bag of lunch, climb round the rock and down to the water.

The picture I find is one of some delight. This pool is indeed larger than the others, maybe 50 metres in length. It starts where the stream flows from a small rocky waterfall, stretches out between the boulder on one side and a narrow slope covered in oleander on the other, and snakes away into a shallow tail before dropping out of sight. Almost half the surface is covered in water-lilies, their dark leaves contrasting with the pale green of the pool. Dragonflies buzz restlessly among them, alighting for seconds before rushing to some new point of vision or display.

The huge boulder has, as I thought, isolated the stream from the road so that even though traffic is infrequent, the place is utterly private. The rock is sculpted and hollowed along the edge of the pool, smoothed and rounded by generations of floods into a ledge ideal for diving from or simply lying beside the water. High above, the sides of the gorge, probably 100 metres apart, appear almost to touch, allowing only a thin line of blue to show between them. The sun, practically overhead at this time, scorches in, catching most of the water but screened in places by isolated outcrops.

The gorge is completely still. Despite no discernible wind, the surface of the pool sparkles with small ripples whose reflection catches the overhanging faces of rock. It is indeed a perfect spot. As I gaze, the beauty of the scene combines with the silence and isolation to create an intense feeling of mystery. I find myself thinking of the streams in mythology where gods and spirits played beyond the ken of man. The only thing missing is a nymph or sprite to complete the picture.

How silly, of course, to forget that I am in Morocco. I have walked upstream for a few moments to take a photograph. At a suitable spot I turn and notice to my great surprise the brown body of someone who has appeared from nowhere and is now lying on the ledge by the pool. I take a picture and then walk back to find out who on earth fate has placed in my path this time. It turns out to be Hassan, a youth of about 16 with unusually curly hair.

'*Bonjour Monsieur. Ça va?*' He smiles up at me.

'*Oui, ça va bien,*' I sigh.

'You like to swim?' he asks in bad French.

'Yes.'

'Me too.' He gets slowly to his feet.

'I thought you might,' I say half aloud in English. 'Is it safe? Are there snakes or anything?'

'No it is good. But be careful of the rocks, they are slippery.' He waves me to enter from a particular rock at the head of the pool, before diving into the middle himself. I follow, finding the most beautiful water, warm but not too warm, and so much softer than the sea of the last few days. The pool is a little over a metre deep, making it easy for tentative toes to reach down and scrape coarse sand on the bottom.

For some time we swim around or float. The pool is a magical place, the only sound being the splashes of our strokes and the slapping of disturbed waves against the edge. Water lilies rise and fall, dragonflies skim, reflections flicker and dance across the rock-face. I cannot say I am totally surprised when after several close encounters Hassan's legs brush unmistakably against mine. Without a word he turns to see my reaction, dark eyes fixing me expectantly across the surface.

Moroccan water sprites do not appear out of the blue without reason and my antennae have been alerted from the moment I saw his uninhibited posture on the rocks. But I am not at all concerned. The boy means no harm, he is trying it on.

As we circle the pool I wonder what form his next try will take. For some minutes he remains in the deepest part, watching with all but his head submerged. Then he swims to the side and pulls himself out. Facing away he stands up. When he turns I get my answer. Quite unmistakable in all its glory is something most Europeans would find impossible to achieve after ten minutes in a cold mountain stream. No attempt at concealment, in fact quite the opposite. In small trunks he is flaunting himself. For one so young his brazenness is surprising and his libido nothing short of remarkable!

'Hassan,' I say in a mock-serious tone, 'you are a bad boy.'

His eyes meet mine very directly, the suspicion of a smile playing across his lips.

85

'Yes.'

I have been working in the desert for a long time – but not that long! In place of what he offers I suggest lunch. As I busy myself making sandwiches he stands watching. Maybe he is still trying to shock – or even boast, although his amused expression suggests it is now a game. Eventually he turns and dives in again. When he next climbs out I am relieved to find the problem diminished.

He tells me that his main job is at his brother's stall selling fossils and mineral samples, but he also likes swimming with tourists.

'Yes,' I say. 'It must be fun.' I do not, of course, mean it. I can think of nothing more frightful than sharing this perfect spot with visiting Europeans. It would be fun though to see their reaction when he struts his stuff!

Despite his poor French we find plenty to talk about until the food is finished. Then, while I clear up he stretches out again in the sun. Taking this as my cue to leave, I have a last quick dip and get dressed.

He asks if I will take him with me on my trip to the falls, but I decline. With the intention of spending the night, I can see few advantages and a number of rather obvious pitfalls in having such a prurient young man as a travelling companion. I offer instead to give him a lift some of the way, but he prefers to stay by the stream.

As I head back towards the real world I steal a last look at the scene. The secret gorge, the hidden mysterious pool and the sprite now lying abandoned in the sun. I have no idea where he came from, but it seems fitting he did so and I am glad.

'The high Atlas... stretch from the Atlantic coast across Morocco and Algeria into Tunisia.'

Agadir area. 'To me it is a sort of paradise in as much as I can think of nowhere I would rather be.'

Tarhazoute. 'The fleet is in silhouette as it draws ashore. With the loss of light all colour fades...'

Immouzer. 'I turn and notice the brown body of someone now lying apparently naked, by the pool.'

Tarhazoute. 'Soon we are sitting round a plate of unspecified food...' The author with Tahib and Ahmed before the fishing trip.

'One of the other barques... comes over... to compare notes.'

Azrou. 'The unmistakable outline of a magnificent Atlas cedar...'

Zianie. 'At one point we come to a ford...' The *chariot* with additional passenger.

13

Mountain Music

Hear her strange lutes on the green banks
Ring loud with grief and delight
Of the dim-silked, dark haired Musicians
In the brooding silence of night.

Walter de la Mare

Leaving the shelter of the gorge, the road climbs again, red rock and soil giving sustenance to small conifers, bushes and herbs. Even after such a small increase in altitude the atmosphere feels clearer, the sun hotter. As I progress, the vegetation thins. Further ridges of mountains come into sight, most running at a consistent height but some unaccountably thrusting individual wild and rocky fists towards the sky.

Being near where the snow lies in winter, the extremities of temperature endured by these hills have left their mark. Everywhere is cracking, splitting, crumbling. Huge seams have torn into each outcrop, leaving isolated stacks poised to collapse at any minute. Boulders and shale litter the valley floor where they fell in the heat or cold of earlier years. The earth's surface seems racked in pain – a fight to the death with no quarter given. Impressive rather than beautiful. Without the majesty of proper mountains yet strangely compelling so that each new corner unveils a spectacle to stir the senses.

After a stiff climb the hills level onto a plateau of less tortured ground where pine trees, probably indigenous, crowd the road. No traffic, except the odd taxi of returning tourists and a few overladen lorries belching diesel as they labour on their way. At the sign 'Welcome to Immozer' the first houses appear near the road.

My guidebook shows scant accommodation so I decide to go straight to the main hotel to see what is on offer. The Auberge des

Cascades turns out to be an unexpectedly charming place surrounded by an elaborate and sweet-smelling garden which clearly suffers from no lack of water. Situated on the edge of the village, its large terrace looks out across the valley of the falls into a haze of inaccessible mountains beyond. After several nights' sleeping on the floor, my resolve crumbles and I decide to take a room. Neither am I disappointed when the one I am given opens onto a veranda with an even better view of the mountains than from the terrace beneath.

🌴 🌴 🌴

It is by now three o'clock, leaving about three and a half hours of daylight. Rather than simply driving to the falls I decide to walk the 4 or so kilometres down into the valley in order to absorb something of the atmosphere of the place. This I duly do, arriving an hour later at a thick grove of holm oaks and olives marking the course of the stream.

My guidebook makes the layout so clear that I feel I can easily explore the falls on my own, but this is not to be. As a result of a scarcity of tourists, my arrival precipitates a row between several young amateurs as to who is to have the pleasure of escorting me. I am not included in the debate as my preference is clearly irrelevant. The idea that I might care to walk round alone is inconceivable. When eventually I start off I am taken in tow by two pleasant youngsters, one of whom is apparently dumb as he does everything by gestures and never says a word.

The falls are a great disappointment. The sight is spectacular, the course of the stream falling 50 metres or more down huge slabs of polished rock into a series of deep blue cauldrons. However, since rain has not fallen here for three years, the water has dried up altogether on the falls, with just a trickle oozing out at the foot of the rock-face. The cauldrons are reasonably full but three years of tourist, and more probably Moroccan, litter with nothing to wash it away has created an unattractive sight on closer inspection.

It is easy to see how impressive the falls would be, locals and litter permitting, with water spraying out and cascading down the side of the rock-face. Even now a mass of rich flora grows at the foot, ferns and mosses clinging optimistically to the old water course. But without water it is something of a sad sight and I hope and pray that such a drought cannot last forever.

From the falls, the boys lead me through a picturesque grove of ancient olives, before pointing out the 'Berber route' back to the village. This involves a steep climb up rock and rough scrub but will

88

make the return journey a lot shorter. With the daunting words *'attention des serpents'* (look out for snakes) ringing in my ears, I set off up the hill, stopping for a sandwich in sight of the top.

On arrival back at the hotel I make enquiries about supper. It seems that the group of people having lunch on the terrace when I first arrived were all day-trippers and only one Frenchman and I are staying overnight. This sounds a bad omen for dinner and anyway it all looks too civilised, so I book out. After a swim in the hotel pool, deserted and heavy with the scent of lilies, I drive out of the village to a quiet spot from which to watch the sun set over the mountains.

It is dark by the time I get back. With no electricity the village is blacked out. The café I had previously noticed in the main street now looks closed, the only light being the lamp of a small general store. When I ask the shopkeeper where I can get something to eat, he redirects me to the original café, telling me to go inside.

Pushing open the door, I find a room partially lit by an oil lamp whose beam is not visible from outside. The place is empty except for two men behind the counter playing chess. They look up as I enter, mumbling the usual greetings in a mixture of French and Arabic. I ask what is available. The proprietor indicates a *tagine* cooking on charcoal which would presumably have been his supper had I not come by. He lifts the lid to reveal a succulent stew of goatmeat, vegetables and olives ready to eat. Sitting me down at a low table with a candle and rough bread, he serves the food in its earthenware container, standing by while I try it. As expected it is delicious and a perfect adjunct to several glasses of Johnny Walker consumed watching the sunset.

After I have bought him and his friend a Coke, we talk for some time about life in the village. It seems that his friend is the local butcher so I am able to make much of his product. The room, which is almost dark, is large, with a fireplace in the centre. When I ask if they have snow in winter they say they do and that the fire is lit almost permanently. It is easy to imagine how cosy the room would be in the candlelight, embers glowing and the smell of pine logs, placid mountain people wrapped in blankets and turbans discussing the ways of the world as, outside, snow blows in from icy wastes.

I tell them the village appears empty. It turns out that tonight there is to be a concert in the other village down by the falls and everyone in the neighbourhood will be going. Apparently a local man who has made good in France has hired a band of Berber musicians. Would I like to go? If so, surprise surprise, I can take them with me in the car. The answer of course is yes on both counts, and the next thing I know the three of us are heading down the hill where I walked that afternoon.

We pass the small number of houses that comprise the village then take a dirt road through olive trees. No other cars are in evidence but every few metres small groups of women and children, wrapped in djellabas, are walking in the same direction. They stop to let us pass, their eyes large and quizzical like deer caught in the head-lights. Eventually I notice a brighter light, realising as we approach that a proper stage with floodlights has been set up on what must normally serve as a football ground.

On instructions from my companions, we pull in beneath olive trees a short distance from the stage. I get out. It is on the cold side but little can be done about that. A strong scent of fig trees and dry earth mingles with the acrid smell of dung. Groups of children run about, shouting excitedly in the gloom, while a line of older men sit silently along a stone wall, cigarettes glowing as they watch the vil-lagers arrive. Through the olives behind where I am parked stands a small mosque. Moon and stars provide enough light to make the white-washed face of the minaret stand out starkly against the night sky as it watches over this small gathering of the faithful.

More groups appear out of the gloom and shuffle in towards the stage although no one actually sits down. Everyone gets as close as they can without leaving the protective shadows of the olives. They stand or sit observing, one and all in kaftan or djellaba and many young boys wearing white skull-caps which accentuate their beauti-ful faces and wide-eyed curiosity. Everywhere, hushed voices and a pervasive feeling of pent-up excitement reminiscent of Guy Fawkes night before the lighting of the bonfire.

The stage itself resembles a boxing ring, white with red taffeta pinned around the base and a series of Moroccan and Berber flags hanging from the edge of the canopy roof. The brightness of spotlights seems out of place in such gloom; the putt-putting of a generator a regrettable twentieth-century intrusion on the night air.

The concert is meant to start at nine o'clock but things are defi-nitely running late. By half past nine, my appetite for new sights has been replaced by a penetrating chill in my legs. I return to the car and sit with my new friends to await developments.

Hardly have I done so when, on an unseen signal, all the women and small children waiting among the olives move silently forward and sit in well-ordered lines at the foot of one side of the stage. Some have brought rugs but most sit on the earth. Some have their faces showing but many are fully covered and remain so all evening. At the same time a man climbs onto the stage and starts adjusting the amplifiers with the Berber equivalent of 'one, two, testing, testing'. This has the desired effect of stirring some life back into those such as myself who are beginning to wonder if the evening will ever get under way.

Perhaps my ideas of Berber music have been too influenced by earlier experience with Mustafa and his brothers, and by some lads I watched performing on a café television a few nights ago. I am therefore somewhat surprised when a group of about eight middle-aged men in white kaftans climb onto the stage. My surprise lies chiefly in the fact that they are wearing traditional dress rather than the jeans I expected.

Their appearance is the signal for all the men and older boys to appear out of the gloom as if by magic and gather in a large group round the opposite end of the stage to the women. Surprise turns to astonishment when I focus on the band and discover its leader to be none other than the Libyan leader Colonel Ghadaffi, complete with white robes, long ringlets of black hair, dark glasses and a red fez such as might come out of a Christmas cracker. In addition to a large ceremonial dagger round his waist he carries a *rebab*, the curious Arab instrument half-way between a cello and violin, played between the knee and the crook of the arm.

The Colonel enthrones himself on an upturned orange crate whose undignified appearance is soon hidden by his robes. He then proceeds to play one or two notes for the others to tune their violins, banjos, *oudhs* and other unrecognised string instruments. Before they have a chance to get settled he suddenly bursts into a complete repertoire of scales played at such speed that it is quite impossible for anyone to follow. Designed more, I feel, to demonstrate his own mastery of the instrument than to assist his fellows in preparing for the gig, it succeeds magnificently.

Having soon exhausted himself, he then sits in silence while the others resume their tune-up – but not for long. His next ploy is to nod vigorously in time to whoever is playing at that moment. Developing a taste for this, within a short time he has his head waving around frantically, eyes closed, reminiscent of a whirling Dervish. The warming-up of the others is so tame in comparison that I wonder for a second whether at this early stage he has already put himself into a trance with his own musical acumen.

With so many strange instruments and traditional clothes, I soon realise that this Berber music is not going to be the same as the songs for which I developed such a liking on the coast. Indeed the tuning-up is so extensive that I begin to wonder if the concert proper has actually started. Just when I am about to ask, four large girls – women really – shuffle into sight from behind the musicians and start to sway in what might loosely be described as a dance. A few seconds later the different instruments join in harmony and we are in business.

I get out of the car and walk across to a stone wall to listen. To start with, the women dancers seem unrehearsed and, for me at any rate, the ample figures of all but one hold little charm. Neither, in fact, does the music, and I wonder how I am going to survive the evening until my passengers have had enough and are ready to go back up the hill. However, as the act progresses I begin to enjoy it more. The music improves, the dancers change gear, the Colonel starts to develop a rapport with the audience.

I say audience. I should say half the audience. As the evening wears on, the men become noisy and demonstrative, clapping, whistling and shouting encouragement. One or two even climb onto the stage and slip money to the Colonel or, to my surprise, down the front of the only pretty dancer's dress. Ghadaffi is well up to all this and carries on a running conversation with them through the mike when not busily sawing at his instrument.

But throughout all of this enjoyable and amusing spectacle the 60 or so women sit in complete silence, watching intently but only able to express appreciation by ululating at the moments of climax. The contrast between them and the men is stark and extraordinary. A fascinating comment on Berber culture.

At some stage my companions get out of the car and ask if I would like to join the crowd at the foot of the stage. We walk through knots of kids and groups of men only half paying attention, to where the crowd is thickest – perhaps about a hundred men and boys. Despite the cold a great atmosphere of revelry and cigarette smoke prevails. All the joking and ragging one would expect at home with a constant undercurrent of conversation and singing along to favourite songs. I notice the Frenchman from the hotel. As the only Europeans we are the subject of some curiosity to those who notice us in the gloom. Dark eyes stare and then turn politely away when we meet their gaze.

After initial misgivings I decide that the more I see of the Colonel the more I like him. It turns out that he is Mbarak Aisser, a famous recording star from Agadir with several hits to his credit. It also transpires that he is almost blind and the Ray-bans are not the gimmick I originally thought. He is an accomplished trouper. After a slow start the show he has worked up with his musicians and dancers is good entertainment.

Watching the ample women gliding and shuffling to rapturous applause I find myself thinking of the lithe and scantily clad go-go dancers sometimes seen performing in cages above discos in New York. I cannot resist the mischievous thought of the impact just one would make on this particular audience. Probably one of total shock to the women, and savage physical affliction to men with a testosterone level like that of my water-sprite of this morning!

Despite his frail appearance the Colonel has tremendous stamina, showing no sign of flagging. Although not really cold, my jeans and shirt are thin enough to allow the chill to seep into my bones, causing a chattering of teeth. When I can take no more I wander back to the car, where the others luckily agree they have had enough. It is by then about midnight. They tell me the concert will run until three or four in the morning. That will mean some six hours' almost non-stop performing for the band with no luxury hotel to return to afterwards.

We start up and reverse quietly from beneath the olives. As we drive off I notice other figures, mostly with young children, slipping away in the darkness. Further on, our headlights catch two fat hares sitting in the road, forcing a confused dash for the safety of trees. Somewhere along the way we acquire one of the cooks from the hotel. He talks excitedly to my two companions and every so often they break into song, beating out the rhythm on the dashboard. The concert has clearly been a most popular event and one which would have completely passed me by had I not found my way by chance into that café for supper.

I drop off my companions in the village before finding my way back to the hotel. A night watchman unlocks the gate. He leads me by torchlight across the scented terrace and through downstairs rooms now empty and silent in the dead of night.

I fall asleep with moonlight lying across my bed and the sound of distant music creeping up from the valley through the open casement of my room.

14

On the Buses

When those long caravans that cross the plain
With dauntless feet and sound of silver bells...

James Elroy Flecker

The bus system in Morocco is generally very good. Buses go everywhere and are incredibly cheap by our standards, though rougher than most in Western Europe. It took me some time to work out the different types. Top of the range are the big express buses, which are modern, air-conditioned, usually with onboard video and all mod cons. I travelled on these on several occasions and found them excellent. After these come various lower grades, some state-owned, some private venture. Age and condition varies enormously – the more local the bus, the lower the standard. Nevertheless they all worked well for me, including some whose dust-covered exteriors and roofs stacked with luggage and livestock looked far from promising.

In addition to these is something misleadingly called a 'car', which is in fact a mini-bus. Not available everywhere, they are invariably squashed full of as many men, women, children and animals as possible and used for local journeys up to perhaps 50 kilometres.

One of the reasons why I was late in catching on to these was because whenever anyone mentioned 'car', I assumed they meant a taxi. To start with I tried to avoid taxis as there are no meters and few set fees for the long-distance *grands* taxis. When you do not know where you are going it is difficult to negotiate a fair price in advance. Without doing so, you risk being taken for more rides than one, although later I used them extensively with little trouble. It is only in the towns where they have *petits* taxis with meters that the traveller has a real idea of what he is letting himself in for.

It is with a heavy heart that I finally leave the fishing village on the coast. I have stayed there for several visits and made many friends, but eventually the moment has come to move on and see other parts of the country. After a morning in Agadir I pack my things and catch a local bus out to where the boys live to say goodbye. It is not necessary but I am determined to tell them of my plans and acknowledge their friendship rather than simply disappear as if it has meant nothing.

Fortunately when I reach the hut Ahmed and Lahcen are at home and delighted to see me. I give each of them tee-shirts, which is the best I can do from my small luggage. I then say goodbye and exchange the usual kisses that I still find faintly embarrassing but also charming. How absurdly self-conscious and cold the British are. To people like this, and indeed all Moroccans, kisses are given without thinking. (When I finally leave the country, the chauffeur from the British Embassy, whose driving has terrified me on many occasions, gives me a resounding farewell kiss at Casablanca airport.)

By now I have seen enough of the people of the Maghreb to completely revise the prejudices with which I was saddled by armchair experts in England. Yes the men do kiss and hold hands, even policemen and soldiers in uniform. Yes they can be very tactile. They do behave towards each other with an intimacy quite foreign to the British. Living among them, though, I learn something of the completely different attitudes of a patriarchal society. I also witness so many acts of humanity between men that the closeness of their relationships becomes a matter of admiration rather than scorn. Anyone who tries to find a sexual interpretation in this intimacy is almost certainly barking up the wrong tree.

The others come with me up to the road where I plan to catch a bus to Essaouira and Safi and then on towards Casablanca – towns they can only dream of. We sit at the side of the road. True to form, no bus shows for over an hour. By then I have sent them away and wait on my own, thankful for my straw hat to keep off the worst of the sun. By the time a bus finally comes I am hot and hungry, to add to my feelings of sadness at leaving.

This is a smart bus. Stepping up into it I am instantly transported to another world. A radio plays furious Arab music, luckily not too loud. The upholstery is brown, with thin curtains cutting out the sunlight. The interior is dark and cool, even cold, as a result of a powerful air-conditioner hissing audibly at the front. Everyone dozes. Stop the world I want to get off! But I know I cannot. I have to leave this strangely bewitching coast at some stage and return to reality. Now the moment has come.

Something very lovely happens on that bus. Having bought a ticket, I settle on my own near the back. For half an hour the road continues along the coast, so I sit up at the window to look at the unfolding series of deserted beaches, the occasional collection of *barques* drawn up on the sand, small clusters of huts like the ones I have got to know, all cooking in the fierce afternoon heat. I find myself wondering how many other Mohammeds and Ahmeds are living along here in the cycle of poverty I find so depressing. Would I be met with the same friendship by other *pêcheurs*? I feel sure it would be so.

Where the Atlas start to recede the road is able to cut inland, passing endless rough parched fields with no crops, masses of argan trees showing as the only vegetation in the red earth and rock. They are picturesque trees and restful to watch. Gradually my eyelids droop.

When I awake the first thing I hear above the noise of the engine is the hiss of the air-conditioning. But above that is the sound of the radio. I listen for a few moments and realise that a different sound is coming from it. A man is chanting the Koran. His words have such a truly holy quality that I know straight away it can be nothing else. Without accompaniment he sings slowly with distinct pauses between phrases, his voice utterly clear and fine, of a purity which lifts it above the humdrum of life.

I look out of the window. The sun has started its downward path, the light more golden than before. The trees are still there, baking in the heat, throwing long shadows across the cracked earth. I lie in my seat, allowing the scenery to wash over me. The chanting penetrates my mind and its simple beauty uplifts my spirit. It is a moment of divine awareness I will not forget.

I fall asleep again and the next thing I know the bus has stopped. We are in a town, probably Essaouira. The bus is having a problem negotiating a street, jostling with every manner of car, bicycle, donkey and truck as well as teeming pedestrians. In the usual Moroccan way they pay not the slightest attention. A colourful scene, with men and women in djellabas and every sort of headgear.

When the bus finally arrives at the station it seems most people are staying on to continue to Safi. As soon as the doors open, a couple of boys climb on and walk down the aisle, selling items for the journey. One has ice cream, the other, slabs of peanuts held together by thick honey and sold in paper for about 25p each. He seems to do a good trade, but the ice creams less so, which must say something for the efficiency of the air-conditioning. With some Moroccans even the cost of these items becomes the subject of bargaining; small discourses, which in Arabic sound much more hostile than they probably are, go on as the boys progress up the aisle.

Just as they climb off, a different noise develops at the front. An old man in rough clothes is shouting an announcement. It takes me a moment to realise that he is praying for us. He persists, regardless of the reaction of the passengers. While some sit up and appear interested, others light cigarettes and continue talking. When it looks as if we are about to move, he walks up the aisle, taking a collection from anyone he can interest and thanking Allah loudly for each donation. On other buses I have seen cripples do the same thing, taking advantage of a captive audience to parade their disability and hold out their hand.

The sight of cripples and limbless in the street is not uncommon but perhaps less frequent than one might expect in a country with a limited national health service. The number of beggars too is nothing like as great as are to be seen in the Strand in London. Islam has clear instructions concerning the giving of alms. It is part of everyday life. Even the poor will stop and search for something to give to those less fortunate than themselves. I have often watched beggars make their way slowly down a line of shops, always getting a few coins from the proprietor with no thanks expected. Practically speaking, they would probably not want to try it too often, but no doubt they vary their route and spread the load.

The road north from Essaouira is very different from the one we were on earlier. As the Atlas slip behind, the country becomes flatter and greener and more intensively cultivated. Water obviously exists in great quantity because we pass all manner of vegetables as well as wheat, maize and pasture. As a result, more people are in evidence either by the road or working in the fields, usually with donkeys or mules. The bus affords an excellent view, being so high off the ground.

Speeding along, I look out onto a kaleidoscope of Moroccan rural life: lines of women gathering sheaves of wheat by hand in one field, while five minutes later the bus gets stuck behind a combine-harvester; stooks of straw such as have completely disappeared from the English landscape; old red baling machines for those who can afford them; women in dazzling colours winnowing wheat in the wind; four donkeys side by side threshing corn by treading round a central pole. Everywhere donkeys and mules, some weighed down by wickerwork panniers bursting with vegetables, others, hobbled with rope, wait to carry their owners home.

Once I see a boy cantering on a donkey. He is not astride its middle as one might expect, but sitting right back on a bony croup. Not only is there no saddle, but no bridle or reins either. The only method of steering is the usual whack on the side of the head with a long cane. It is hard to imagine how the brakes work.

Ploughing in Morocco is done by a variety of animals. The strangest sight I ever see is a single plough hitched up to both a camel and donkey together. I do not notice how the harness copes with two animals of such different dimensions. I assume they must be the farmer's only possessions and therefore have to be used in tandem, but later I see the same glorious combination several times so maybe there is some more technical explanation of which I am not aware. It certainly looks quaint the first time.

Because of the drought nearer the Sahara, camels this year have come further north than usual for food. Around Agadir and the foothills of the Atlas camels are common, but now quite a few have found their way even to this fertile area. Another amusing sight is to see grazing together in the same field, cows, sheep and camels, all quite unconcerned by each other.

One area we drive through seems to be a centre for growing carrots and for several miles we pass groups of men and women harvesting them. The first thing to see is huge mounds of bright orange. Near these is some form of water-supply and wooden troughs for washing them. The men actually doing the washing wear protective garments made from plastic fertiliser sacks, giving them the comical air of activated scarecrows not unlike *The Wizard of Oz*. The carrots are brought in from the fields by horse-drawn carts and, after washing, loaded onto lorries for transportation to the towns.

Lush green takes some getting used to after the rocky, red harshness further south and I imagine we must have left the Berbers behind in their barren wilderness. The Arabs here appear from the bus to be a happy smiling band, always ready to wave at passing traffic for no reason other than a general *joie de vivre*. Every so often the bus stops for anything from five minutes to half an hour. This is usually an excuse to get out for a leg-stretch among the gamut of boys selling cigarettes, either singly or in packets, and shining shoes.

On one such occasion I remain on board while the woman sitting next to me gets out. She returns with a portion of chips for me, wrapped in newspaper and completely unsolicited. Indeed, apart from smiling at her child once or twice, we have had no contact for over an hour. So rarely do I have contact with women in this country that I am unsure with what degree of friendliness she should be treated. This particular woman, whom I judge to be about 40, has the most lovely unblemished skin. A real bloom, showing none of the signs of age which seem to come to male faces at a sadly early age. I can only assume her freshness is the result of almost perpetual covering of the face from sun, wind and the lascivious gaze of men.

On longer stops, the drill is to go in search of sustenance, which comes in various forms. One possibility is to buy the wherewithal for a sandwich – bread and cheese; for example – and make it up for oneself. Another is to go to a shop and ask the proprietor to do likewise. Typically this will be done by splitting a baguette and slicing a hard-boiled egg into it with salt and pepper to taste. I do this sometimes, having first carried out a cursory inspection of the hygiene of the premises and of the gentleman in question. As with most aspects of this particular facet of Moroccan life, one has to quite literally place one's health and survival in other people's hands.

A third option for food is to buy ready-made sandwiches at a bar. More interesting than this, though, and what most of the more affluent local travellers do, is to go to a butcher, buy a skewer of raw meat, and take it to a pavement stall, where another worthy cooks it over charcoal. I could never understand why the stall-holder himself did not buy the meat and have a few brochettes ready for each bus. Maybe, in an area where there are few fridges, he did not want to risk being left too long with uncooked meat. I do not know. The cooked meat can either be eaten as it is, or placed in bread, or even eaten at a café with a salad of tomato and onion. I sometimes have these salads, despite reservations. As the ingredients are usually chopped into tiny pieces, one has no idea of the state of the raw materials nor the number of other people's plates they have already adorned that day.

Safi is a large town and port with Portuguese and Spanish influences. Having extended my days further south, I do not have time to stop here as I want to look at Oualidia, a village some 30 kilometres further north, which has been recommended by friends. When we reach Safi I ask the conductor how to get to Oualidia. He tells me I will have to get a 'car' which leaves from the other side

99

of town and to get there I will need a *petit taxi*. He asks for a pen and kindly writes out directions for the taxi-driver in Arabic. As a result of his help the transfer is accomplished without difficulty and I eventually arrive at the car just as it is about to leave.

This car is in fact a transit van of which three quarters of the body is enclosed for passengers, with the rear open for baggage. I can see the inside stuffed with people so am not very hopeful of a place, but when I appear the conductor beckons two men out and puts them in with the luggage. This gives me room to squash apologetically in among the remaining men, women and children, and crouch on my bag by the door. We set off almost immediately, soon climbing away from Safi, up onto a small coastal road.

The car rattles and labours with some discomfort. Every so often we stop to drop off, or worse, take on passengers. Gradually I notice another change of scenery as the land becomes more rocky. This time it is pale grey granite, though, rather than the red of the Atlas, and rolling and smooth rather than jagged and mountainous. Clinging to the rock are patches of rough grass scattered with wild fig trees. Clearly grazing land, the whole landscape is criss-crossed by beautifully laid dry-stone walls. The nearest similarity I can think of is parts of the west of Ireland.

Indeed the further we go, the more the scenery reminds me of the Emerald Isle, even though the temperature and rainfall are somewhat different. Despite the gentle rolling nature of the fields, it strikes me as a wild, wind-blown piece of country supporting few people other than solitary shepherds with their flocks of sheep and goats.

After what seems a very long time in cramped conditions, the bus starts passing houses and signs of civilisation. The sea has been visible on our left all the time, but not the coast, due to high cliffs. The water sparkles temptingly in the sun, particularly to me, as I am beginning to find the intimacy of the car somewhat stifling. Actually, it cannot be any better for the locals. Moroccans have a great sense of humour on these occasions and it is usually easy to catch someone's eye and share the misfortune with a wink or a smile. Even so, everyone is visibly relieved when we finally arrive in the centre of the village of Oualidia.

We unravel ourselves from the inside and stand about on the road, stretching our bodies back into shape. The conductor goes to the back and starts lifting off luggage. I have nothing more than my backpack, but as I turn to leave I notice him offload a goat's carcass, its legs trussed together with rope for lifting. He drops it carelessly among the bags. It is only when I look more closely that I notice the unfortunate creature blink.

15

Tariq

All the great courts were quiet in the sun,
  And full of vacant echoes: moss had grown
Over the glassy pavement, and begun
  To creep within the dusty council halls.

Rupert Brooke

I ask directions and walk downhill towards the sea in search of the
Hotel Hippo Campe, which my friends have recommended. Realising
that I have not slept in a bed nor bathed in hot water for six nights,
the prospect of a hot shower and sheets, which until now has not
crossed my mind, suddenly seems like heaven.

Walking on, I become acutely conscious of the smell of vegetation in general and certain strong and delicious scents in particular.
Either side of the road are walls concealing private gardens. Exotic
trees poke up from behind them, long branches and fronds hanging
out above my head. These scents are the first indication of a return
to the civilised world. Where I have come from, scent has been
scarce, and usually suspect. No water can be spared for gardens,
neither do *pêcheurs* have the money or time to contemplate
such luxuries. But here, within easy drive of Casablanca and with
plentiful water, people have the wherewithal to beautify their
surroundings. Nearing the hotel, I begin to consider this difference.
On the one hand the air is deliciously fragrant, something I now
realise I have really missed. But on the other the very fragrance
indicates domesticity, civilisation. The place and people have been
tamed.

My hotel is rather curious, consisting of a main building with
reception and dining room; a garden massed with colour and scent;
then three lines of bedrooms somewhat like military barrack-blocks.
Hardly a soul is to be seen. I am not disappointed by my room.

Simple, spotlessly clean and, yes, a shower, bath and proper WC. The porter who has directed me hovers at the doorway.

'Thank you,' say I, 'I will give you something later as I do not have any change at the moment.' I have carried my own luggage so he has done nothing more taxing than show me to my room.

'Could it be this evening please as I am not here tomorrow?'

'*Bien sûr.*' I smile at his cheek.

It is six fifteen. I reckon there is time to walk down to the sea to get some idea of the layout of the place, and then have a long bath before dinner. I open a bottle of wine, fill the tooth mug and drain it before heading out of the hotel.

🌴 🌴 🌴

Oualidia overlooks a large sandy lagoon protected from the sea by a reef through which there is only one entrance. At low tide the lagoon is virtually dry, showing the most lovely golden sand. But when the tide comes in, it does so at great speed covering almost all the sand, and creating a large sea-water lake. In the evening light I walk past this lagoon towards where ferocious waves pound the protective rocks beyond.

'*Bon soir, Monsieur.*' I know Morocco too well to expect to be allowed to carry out this reconnaissance on my own. And yes, there he is, a boy of about 16, in jeans and faded black tee-shirt, smiling as he appears from nowhere.

Inevitably we start talking. Do I want a guide? He knows the history of the area. Would I like to see *les grottes*, the caves? As he talks I assess him as harmless, intelligent and personable, so I hire him.

He tells me that the best *grottes* are some way down the coast, but that there is one nearby. I say I should like to see it, so, without pausing, he starts to climb up onto the reef which forms the barrier from the open sea. The rock is coral, twisted and sharp and difficult to walk on. My admiration bounds when I realise my friend is barefoot. Razor-sharp rock seems to make not the slightest difference to his progress – he is still quicker than me. On reaching the top we look down onto a seething mass of waves crashing against rocks and rebounding into each other with frightening force in a furious caldron of spray. The noise is overwhelming.

I cannot make out why the sea should have such a swell when practically no wind touches my face. Looking south along the coast, an amazingly rough scene of waves and spray reveals itself for which there is no obvious explanation. It gives the lie to my thoughts of domesticity inland. This part of the coast of Africa is wild and spectacular, particularly in the evening sun.

After giving me the chance to absorb the sight, my friend beckons above the roar to follow. We drop down on the seaward side and suddenly come to a hole in the rock just large enough for a man to squeeze through. Indicating this as the entrance to the cave, and warning me to watch my head, he leads the way.

The first thing I notice is how the roar of waves fades as soon as we get into the narrow passage. I follow my guide, stooping to avoid the glistening rock, the light growing dimmer as we progress. After perhaps 20 metres the sound of the sea returns and the tunnel opens out into a cave about 5 metres round and just too low to stand upright. We pause in this small echo-chamber and then cross to the mouth. Shaped like a keyhole, it looks out just above the boiling caldron. The boy steadies me as I lean forward to look down.

When I have seen enough I signal to go as it is getting late. We retrace our steps and eventually emerge into the dying sunlight. I am genuinely pleased by the *grotte* and tell him so.

'*Comment t'appelles tu?*' I ask. 'What is your name?'

'*Je m'appelle Tariq,*' he replies.

'OK, Tariq. I must go now, but will you be able to show me the rest of the place tomorrow?'

'Of course.' He pauses. 'Would you like to stay at my house? I have a room in the village.'

At this particular moment I can think of nothing in the world more desirable than the shower and large brass bed in my room in the hotel. I thank him for the offer but decline and we agree that he should come and find me at the hotel tomorrow morning. He has so far proved an informative and pleasant companion – an improbable state of affairs in England but quite normal in Morocco.

I only have one real complaint about the hotel – namely piped music in the dining room. That in itself is not unexpected, but the sadness is that it is European music, French and British. After the wild Berber music of the Atlas I am simply not ready to be drawn quite so speedily and conclusively back into the world from which I have purposely escaped. True, the whole feel of Oualidia is different from further south. But the wildness of the sea has left me with some encouragement that things African might continue to prevail over things European. The music belies this. It is a disappointment.

Next morning I head for the dining room feeling well rested and happy. Hot sun highlights the colours and scent of geraniums, roses and lilies outside my room. As the dining room is empty I ask to have coffee on the veranda, and am soon sitting on my own at a small table looking out across the lagoon. The tide is out and the sand a deep yellow with one thin channel of water threading its way inland up the creek. Not a soul moves anywhere. Immediately below me, rocks and pools give off that strong smell of seaweed reminiscent of childhood holidays. I soon spot Tariq sitting among them.

When I join him he asks if I would like to see oysterbeds up the creek. I agree, so we pick our way along the edge of the channel heading inland. Almost immediately I am surprised to find that just along the coast from the hotel stands a strange sight – namely a small, semi-ruined and overgrown palace. It turns out to have belonged to King Mohammed V, grandfather of the present King.

No fence or wall protects it so we are able to wander at leisure around the deserted buildings. The doors to the main rooms are locked, but we spend some time looking through windows and climbing outside terraces and staircases. The buildings, of an attractive yellow stone, do not appear to have been unused for all that long, perhaps 20 years. They would be easy to resuscitate, but for what? King Mohammed already has four palaces to my certain knowledge and probably more. Tariq says he thinks that latterly the palace was used as a hospital or convalescent home.

The oysters disappoint slightly in that, apart from various marker-buoys, the shellfish themselves are kept in wire cages under water. The only ones we see are a few hundred in boxes, waiting to be scrubbed and shipped off to the restaurants of Casablanca, where, in my other world, I sometimes enjoy them. A small team of women cleans and packs them.

My guide asks if I still want to see the larger caves, and when I tell him yes, we set off down the coast. Annoyingly a large bank of cloud has come into sight, blocking out the sun and reducing the temperature significantly. I am hoping to swim as Tariq tells of a good beach near the caves, but without the sun the prospect fades. We replace our shirts and walk on.

Tariq says he is still at school. Quite how he is therefore able to spend the day guiding strangers round the beach, I cannot imagine. He comes from further down the coast and lives on his own in a *chambre* in the village. In his spare time he goes out with the *pêcheurs* to earn money and, more improbably, learns karate. Extremely self-possessed and no fool, I notice he has blue eyes, which is not uncommon amongst Berbers but comparatively rare in Arabs like him. When he grows up he wants to study *médecin*.

We walk for some way in silence. Houses cluster around the lagoon and uphill inland to the main Casablanca road where the bus dropped me yesterday. Now we head south along the coast, leaving buildings and civilisation behind. Our route takes us sometimes along the high-tide mark and sometimes through sand-dunes covered in reeds and rough grass. Always on our right is the coral barrier beyond which a furious sea crashes and leaps with unexpected ferocity. The ground inland must be brackish as fields beside the escarpment turn into unkempt marshland at sea-level. No one is about because no one has any reason to be there.

The other *grotte* has a similar entrance to the one of the night before and I can see that it too will take us out to a vantage point above the sea. I turn to Tariq for directions and am surprised to see his arm in the air in a wave. Looking the other way, I notice two men standing on the coral breakwater, not far off but hidden during our approach by a small headland. They are the first people we have seen for ages. Tariq waves again and they acknowledge.

Quite suddenly I feel a frisson of apprehension. He has known since last night that he and I will be coming to these caves this morning. We are now a long way down a deserted beach. No one has seen us come there, and no one knew where I was going when I left the hotel. Supposing these two men are in league with the boy? Suppose he is the bait in a rather nasty trap that at best will lead to a confrontation in the cave, at worst a watery grave on this wild coastline? A body would not last minutes in that boiling caldron before being smashed against the rocks and torn apart even before the sharks arrived. I pause. Tariq, who has already started down the narrow tunnel, turns. Some sixth sense seems to tell him of my doubts. For a second he looks quizzically into my face. Then he smiles.

'Come,' he says. 'Don't be afraid.' He stretches out his hand.

My penchant for living dangerously has always been tempered with an instinct for self-preservation and something of an ability to assess character at a glance. If it is true that your senses are heightened the moment before you die, I feel like that right now. In the brief second that I stand at the mouth of the passage, I register the distant background of flying spray and white surf, the nearer silhouettes of the two men watching from the rocks, and immediately to my front, Tariq's smiling face and outstretched hand. Of a sudden the atmosphere seems unnaturally intense. I hesitate. He speaks again but his voice is carried away on the wind. Still I pause. At this precise moment a shaft of sun breaks through the cloud, changing the sea from grey to pale green and sending a burst of warmth onto my face. Is it an omen? I turn to the entrance.

The start of this cave is spectacular. Narrower and longer than the other, the hole drops steeply. Every now and then I glance behind me. It would be difficult to hear anyone approaching, so great is the roar echoing up the rocky passage. I wonder how easy it would be to defend oneself in such a confined space. Probably not impossible, provided the others have no weapons, although if Tariq is with them he will be at my back when I turn. I do not think he is armed as there are no unexpected shapes in his jeans, but although still a boy he looks wiry and tough – and there is always the karate factor.

The stone walls and ceiling glisten with moisture. I follow close as we crawl on hands and knees over damp sand and rock. The further we go, the darker it becomes, until we reach the cave proper. Then suddenly the passage opens into a much more substantial chamber than the one yesterday, with a large mouth at the far end above the sea. Every few seconds a dull thud from below precedes a cloud of spray shooting across the opening. After examining the chamber we crouch by the edge and look over. The sea is smashing against rocks about 3 metres below us, pushing and sucking at barnacles and weed. For a moment all is clear, then another wave crashes in, smothering everything in foam and roaring up with consummate fury.

I glance once more across the cave into the gloom of the tunnel. Not a sign of anyone. It is far too noisy to talk so I get out cigarettes and light a couple, passing one to my guide. He takes it with a nod and sinks back against the rock, gazing seawards through a veil of smoke.

For a few moments I contemplate him. I do not know why but for some reason he does not seem quite as vulnerable as my Berber friends further south. I reckon he is more intelligent than them. Whether it is that, or whether it is simply that I have not seen his home and the conditions in which he lives, I am not sure, but somehow I do not feel the same concern for his future as I do for theirs. Who knows? Before I leave he tries again to persuade me to extend my stay and spend the night in his room. I would like to do so if only to complete the comparison with the other *pêcheurs*, but my programme will not allow it this time.

We eventually emerge from the *grotte* to find the sun making a valiant effort to break through. My earlier worries seem unfounded as the two men have disappeared. Tariq takes me to a place where waves have undermined a small cliff, creating a natural blow-hole. With every wave a blast of sea-air expels itself with a groan of considerable force up at our faces. He waits until just after it has done

106

so and then packs the hole with small pieces of driftwood. A few seconds later the wood shoots out scattering for about 20 metres across the rocks. A clever trick.

🌴 🌴   🌴 🌴   🌴 🌴

Time is marching on. We head back, but when the sun finally comes out, decide to stop for a swim after all. We choose an isolated spot a little like a miniature version of the lagoon in front of my hotel, with only a narrow entry and exit to the ocean. Even here the sea boils with more unaccountably large waves, but I am confident that should anything go wrong we cannot be carried far. Also, inside the reef there are probably no currents.

Leaving our clothes on the sand, we run into the water. Tariq turns out to be an unadventurous swimmer and soon gets out to lie in the sun while I have an exhilarating quarter of an hour battling with the waves. Suddenly I realise I must grab lunch and start thinking about my bus.

Bread and sardines are bought at a small shop, then we sit beside the lagoon eating and talking. The boy points out another one of those creatures I prefer not to contemplate when swimming. This he calls a cat-fish, but I know it is nothing of the sort. About 30 centimetres long, at first glance it resembles a black polythene bag floating in the water. Only when looked at carefully is it possible to see a discernible front and rear with, between them, several transparent black wings propelling it slowly along. Whether it is poisonous or not I do not know, but it has a most sinister appearance and I am glad we did not find it earlier.

Having packed my bag and settled up at the hotel, I walk with Tariq back up the hill to the bus stop. I pay him for guiding me and send him happily on his way with a promise of copies of the photos. He is a likeable young man with a certain charm and has been an excellent guide. Without him I doubt I should ever have seen the caves as they are not mentioned in any of my guidebooks. I would probably not have explored the palace either.

I have one final unexpected incident in Oualidia while waiting for the bus. In my experience if you ask three different people the time of the next bus you will get three different answers. I therefore do this and work out the average. I conclude that a bus for Casablanca should be along in about half an hour.

'*Allemand?*' By now I am beginning to feel rather like Clint Eastwood in the film *Coogan's Bluff*. He plays the part of an Arizona agent who chases a criminal to New York. Because of his stetson,

107

all New Yorkers open conversations by saying, 'Texas?' to which he replies with an increasingly long-suffering grimace, 'No, Arizona.'

'*Non, Anglais.*' I turn to see who is after what this time. A fine-looking middle-aged man in djellaba sits behind the counter of a kiosk.

'*Veux-tu un café?*' he asks. I accept and we fall to talking. He asks what I have been doing and I explain. He then tells me something I find rather fascinating. Apparently this part of the coast is one of the main migration routes for various birds flying between Africa and Europe. I forget exactly which is the optimum month, but for a few days each spring, he says, the lagoon is a staging post for literally thousands of flamingos. At low tide you can hardly see the sand for the mass of birds that stop over. It sounds a wonderful sight and I make a mental note to try to return sometime and see it. To my complete astonishment he then starts on a different tack.

'I expect you've got shares in the Channel Tunnel?' Bearing in mind we are in an insignificant country village in Morocco and the conversation is in French, I wonder if I can possibly have heard him right. But I have. As it so happens, I bought some of the shares at the top of the market and have watched them collapse in value ever since, but the last thing I want on holiday is worries of this type. As the bus seems reluctant to appear I delve a little deeper. My new friend, I discover, works in Paris and is just home for a holiday. In this context his original question seems less odd, but even so it takes me completely off-guard.

16

The Zaiane Highlands

His season is not all delights
Nor every night an ecstasy!

Laurence Hope

Perusing the pages of *Rogerson* while sheltering from the sun on some wild deserted beach, my interest is raised by his descriptions of the Zaiane Highlands. This area, starting about 100 kilometres inland from Rabat, is renowned for farming and horses. What attracts me more is his belief that it has virtually escaped the attention of tourists.

This time I take a civilian flight from Laayoune up the coast to Agadir, stopping for a short while at Tan Tan, a tiny landing-strip which cannot have changed much since the pioneering days of Saint-Exupéry. While mail from Laayoune is unloaded we are allowed off the prop aircraft to stretch our legs in the evening sunlight. There is a round flight from Agadir to Laayoune three times a week, but what on first thoughts may seem a dull journey, especially for the pilot, is invariably enlivened by the unrelenting attention of the wind.

From Agadir I get an onward flight to Casablanca, arriving after dark and being forced to wait while a planeload of holidaying Egyptians fight their way through immigration. On the flight I have been befriended by a Moroccan bank manager who volunteers to give me a lift to the city centre, and also tells of a reasonable hotel. As we talk I become increasingly interested to see what car he drives. He has a daughter being educated in England and he himself has travelled extensively in Europe and Asia, so is he a fat cat or what?

Luggage in hand, we soon meet his wife, a smiling woman of about 40, and head out of the airport building to find the mysterious status symbol. In the car park we are assailed by a mass of boys and youths, which he disperses with an ease I have yet to master. Suddenly he is unlocking the door of a small Fiat of no significance whatever. Well, if this successful member of the professional classes travels in a Fiat, who is it who drives the big Mercedes? They cannot all be cousins of the King!

These are a charming couple, most anxious for me to enjoy my stay. In the centre of Casablanca they drop me off, having found and briefed a taxi-driver. The man waves goodbye with a 'The hotel is about five minutes,' which might be true had the taxi in question not previously been the subject of a serious accident which prevents it moving in a straight line. Forward motion is crabwise, the rear wheels tracking to the right of those in front, and an ominous scraping sound coming from underneath. Anyway I am now committed so just have to hope we arrive before the conveyance collapses.

My intention next morning is to hire a car to explore the Zaiane district, *Rogerson* having advised that buses are not ideal. However, a trip through the pulsating rush-hour traffic of Casa to a firm recommended by the concierge proves abortive due to the exorbitant price. Eventually I catch an excellent train to Rabat and transfer to a bus which sets off almost immediately. My plan is to take the main road to Meknes as far as Khemisset and then find a smaller bus to take me via Maaziz into the centre of the Zaiane region. As usual this is tempting fate, but at the same time it lays me open to unforeseen encounters on the way.

It is only an hour later that I find myself in Khemisset, the subject of many shouts, whistles and grasping hands as I am offloaded from the main bus and rushed to a rough old charabanc, roof piled with luggage, black diesel belching from the exhaust as it stands waiting to leave for Maaziz. Just as well I have already removed my backpack, as the interior of the new bus is so crowded that I can barely squash up the steps. This is real peasant transport, everyone in robes and turbans, the aisle blocked with sacks and bags. By now we are moving, our horn blowing an *au revoir* as we weave through people and cars to the exit from the bus station.

Straight away the conductor starts reorganising things, squashing a man up here, putting a boy on the floor there, stowing a bag there. An old-timer offers me the edge of his seat, on which one cheek finds some sort of sanctuary although it may not survive the whole journey. We are already on the open road, groaning along at a steady speed.

'*Monsieur, ici,*' a youth is beckoning from half-way down the aisle. Is he talking to me? Yes, I think he is. He signals again, so, thanking the man and unravelling my backpack from the sandalled feet of several neighbours, I struggle down the aisle, trying not to crash into my fellow voyagers.

'*Ici.*' My new friend indicates a small space beside him into which I sink, propping the backpack on my knees. We shake hands and I learn that he is another Hassan, a student from Fez.

'Where are you going?' he asks.

'I am not sure,' say I. Open-ended travel is hard to explain to Moroccans, partly because they will only board a bus to get to a specific place and partly too because they know perfectly well that any European can afford to travel in greater comfort. 'I am going to Maaziz to start with, and then on towards Khenifra.'

'The bus finishes at Maaziz,' he says.

'Well, I'll stop the night there then.'

'Where will you stay?' he asks. This sort of interrogation may sound annoying but in fact it is not. My companion seems genuinely interested. He is perhaps 18 though it is hard to be sure behind wrap-around dark glasses.

'I'll find a hotel,' say I. 'Can you recommend one?'

'*Monsieur*, there is no hotel. You are welcome in my house.'

I have a feeling he is speaking the truth and there probably is no hotel. Certainly *Rogerson* does not mention one. It is now about four o'clock. In jeans and white shirt he looks genuine enough, so I thank him and agree to stay at his house. The offer accepted, he falls silent, so I am able to look out at the countryside. Round here is rolling earth, some ploughed, some barren, too dry to support anything more than wisps of grass turned to hay where it stands.

We reach Maaziz about an hour before last light, but when everyone else gets up, Hassan tells me to stay put. We apparently have further to go.

This time of day is always busy, with workers buying the evening meal on their walk home. The bus takes an age to negotiate its way through stalls teeming with people while everyone on board stands in the aisle ready to get off. Eventually it stops with an almost audible sigh. As the others unload I enjoy looking at the bustle of a small market, people choosing vegetables, stall-holders fanning the flies off meat, old men clutching bundles of mint, donkeys everywhere. The sound of traders shouting their wares mingles with the general buzz of activity and the wailing of music. For a moment I contemplate a rack of dead chickens slowly putrefying in the heat and dust.

When the bus moves off, Hassan and I are the only two passengers left. We are going, he explains, to his sister's house the other side of the village. Leaving the buildings, we cross a bridge over a substantial river-bed with little water, and as I turn to look back, the bus halts. Soon Hassan and I are standing together on the side of the road while the bus disappears into the hills beyond.

The first impression is of silence. The village is visible beyond the bridge, but it must be a mile away so no noise comes from there. Trees grow along the edge of the river but the fields around us are empty, the only sound being the twittering of sparrows preparing for bed. Nearby, the only feature is a substantial house on the other side of the road, surrounded by a luxurious orchard and stone wall. Surely he does not live there, although if he does not it is hard to think why we have got off. Have I really fallen so squarely on my feet?

'Come,' says Hassan, picking up my backpack with typical Moroccan courtesy. We walk through smart gates and round to one side. The building looks deserted but delicious smells come from the surrounding vegetation. And then, yes, there it is, a small hut in the garden with a girl working outside. As I had half expected, Hassan's sister is married to the *gardien* of this property, whose owner is a government official in a nearby town. Also sharing the hovel are the girl's baby son and another young woman.

Hardly have we arrived and been introduced when the *gardien* himself arrives on a bicycle, apparently undaunted by the sudden appearance of his brother-in-law with a middle-aged Englishman. The hut is divided into two rooms and we are shown into one, where rugs and cushions are quickly laid out. Conversation in Berber follows between the men while I have my first look at the women. Both about 20, they have charming faces, clean hair, rough clothes and a manner at the same time outgoing and welcoming, but also shy and reserved. Apart from the odd 'model' in Agadir and a few chance encounters with more worldly women in towns, this is my first experience of meeting unspoilt Moroccan girls. Impressions are favourable.

Hassan's brother-in-law is going by bike to buy food in the village. I offer money but they will not hear of it. Hassan comes to sit with me, carrying in his infant nephew, who is quite delightful both in appearance and manner. With big brown eyes, he already shows signs of Moroccan inquisitiveness, approaching me quite unafraid and playing with my belt buckle. These Moroccans are not dark-skinned and I am sunburned; even so, this child cannot possibly have seen anyone of my colouring before. Nevertheless he gurgles and smiles and I am soon captivated.

When Hassan takes over with the child, I start to speculate on two more mundane subjects. The first is, how will we sleep tonight?

There would seem to be three possibilities: either husband, wife and child will sleep in one room, while brother, companion and European bent on discomfort, sleep in the other; or both girls and child will sleep in one, while the men sleep in the other; or brother, sister and child will sleep in one and the rest of us in another. Because of the segregation of men and women, this mélange presents an interesting conundrum.

My second speculation revolves around the location of the loo. I am able to resolve this quite soon when I feel the need for a pee. I ask Hassan and am told to go anywhere in the garden. This is not quite what I hope to hear but not altogether surprising.

It is now dark. Hassan has lit an oil lamp for the girls, who are washing and changing the child prior to bed. A feeble light penetrates my room but not enough to stop my eyelids from drooping. Just as I drop off the *gardien* appears triumphant from the village, carrying our supper into the other room. When the child's ministrations are finished, I look in, to see, lying on the block of wood where the nappy-change had just taken place, one of those dear old putrefied chickens!

Luckily my horror is distracted by Hassan's appearance in my room with his brother-in-law. Another lamp is lit and the *gardien* produces a small silver pipe, which he fills with hash. Laughing, he lights a match and draws on the pipe until the room is filled with smoke. For some time he lies puffing and watching while Hassan and I discuss the ways of the world, our perceptions no doubt enhanced by passive inhalation.

I have been in Morocco long enough to take most things in my stride, but I must admit to being a little surprised when Hassan stands up and uncovers a television. How, I wonder, can this possibly work? Surely not on kerosene. My question is answered when he produces a flex, which he connects up to a car battery I had not noticed in the other room. Soon we have black and white football, the picture good but the volume excessive. Actually it is something of a relief as the effect of constant chat in French is beginning to tell and the night is still young. But hang on, what is happening now? I don't believe it. The *gardien* is kneeling to pray in the corner of the room while, 5 metres away, a game of international football is being played at full volume. Oh well!

The chicken is better than expected and I manage to forget where it has been prepared. Afterwards, when the telly has been switched off, I go outside, partly to give them the chance to prepare the rooms for sleep, but also to recce a suitable loo should the chicken strike back. In bright starlight I stand in the orchard, suddenly conscious of the fragrance of watered vegetation and the freshness of the night air. The only sound is the distant barking of dogs, the only sight the long, low silhouette of hills and the twinkling of lights towards the village. This is the beauty of Morocco. Last night I was in the hurly burly of Casablanca, and now here I am in total tranquillity.

When I get back to the hut, the door to our room is half closed and I can see shadows moving about inside. I push it and find everyone busy preparing for the night. More cushions and a couple of blankets have appeared, although I for one will not need them. Hassan indicates an area of rug to me and places a pillow at one end. Gradually movement subsides. I occupy my space, then the *gardien*, then Hassan. Finally the two girls come in with the child, each taking the remaining space on the floor until the one option comes about that I had never considered – we are all to sleep together!

Perhaps there is 30 centimetres between each of us. Curiously, I soon drop off despite the hardness of the floor, although I wake several times in the night and lie listening to the breathing of my companions. I know that Berbers are less concerned about the segregation of women than Arabs, but in all my adventures in Morocco I have never before slept in the same room as a woman. I wonder whether having me there has given rise to any quandary or whether they have treated me exactly as they would a local visitor. I feel it is the latter which is faintly flattering.

Next morning the girls are up first, my reveille being sounded by the roar of a gas cooker heating water for the child. I lie for a while, allowing the others to do whatever it is. Sun streams in through the door while cockerels crow nearby. The *gardien* leaves early on an unspecified mission, while Hassan remains horizontal beside me. He is a student taking a few days off, so he has every excuse to relax.

I am pleased when his sister brings in the child, sits down with her back against the wall and uncovers a full breast. Without the slightest hesitation she feeds in front of me, first one breast then the other, skin unblemished, bosoms perfect. I say pleased because I feel that by so doing, her lack of shyness shows again that I have been accepted.

🌴　　　🌴　　　🌴

I am in a dilemma as to what to do regarding my travels. In some ways I feel that I have had a good experience with these people and now I should move on if I want to see more of the Zaiane area.

114

Equally, hurrying through endless villages, one only brushes the surface and perhaps I should spend longer in this welcoming company to find out more about them and their lives. My dilemma solves itself when Hassan announces, 'Today we go *à la campagne*.'

Oh? What exactly does that mean? To the country? After my night in Casa I feel I am already in the country. When he adds, '*Dans le chariot*', my suspense is complete.

At his bidding I accompany him the mile or so back to the village to see what will transpire. On the way we cross the river, which by now I have discovered to be the headwaters of the Bou Regreb, the famous river which flows into the Atlantic between Rabat and Sale, where on other trips I have admired it from the British Embassy. Up here it shows the potential for greatness, with a wide bed and substantial bridge, but at this time of year the level of water is only that of a stream.

The village is not interesting, consisting of one main street lined with shops. It is clearly a centre for farmers, and beneath a thick coating of dust most buildings are modern. The river must bend because we meet it again at the other end of the street, and Hassan tells me to wait by the bridge. Unsure where he is going, I swing my legs over the wall to await his return.

Slightly to my surprise three boys are bathing naked in the river just below me. Surprise, that is, because they are approaching puberty and previous experience has shown Moslems to be modest in this regard. But rather like the girl breast-feeding her child, I see this as a much more natural glimpse of rural life than normal. Needless to say these three are typically athletic, carrying out running dives and somersaults into water that looks dangerously shallow and hideously filthy.

Hassan calls me from the road. He is standing beside an ass pulling an open cart remarkably like, yes, a chariot. At the reins is a Berber youth of dashing appearance. I have no idea as I shake his hand that he is about to be responsible for one of my worst moments in all Morocco. I stand beside him while Hassan perches behind us. The plan seems to be to return to the hut, collect our things and then go *à la campagne*. For a while we trot down the street, the driver clicking his tongue and swishing an encouraging stick across the ass's quarters. The rough old chariot travels well even though the wheels look as if they may have come off a child's pram.

In the village are other horse-drawn carts as well as a number of cars and trucks. As we reach the outskirts, the road starts to slope to the river and it is now that the driver flicks the ass extra hard and jerks the reins to induce a canter. My vivid imagination goes into

115

overtime for two reasons; one is that the ass is not shod, so its spindly legs could easily slip on the sloping tarmac; the other is that he insists on driving down the line where tarmac ends and hard shoulder begins – in other words, down the roughest bit of going anywhere. Apart from one leg being marginally higher than the other, this also gives the ass the opportunity to stumble on the many holes and bumps which mark the line.

'Hep, hep,' he shouts, smacking the ass's arse with far more force than necessary. By now it is cantering freely, the wheels rumbling, the box trying to lead off to the left. 'Hep,' he cries, shaking the reins in a way which prompts me to fear for the animal's balance.

'What is your ass's name?' I ask nonchalantly as if jaunts of this kind are quite normal.

'It's an ass,' he laughs. Moroccans clearly do not humanise their beasts of burden the way we do.

As we get into a full gallop, there is nothing I can do but hold tight and try not to think of the reasons why our ass must surely fall, pitching us out at speed onto the tarmac. Is there a hospital in the village? Forget it. An ambulance? Don't be funny. The bridge is coming up and I can see our destination beyond, but this boy is now really enjoying himself. 'Hep, hep.' Still we career along, the horse shaking its head every time his whip strikes. Are we going straight enough to make the bridge or will we hit the side? Phew! After a nail-biting few minutes we are suddenly on it and at last he is slowing down.

It is a bit awkward being the only one who has noticed anything wrong. Hassan gets off, smiling as if all is normal, and I cannot possibly explain to the girls the nightmare I have just been through. Eventually we place my backpack onboard and say goodbye. They still refuse to take any money and it is at a walk, thank goodness, that we start to follow the river upstream.

The water is low, but the *oued* either side is wide. In some places the track takes the dried-up river-bed, necessitating frequent and severe beatings of the ass as it struggles to pull us over boulders avoidable by those on foot. In other places the route takes us up out of the *oued* to a dusty track between hedges of bamboo or cedar.

The sun is now well up in the sky, birds singing and the wheels of our dear old buggy creaking along behind the plodding ass. At one point we come to a ford, giving me the opportunity to jump down to take a photo. As I return, the chariot is brought to a halt behind a particularly large rock.

'Hep, hep,' calls the driver, laying into the ass's quarters.

'Why don't you get off?' I ask, it being obvious that progress would be a lot easier if the cart were lighter.

Hassan shakes his head and the driver beats the animal again without reply. After a painful expense of effort, it eventually strains the chariot slowly up and over the obstacle, only to be beaten again to encourage it once more along the path. Oh well, let's hope there are no more large rocks. I climb back aboard.

After leaving the river-bed we walk pleasantly along a dusty track between fields. The sun is hot, the motion of the chariot sets a pleasant rhythm; small birds twitter in hedgerows. The regular sound of the ass's feet combines with that of the wheels to make me feel drowsy. My perch is not comfortable but I could easily snooze, except that we suddenly stop at a well, hidden from view beneath the leaves of a large fig tree. Leaving the chariot unattended, our driver pulls on a rope which brings to the surface an ancient bucket spilling water onto the dusty earth.

'Here,' he says, offering it to me.

What do I do? Does one drink from the bucket or ladle it with one's hand? With a sign of deference I offer it to Hassan who raises the bucket to his lips and drinks. When satisfied he drops it back into the well, offering me a full one a few seconds later.

It is not long before humans and ass are refreshed and we are on the move again. Immediately to our front I can see a mass of tall cypress trees with attendant shadows. Beyond them the ground rises to a line of rolling hills showing only rock and bare earth. Cultivation is clearly limited to the edge of the river and even in this part of Morocco I suspect we are technically in desert.

I am still contemplating the scenery when we reach the cypresses and I am able to see that they are planted as breaks to provide shade. Apart from the distinctive smell of resin, I start to detect another altogether sweeter and more seductive scent. Starting in pockets, it gradually fills the air until the atmosphere becomes intoxicating. Unable to contain my curiosity, I jump from the chariot and run across to the nearest field. Yes, I thought so. The crop in this entire field and all the others around is jasmine, now in full flower, the dark green foliage covered in cascades of small white flowers. I am not sure for what reason it is grown other than the manufacture of perfume, but the next ten minutes are made quite unforgettable by the magic of the heady smell.

My companions show no sign of interest when I comment on the jasmine. As on many previous occasions I wonder whether they appreciate such commonplace beauty. My faith in Moroccans is such that I believe they do, although in a less demonstrative way than someone like me, for whom it is such a novelty.

When the cypresses and jasmine fall behind, we continue to

follow the edge of the *oued*, soon finding ourselves in country more hilly and less cultivated. The last real vegetation ends with an enormous fig tree, after which we take a pathway climbing steeply onto the back of the first real hill. To our left the river winds on, its yellowy water bounded by green scrub. Ahead lie nothing but crests of rough, red hills heading into the heat haze. Climbing here is less restful than the path beside the river and I am beginning to wonder where exactly 'in the country' we are going, when a small white building comes into view quite close.

'There is my home,' shouts Hassan, pointing. 'There are my parents.'

17

Pastoral Pleasures

Sweet to ride forth at evening from the wells
When shadows pass gigantic on the sand...

James Elroy Flecker

It is hard to imagine the thought processes of a couple of poor farmers in the hills of Morocco when their son arrives home un-announced, accompanied by a European twice his age whom he has just met on the bus. Whatever goes through their minds, not a trace of surprise crosses their wizened faces. I am welcomed inside with a courteous handshake and an indication of somewhere to sit. Maybe the ensuing conversation in Berber explains me away, but I am given barely a glance.

The single-storey hut forms one side of a U-shaped courtyard. I later learn that the parents sleep in an adjoining room, while opposite is a kitchen with the usual gas cooker and vessels of water. Dogs and chickens wander inside and out. Nearby two decent-looking horses stand sleeping in the afternoon sun. Between the buildings a gum tree provides shade and beyond it the ground falls away sharply into the valley. The surrounding land supports scrub, which increases towards the river.

As usual, our arrival is celebrated by a tray of mint tea, which the father pours laboriously while we all watch. Neither parent speaks French so I relay my surprise and pleasure through the boy. As most of my brief comments become long sentences in translation, I find myself wondering what on earth he is telling them. Almost immedi-ately I strike up a rapport with the mother, who watches me intently and smiles when I talk. She is probably not many years older than me, but hard work and sun have taken their toll. She has a charm-ing expression which immediately makes me warm to her.

After tea, Hassan tells me we are to accompany his father to the river to water the crops. Soon we are standing among small fields of aubergine, peppers, potatoes and onions, all growing in a complicated pattern of terraces and mud channels so that water introduced at the top can reach each of them as it flows down the slope. In the middle of the garden, which may be about a hectare, stands a corrugated shed housing a well and diesel pump. An old hose leads up hill to the top channel.

Hassan goes to the engine, primes it and winds the crank handle. With a slow splutter it comes to life, turning, as it does so, a long canvas belt to the pump. Chug, chug, chug goes the engine; whirl, whirl, whirl goes the belt. As it fills with water the hose expands and snakes its way across the ground like a waking monster. But hardly has the process begun before the engine roars and a smacking sound nearby indicates that the belt has snapped. Hassan bounds across to stop the engine.

Without a word, his father gathers the belt and winds it back between engine and pump to rejoin it. This must be a regular occurrence as he already has a needle and thread with which to stitch the two ends together. Hassan and I stand watching until the crank handle can be wound and the engine re-started. Phut, phut, phut it goes as the belt once more begins to turn.

The join has left a lump in the otherwise smooth belt. For several minutes we stand transfixed by its progress, me fearful each time it reaches the pump that it will either slide off the fly-wheel or snap. But the farmer clearly knew what he was doing and this time it works.

Soon water reaches the top channel, but just as I make my way round the small fields to see what is happening, Hassan shouts and I realise the hose has split; water is streaming onto the path by the pump. Oh dear, must these poor people struggle for everything? Once again the pump has to be turned off while another length of hose is found to repair the split.

As soon as the engine stops, the valley becomes totally silent. The sun is now off the garden, having sunk below the hills, its departure leaving us in the soft violet light of evening. Already some water has dissipated, coaxing from dryness a smell of damp earth and vegetation. Were it not for the capricious nature of belt and hose, watering this small patch might be a real pleasure. Anyway, Hassan has now gone back to the pump to try again.

Once more the engine coughs its way to life, the belt turns and the hose fills. My eyes switch between belt and hose as I try to anticipate the next drama, but this time all is well. Soon the hose stiffens beyond the danger area even though dribbles appear from several holes. Hassan and I are now at the top, where water pours out and speeds along the network of channels. I soon grasp the technique, which is to stand, spade in hand, by the first crop, having blocked off the main channel and opened an entrance. Diverted water floods in, spreading wide and creeping through the roots to the far side, at which point a shovel-load of earth is used to block off that bed and redirect the flow along the main channel. At the next bed the process is repeated.

Somewhere in my mind is the eternal question of snakes. I wonder whether any live in what must be a tempting home near the river, and if so, whether they will be disturbed by the water. As it seeps through thick roots of mint or swirls round stems of peppers, I watch. But nothing moves. Satisfied that all is now working, Hassan's father heads back to the house.

The two of us work well together; I am able to anticipate the next move of my companion. Little is said as we are both absorbed in getting water to every bed before dark. When all is successfully completed, we turn off the engine and I walk with Hassan through the beds, gathering aubergine and peppers to take back to his mother. By now the light has faded and, with the engine off, a quietness returns to the valley. The smell of damp earth sweetens the evening air.

Back at the house a lamp is alight in the kitchen where Hassan's mother is working. Another hisses in the main room so I accompany him inside and take a few moments' welcome rest. Without electricity the pace of life is dictated by the sun and I know it will not be long before we eat, leaving the whole evening ahead of us before bedtime. This period, between about six and ten in the evening, is often difficult for me as I cannot sleep so early. At the same time, without proper lighting it is impossible to read, the only alternative being endless conversation in French. The pleasure of this depends on the company but with Hassan's parents, who do not speak French, I know the evening will be a long one.

I must be making a good impression because this time, instead of being waited on in the main room, I am bidden by Hassan's father into the kitchen. I say kitchen; the room is in fact just a small area with water containers and gas-ring stove. Mama is cooking couscous, kneading a large bowl and sprinkling the already heated grains with hot water. For several minutes I watch her hands circling the bowl, gathering up the cous-cous and letting it fall back until it reaches the right consistency. When satisfied, she turns it out into a pot covered with muslin and props it on top of boiling water to retain heat while she prepares the vegetables and meat.

121

I doubt she has had many such audiences, something which is borne out by the number of times she either mutters to me in Berber or simply catches my eye and chortles to herself. She is a truly lovely person, her skin gnarled, her head covered in a scarf which periodically falls forward and has to be pushed back over one shoulder. Cous-cous is basic fare but she is preparing it with real care and affection, leaving me in no doubt that I am an honoured guest.

Things change a bit when another man appears, his arrival announced by the furious barking of dogs I have earlier noticed round the buildings. He pushes in through the door, swearing at them. In the lamplight we shake hands. To me the night is still warm, verging on hot, but he is wearing a thick wool burnous which he keeps on as he squats by our host.

In some ways his arrival is a relief as it allows a Berber conversation to develop between them, leaving me to watch and listen without having to make an effort. At one stage I ask Hassan what they are talking about and he tells me they are discussing the problem of splitting their land to give an equal amount to each son. It seems their plots will become too small to be viable if they are split, but at the same time each son must have his share. When I tell them of the practice of primogeniture in England they both click and tut their understanding, nodding politely at such a novelty.

I have eaten cous-cous on many occasions both in Morocco and London, but I think I can safely say that Mama's this evening is the best ever. It is with drooping eyelids and a full tum that I am finally able to retire to my patch of floor in the main room, pausing outside to sniff the night breezes.

I awake next morning to the sound of a rampant cockerel beyond our window. The first crow is so loud I wonder if he might not actually be in the room, which is quite possible as the door and shutters have been open all night. But no, he is strutting around outside as I head for the bushes. The dogs are not in evidence now, but on my return I have the unnerving experience of being spotted for the first time by dogs to whom one is a complete stranger. And these are not dogs kept as pets, but guard dogs, which bound forward, fangs bared, barking ferociously. My immediate action, learned from watching Moroccans, is to gather stones and stand my ground. The noise itself, now a murderous snarling, is terrifying, but what else can one do? I thank my lucky stars that this particular call of nature was not necessary in the dark as then the dogs really might have attacked. This time they take note of my weapons and allow me back unmolested.

Our morning activity decides itself when Hassan's father comes in to say that his flock of sheep and goats has wandered down-stream and would we go and drive it back. This gives Hassan and me an excuse for a long walk through scrub and dried grass, and an enjoyable time trying to coax animals of a very independent nature in a certain direction. Walking across rough ground in the sun is hot work and my mind starts turning towards a swim. I leave Hassan for a moment and go over to the river to see what it looks like. From a distance I have noticed thick green shrubs similar to mangrove bushes, growing along the banks. Do they harbour snakes? Almost certainly.

The river here is perhaps 10 metres wide. My approach brings about a series of splashes but, as no birds show, I peer at the water trying to see what has caused them. Were they water rats or voles or something? It takes me some time to discover that the disturbance was made by terrapins who have been resting on the bank and are now hanging in the water with bodies and shells submerged and just their heads breaking the surface. This is the first time I have ever come across terrapins and I know nothing about them. They look exactly like tortoises with shells the size of a good Cornish pasty.

'Hey.' Hassan is calling so I head back towards him, gathering up a break-away group of goats on the way.

'What about a swim in the river?' I ask.

'Of course. We can have one this afternoon.'

Our shepherding duties completed, we climb the slope back up to the farm for lunch of mint tea and bread dipped in olive oil. Hassan's parents do not join us. They have spent the morning skinning and butchering a goat, cutting the flesh into strips which are now draped over poles to dry in the sun. Although not offered a sample, I presume it is chewed like biltong as an emergency ration when working away from home. Being so far from a village, Mama also has to bake her own bread and we are now confronted by the end product, which is rough but edible, while around the farm the smell of her oven fire lingers enticingly. After eating we go indoors for a snooze, leaving the country outside to shimmer in the long, still heat of midday.

I am woken by a bluebottle landing on my face. Hassan is still asleep but wakes when I stand to look out of the window. Soon we are once more heading downhill towards the river, where we walk for some way until the mangrovy scrub gives way to rock and shingle and a perfect pool appears.

'You want to swim?' asks Hassan.

'Yes please.' The walk has reminded me how hot and dry we were before lunch and also that, apart from shaving, I have not washed at all for three days. I cannot wait to get into the water, but what about the terrapins and other reptiles?

'Are there snakes or anything?' I ask my companion, who is now undressing.

'No. It is fine. No problem.'

Soon we are wading in our underpants into the water. The temperature is ideal – warm but refreshing. I wonder for a moment what lies upstream in the way of villages and sources of pollution, but the water feels so fresh I conclude that if anything unpleasant has got in, it will have dissipated by now. This water must start from a spring further up in the hills.

The pool is deep enough to swim and it is not long before I find myself trying to ambush terrapins as they float about ahead of me. It proves difficult as they are shy and very alert, particularly to the huge white whale which has suddenly spluttered into their midst. Eventually we pull ourselves onto a flat rock and lie in the sun, revelling in the freshness of the water and the silence of our secluded pool. Hassan tells me that last year he saw monkeys in the trees nearby.

Before we head for home, Hassan wades ashore and fetches soap, which we share for a thorough wash. It is a pity to see our lovely pool streaked with suds but they soon disappear and cannot do much harm. We stand about for a bit to dry in the sun, and then dress and walk back to the farm, wet knickers in hands.

After two days I broach the subject of leaving. Once again I am in a dilemma. On the one hand the slow pace of life on the farm is seductive and I am getting a rare experience of genuine Moroccan life. On the other, I am still nearly 500 kilometres from Marrakech and another 200 from my final destination of Agadir. Relying, as I am, on local transport, I feel I must go soon or I will never get there in time to have a few days on the beach.

Hassan is surprised when I talk about leaving. He tells me I can stay as long as I like, but I steal myself to be firm and say I must leave tomorrow.

'Tomorrow is the souk in Maaziz,' he says. 'You must see that.'

Eventually we agree that I will go with them to the souk and then continue on my way by taxi.

Back at the farm, Hassan's father is preparing for an early start. A cart has been brought out and loaded with large sacks of grain. Boxes of aubergine and peppers stand nearby. I learn that we are to leave before dawn in order to arrive in the village in good time, and so it is, next morning, that I shave by candlelight and then watch the hitching-up of a horse and the final loading of boxes by lamplight. A cacophony of barking greets the arrival of our guest from last night accompanied by a slender youth who is presumably one of his sons and heirs. The old man wears the same burnous and a skull cap, his son jeans and white tee-shirt.

Mama has watched us loading, every so often giving instructions or moving forward to help. Despite the usual segregation of the sexes there is little doubt where the power lies in this family. When the moment arrives to go, I shake her rough hand and get Hassan to thank her for her kindness. I shall never see her again, but I will remember her for the simplicity of her lifestyle and the kind dignity of her face.

Because the cart has only two wheels it is important to get the weight distribution right. Once in the shafts, the horse stands patiently while adjustments are made, everyone apparently an expert on the subject. When all is done the two fathers sit at the front facing forward, Hassan and I sit at the back facing backwards and the boy is left to follow on foot. This seems unfortunate as we have a long journey, but it is not my affair. As we start towards the river, the first signs of dawn are streaking the eastern sky.

After a night of comparative cold, scrub by the river gives off a strong smell of vegetation, permeated every so often by scents of strong and subtle sweetness. No one talks. Propped against a sack and lulled by the rhythm of hoofs and the turning of wheels, I soon find my head sagging. To start with, I resist, but before long I sleep until bounced back to life by a large rock in our path. By now the sun is perched on the horizon, a blinding orb spreading warmth and life as it chases away the last pockets of the night.

The boy is walking just in front of me. I have a twinge of guilt at having taken his place on the cart and then slept while he walks, but as with many Moroccans he is probably a lot tougher than he appears. When he sees me looking at him he gives a charming smile with no hint of rancour. It is another hour and a half of walking without halts or water before we finally reach the first houses and offload a couple of sacks, making room for him to squash in between us.

From someway out, traffic both on foot and cart has built up as everyone heads for the souk. In the centre of town we turn towards eucalyptus trees thronging with people, where we pull into the shade and halt. It seems the cart will be left here while the two men try to sell the produce. Hassan and I are told to guard it while the youth is loaded with a sack which looks far too heavy, and he and the others disappear into the crowd. Hassan volunteers to watch the cart so I can explore.

Although I have frequently seen village souks at a distance, this is the first one I have looked at closely, and from the initial impression of milling people I gradually determine a kind of order. It seems that each commodity is allocated an area within the souk, so that the total patch of perhaps 3 hectares is divided into blocks selling vegetables, household utensils, clothes new and used, farm machinery, donkeys, asses and horses, chickens and turkeys, and everything else you can think of. I have started among the vegetables.

Canvas canopies cover each stall to keep off the sun. Beneath them, piles of every imaginable vegetable, fruit and herb are displayed, most neatly, others simply dumped on the ground. Some are of the highest standard of quality and freshness, others the opposite. Among the veg squat men and women in djellabas, accompanied by the inevitable children, while already a mass of women are bending and haggling, fingering produce and shouting the odds as they bargain with the sellers. This undercurrent of conversation forms the backdrop to shouting from every direction by men and boys advertising their wares.

The clothes area absorbs me for some time until I stumble across a row of stalls selling farm implements of a type which in England would have long since been consigned to a museum. Beyond them an open area is filled with donkeys standing hobbled and uninterested in the sun. Some are saddled, others not. All wear worn headcollars, their ribs protruding through filthy coats, legs painfully restricted by twisted ropes. Here and there men discuss a particular beast, the conversation exaggerated in typical Berber fashion so as to sound positively hostile even though the point under discussion is probably quite trivial. Teeth are examined, legs picked up, eyes peered into, and still the poor donkeys await their fate unmoved.

Live turkeys, rabbits and chickens form another line of stalls, which I am hurrying through when a small crowd attracts my attention. Looking over a couple of turbans, I discover a pen of chickens scratching in the earth while a queue of men wait to collect something from the salesman nearby. I soon realise that it is the chickens which he is selling, only the ones being carried off are dead, plucked and oven-ready. Oh dear. Not a pretty sight. As I watch, the salesman reaches into the pen, scuffles round amid a panic of feathers and squawks and traps a chicken in his large hand. Within seconds he has cut its throat and hung it upside down where scarlet blood runs freely over white feathers and splashes on the dry earth as the last moments of life are flapped and jerked away.

How long does a chicken take to die like this? Less than 30 seconds I hope, because by then he has removed the lid from an oil drum of boiling water and armed himself with an old towel. The twitching chicken is grabbed by the neck and held in the water for a few seconds. Then it is pulled out and drawn through the towel so tightly that the feathers slide off the skin and the bird is rough-plucked in a matter of seconds. With well-practised ease he shakes open a black polythene bag, dropping the bird into it with one hand as he accepts money in the other.

My feeling of revulsion is accompanied by one of fascination at the consummate skill with which this whole process is accomplished. My conscience is slightly salved too by the realisation that this, or similar, is going on every day in souks all over the world. I stand for several minutes watching, discovering that it takes less than three minutes for the chickens to progress from pen to bag.

Glad to be back amongst inanimate vegetables, I am returning to where Hassan guards the cart when another group catch my eye. This time it is a dozen or so youngsters crowded together in a circle. It takes me a moment to grasp what is going on, but their spellbound expressions and undivided attention soon direct my gaze to an old man who with slow voice and exaggerated mannerisms has them hanging on every word. The village story-teller. As I study their faces I am struck by the charm and innocence of such a scene, one which would be impossible in Britain. It is only in societies like this, I suspect, where old people are still revered and television has yet to penetrate, that such simple entertainment can still command an audience.

I must have been away for about an hour and am now getting worried about Hassan. I have also been on the lookout for something to buy his mother as a token of appreciation. Food would be pointless and nothing else has caught my eye. Luckily, just as I am starting to find the problem too difficult, I spot a stall selling glass-ware. Soon I am hurrying back to the cart carrying a box of glasses decorated not to my taste but probably acceptable to her both for offering mint tea and more particularly for the gesture. Hassan looks suitably pleased. Perhaps he can already imagine them impressing the next guests he unexpectedly invites home!

I do not have time to wait to say another goodbye to Hassan's father. When his neighbour's son reappears we leave him watching

127

the cart and Hassan leads me through the souk to the main road, where he soon flags down a long-distance taxi. At the last moment I try once more to give him money but he resolutely refuses. He has become withdrawn and silent and it dawns on me that, like the fishermen on the coast, he is genuinely sorry to see me go.

From the edge of town the road stretches dead straight for at least a mile into the hills. I am bound for Oulmes, where springs provide the 'source' of bottled water sold throughout Morocco. The journey is to take me through glorious limestone hills covered in forests of cork and holm-oak, with virtually no one to be seen away from the villages.

As I head off to a new adventure I watch in the mirror while Hassan's figure recedes. He is still gazing after us when we finally disappear from sight.

18

Travel

God be thy guide from camp to camp: God be thy shade from
  well to well;
God grant beneath the desert stars thou hear the prophet's
  camel bell.

James Elroy Flecker

Because I adore Morocco I may be accused of painting too rosy a
picture of some aspects of life for the traveller. So much depends on
one's attitude.

In common with Britain, minor officials and staff in shops can be
marvellously irritating. The disengaged stare into the middle distance while apparently serving you, or endless chat on the telephone
while you await attention, are not exclusive to Europe. I am refer-
ring in general to assistants in the larger towns. The poor and country folk tend to be more attentive but more easily foxed by difficulties
of language.

Also as in continental Europe, queuing is unheard of. The hapless
traveller must be either very patient or quite firm about forcing his
or her way towards a crowded counter. Even when you reach the
front, others will shout in Arabic over your shoulder, normally
snatching the attention of the assistant from under your nose. This
sort of thing can drive you demented and I can suggest no antedote
except, as I have said, firmness and patience and a good measure of
what Edith Wharton describes as 'the fatalism necessary to the
enjoyment of Africa!'

Shop assistants – normally male – particularly at peasant stalls,
can be incredibly young, perhaps under ten years old. But worry
not. Boys of this age are usually extremely able. On the other hand
one of the sorriest sights I have noticed recently in Agadir is a fast-
food shop similar in all but name to McDonald's. The counter is

tended by exquisite young Berber girls such as I have seen so often at a distance in the mountains. But instead of traditional clothes and hennaed hands they stand decked out in European trousers and absurd cardboard sunshields like girls in McDonald's anywhere. A sad sign of changing times.

On one leave I decide to visit the coast south of Agadir. I like the beaches and villages to the north, but want to find out how the absence of mountains affects the coastline nearer the Sahara. From *Rogerson* I choose as my target the village of Mirleft, which he describes as being within walking distance of five beaches. It is not on a main route so getting there will involve a bus trip to Tiznit, after which I will either have to try for a 'car' or else take a taxi. I therefore find myself with a morning to kill in Agadir, before catching the afternoon bus.

Soon I am heading for the village of Tamraht, famous for banana groves which line the *oued*. On local buses one boards by a door at the back, buys a ticket from a conductor wandering around inside, and exits via the door by the driver. This one is crowded so I squash in and stand among a group of men. Suddenly, loud Arab music. I had not spotted four young musicians near the front. Now they burst into song, one playing a flute, two banging drums and one a tambourine.

They play with real fervour, swaying and dancing until the whole bus is enthused. One of them has an impish smile. While the bus races along, he carries out a solo dance of great allure down the central aisle, ending by waggling his bottom towards us in a manner which leaves little to the imagination. Women warble, men cheer, everyone claps. It is so gloriously Moroccan that when the hat is passed round I am more than happy to part with a few coins.

From the village I find my way down onto a large beach empty except for two families some way off. I have a long swim and then stretch out on the sand to sunbathe. Children play in the shallows while the women, fully clothed, swim in a group further out, one even with a scarf over her head. Moroccans normally bathe segregated, the women with arms and legs covered. Bikinis are rare away from tourist centres.

I may not have mentioned elsewhere that the months of July and August see a complete transformation to the beaches around Agadir, and probably all along the coast. Literally everyone descends onto the sands for their holidays, most bringing tents, campers, caravans, tarpaulins, rush fences, cardboard boxes or anything else to enable them to sleep out. I am not just talking about the prosperous. This is everyone, penniless school kids, students, labourers, even clerks, salesmen, government officials.

The result is a seething mass of bodies every bit as concentrated, but a good deal more elegant, I should imagine, than Blackpool sands on August Bank Holiday. Sport of all kind goes on amongst the crowds, adding to the general confusion of swimming, cooking, washing and all the panoply of beach life. I will not mention sanitation arrangements as there are none!

If this book inspires you to visit Morocco, please do not think of doing so in July or August.

Anyway, on the day I am describing, I am lying in the sun, my head turned to one side, vaguely watching distant figures playing in the sea. At some stage I notice a boy making his way along the tideline, carrying on his shoulder a heavy bag. When he reaches the families he opens the bag and they all peer in. What has he got? Whatever it is, no one seems interested.

Eventually he steers a course for where I lie pretending to sleep. Dark-skinned in baggy shorts, he must be about 14. As he approaches I sit up.

'*Bonjour, Monsieur.*'

'*Bonjour.*' I soon discover he cannot speak French. He rests the bag on the sand and beckons me over. Inside are beautiful fresh fish – tuna I think, their scales flashing blue and silver in the sunlight. He smiles and starts talking in Berber. The message is fairly obvious. The fish look quite excellent, but of course I have no use for them now with nowhere to cook and a bus trip down the coast beginning in two hours.

As best I can I signal my admiration for the fish and my sadness at having no use for them on this occasion. A moment later I find myself using the same signs to refuse a much more personal item he offers me quite casually from the folds of his shorts. *Vraiment.* It is true!

Back at the bus station I buy a ticket to Tiznit and then sit at a café with a glass of coffee until the bus arrives. Eventually we are off, although I know from experience that our first stop is only a few kilometres away at the main depot at Inezgane, a suburb the other side of Agadir.

The first time I saw Inezgane was when the UN General and myself paid an official visit to the Moroccan army in Agadir. Part of our time was spent on a guided tour of the town which included this particular suburb. I have since been there often and found it most fascinating. As the main bus and taxi depot for Agadir, it attracts a

131

mass of poor, either in transit, or more likely living there, somehow hoping to profit from the wealth of passing tourists. Fifteen or twenty buses fill the bus park at any one time, departing not only to all parts of Morocco, but also to France, Belgium, and Algeria.

Beyond the bus area is the taxi park. This is well worth a photograph, being the gathering point of perhaps 200 or 300 blue Mercedes cabs. Old, dented, with ferocious mileages on their clocks, they wait in lines, being pushed by hand to the head of the queue so as to save fuel.

The combination of both modes of transport in such profusion supports the corps industry of Inezgane, namely hustlers preying on travellers. Amongst a plethora of barrows loaded with anything from prickly pears to imitation Rolex watches is a mass of urchins from about eight to twenty, offering to clean your shoes or sell you just about anything you can think of. Most are somehow connected with one of the barrows. When a new bus comes in, they swarm to the door to climb on and pester the occupants. When no new bus is in sight they mill around, adding to the throng crowding the pavements. Old men, young men, kids, beggars. No women except those in transit.

The poverty of the area is unmistakable – somewhere not to linger unless you are relatively confident about protecting yourself and more particularly your luggage. That having been said, I have spent many hours there with no ill effect – a most absorbing spot for a compulsive observer of the human condition.

What a relief it is when at last our bus sets off for Tiznit. We have been delayed longer than I had expected and, not knowing how I will make the journey from Tiznit to Mirleft I have been anxious to get moving as soon as possible.

Everyone travelling by bus carries a bottle of mineral water. Soon I am sitting by a window, water bottle on lap, watching the suburbs of Agadir being replaced by walled orange groves then sparse plantations of eucalyptus. Flying into Agadir airport is interesting, partly because of the rapid descent the aircraft has to make from the height of the Atlas, but partly too because of the patchwork of very green and prosperous-looking farms which can be seen scattered across the otherwise brown Sous plain. At ground level now, though, the countryside looks dusty, the green richness of orchards and olive groves hidden by high mud walls.

Still without an adequate map, I am roughly following the route south, with the sea to my right and the low rolling foothills of the Anti Atlas ahead and inland. This, the only road down the coast of Africa, leads to Laayoune, my place of work on the edge of the Sahara, and then on through Mauritania, Senegal and ultimately West Africa. The route, in fact, of the Paris to Dakar Rally. The surface is excellent, but barely wide enough for two lorries to pass without using the shoulder.

The bus drives at great speed, overtaking with only inches to spare, hanging for ever on the wrong side of the road when engines of equal power fight a slow-motion duel. The roof is open, allowing warm wind to rush through. Sun curtains sway, the world flashes by, morale soars. But not for long.

At a large crossroads we mysteriously turn left instead of right, slowly weaving through a collection of ugly modern buildings. Soon we pull through gates into a huge hangar to park beside several other buses. The driver switches off and jumps out.

Without explanation we suddenly find ourselves not speeding towards Tiznit, but stationary on the wrong road. Enquiries disclose that the bus is now to be fitted with a new fuel tank. This means draining and removing the old one, taking it out and inserting a replacement. There was no mention of this when buying my ticket.

Inevitably the tank is not new at all. I get out to watch and see a funny old welded drum being eased into the undercarriage of the bus. The whole episode takes perhaps an hour. A typical example of why it is no use trying to hurry when travelling by public transport.

When the long wall and palm trees of Tiznit finally appear it must be well after four. The bus swings through the grand main gate, coming to rest in a picturesque square teeming with people. I get down, backpack on one shoulder, to survey the scene.

'*Monsieur, Monsieur*, what do you want? You want hotel? My cousin has good hotel? You smoke?' The usual calls come from not one but several youths hanging around the bus stop.

'I want to go to Mirleft, please.'

'Mirleft. I come from Mirleft. I show you, *Monsieur*, come with me.' Soon I find myself following a young man in the direction of the main gate through which our bus has just driven.

'Where are we going?' I ask my guide.

'You need taxi for Mirleft. Come. You have cigarette?'

The youth seems genuine although I am wary of leaving the town centre to head off across wasteland outside the wall. As luck has it

133

I notice in the distance a number of taxis, so feel reasonably confident that things are all right. Even more luckily, a 'car' or small bus halts on the road just in front of us, with a sign saying Mirleft in the window. Denying my disappointed guide a commission from a taxi driver, I tip him and clamber aboard.

Leaving the town, the road crosses dull flat fields before winding its way into the hills. Away from the main route the volume of traffic drops to a trickle. Apart from wayside houses the land is desolate, turning to rock and scrub as we reach the hills. Occasional flocks of goats or sheep can be seen picking amongst the stones, but on the whole we are crossing desert, now reddish-brown in the setting sun.

Towards Mirleft, by which time it is dark, the conductor comes and sits beside me. We have already had some banter at the beginning of the journey when he and another man discussed me very obviously in Berber – good-naturedly with many smiles. In French he asks where I am from, giving the usual look of surprise when I tell him.

'You have a sister?' he asks.

'No, 'fraid not. Why?'

'English girls very nice. Very nice.' As he warms to his subject I think of a number of replies loosely based on the fact that had I a sister I would rather hope she would not consort with the bus conductor from Mirleft. But I nod agreement and we slap palms in a 'high five' to cement our friendship.

'Where you stay in Mirleft?' he now asks. I tell him it is my first visit and I have no plan.

'Hotel Atlas very good. You stay there.'

I fish in my backpack for *Rogerson*, discovering that there is indeed a hotel of that name though not strongly recommended.

'OK, thanks.' I decide to get clear of my advisor and then see for myself what is available. In fact the village consists of just one street, bordered each side by a colonnade of shops. The bus stops outside the Hotel Atlas, which is full of people – a popular spot.

In the dark, Mirleft has something of the feel of a Wild West town when the stage arrives. The horn has already alerted the village, and men are running out to offload boxes and freight. Youths appear, selling drinks and cigarettes. Passengers climb down to stretch their legs. The front of the hotel bustles and blazes with light, while Arab music wails within. Although I cannot see the sea, the night air clings, warm and salty.

The hotel stands half-way down the street. Beyond it few lights show, although in some places beneath the arched colonnade solitary bulbs hang above stalls, illuminating merchandise as well as shadowy figures shuffling for home. Off-stage, children call to each other, appearing suddenly as they rush about in the gloom. Above the roof-line I can just make out the silhouette of a rounded hill capped by an old Foreign Legion fort which keeps sentinel over the town.

The Hotel Atlas is owned by the brothers Ahmed, Hussein and Mbarak Boulash. Above the noise of the music they greet me warmly, stretching hands over the counter.

'Welcome, my friend. How long you stay? You like to see room?' Looking at a room before taking it is standard practice, so I follow one of the brothers upstairs and along a passage. The room is not smart but quite adequate, with a bed, blanket and rush-matting floor. Unfortunately this one faces inwards, the window opening into the passage.

'How much?' I ask. It turns out to be slightly under three pounds a night, so, without further ado I accept. On the way downstairs he indicates doors to the loo and *douche*. It all seems perfect.

By the time I am down the bus has gone and the front of house is calm. I order supper and choose a table on the pavement. For once no one joins me, although several kids find an excuse to pass backwards and forwards in order to observe. Seeing their poverty tweaks my conscience as I sit surrounded by food and bottles of Coke. It is salved slightly when a boy of about 12 sidles up with a shy, '*Monsieur, une cigarette, s'il vous plaît.*'

Normally boys of that age sell what they cadge rather than smoking it themselves. Naturally I oblige, making an instant friend.

One of the best things about the hotel is that it has electricity. After supper and a short walk in the street, I retire to my room, pour a large whisky and lie on my bed to read.

Gradually the sounds of music and conversation die as the village prepares for the night. Once or twice I hear people in the passage outside, but the hotel seems almost empty. Before sleeping I head for the bathroom.

Oh dear. No running water.

When the brother had waved towards the *douche*, I had been naive enough to believe it. However, as soon as I switch on the light I notice the smart porcelain basin has no taps or plug. A barrel of water with ladle stands nearby. The shower too has a base and curtain but no head. With gathering misgivings I continue my recce to the loo. In fact there are two, both just a hole (called, I am reliably informed, a Turkish toilet) and bucket of water, which is all I could reasonably expect. I cannot resist a smile when I notice written in chalk above the door of one '*Pour les petits besoins*' (for small needs).

135

I wake early from noise in the street, and then become conscious of someone busying themselves outside my door. It turns out to be a youth, Samir, whose mission in life is to attend to the first floor of this hotel. At this hour he is washing the floor, but whenever I come or go he is either sluicing the bathroom and loos or replenishing water or generally lurking about the passage. Because of our frequent encounters we develop a good rapport. About 16, with good French and an amusing manner, he tackles these menial tasks with pride, keeping the facilities spotless so their shortcomings are minimised.

The purpose of this chapter is to illustrate some of the hazards for the traveller in Morocco. I will not dwell on Mirleft, save to say that it is not hugely interesting but is indeed within walking distance of three decent beaches and two lesser ones, a picturesque coastal track connecting all five. The beach where I spend most of the day is literally deserted, partly because of an awkward climb down the cliffs, but partly too because it is a 4-kilometre walk from the village. The other beach contains several Moroccan families.

The following day, on advice from Samir, I walk to the third main beach. I think I must be dreaming when I notice the fair skin of a European lying in a bikini on the tideline. Before long I find myself in conversation with a woman of about 40 from Birmingham.

'What on earth are you doing alone on this beach miles from any-where?' I ask, or words to that effect. She tells me she has inherited some money, so has opted out of the rat-race and rented a house here for three years.

'Look in for tea on your way home,' she says as I stand to leave. Sure enough, about four hours later I follow her directions and find myself outside a typical old square building with no windows. I bang on the door. No reply. I bang harder. Just as I am about to go the door is opened by a Moroccan man of about 20, sullen and exceptionally handsome; her reason for being there is immediately explained.

'Is there an English woman here please?' I ask.

He motions to follow, leading me through an outer courtyard, past goats and maize, to a white-washed room from which the girl emerges.

'Hi,' she says. 'Tea?'

She turns out to be pleasant company and not remotely concerned when I steer the conversation onto her relationship with the young man.

'Watching him playing frisbee on the beach is pure poetry,' she says, which I find easy to believe. I can also understand his surly manner when a strange European inadvertently trespasses into their private little paradise.

🌴 🌴 🌴

Needless to say, when the time comes for me to return to Tiznit there is no suitable bus, so I am advised to take a taxi. I have noticed a spot at the other end of the main street where taxis arrive and depart, but it is difficult to decide when to leave Mirleft as no one knows the time of buses from Tiznit back to Agadir.

My last day is beautifully still and hot so I delay as long as possible before returning from the beach to pack up, tip the staff and say a lengthy goodbye to the brothers.

Heading for the taxi, I stop to buy a prickly pear from a barrow piled high with the pale green fruit. Barrows like this are to be found everywhere and indeed the trees or bushes can be seen growing throughout southern Morocco, often used as barriers to stock or humans. Originating in California and only introduced to Africa in the last century, they have a classic cactus appearance with broad spiked leaves and pears growing at the ends. Looking themselves slightly like a distressed gooseberry and consisting mainly of taste-less pips, the main attribute of the prickly pear is a moist interior, revealed when the top is cut off before eating.

Pear in hand, with a mouth full of pips, I arrive to find an ancient Peugeot collecting passengers. A woman and child are already sitting in the front but it is difficult to be sure who else from those on the pavement is travelling. Having discovered the price and put my backpack in the boot, I light a cigarette and await developments.

By the time we leave, a youth has also been put in the front seat astride the gear lever. An old man in turban and djellaba is placed on my left and on my right a boy of about 12, with a horrific scar down his forehead. A prosperous-looking man in middle age squashes in on his right, forcing him almost onto my lap. When the doors are finally closed the seven of us are wedged so tightly that movement is impossible.

Probably the oldest person on board is the driver, also in traditional dress and turban. He seems to know the man on my left and chats away over his shoulder. The child sleeps in the woman's arms while she joins the conversation. Unable to move, I soon nod off.

I awake to find the taxi stationary in a narrow defile. It does not

137

take long to realise that the engine is boiling, steam hissing from the bonnet. The old man chuckles. The prosperous one gestures resignation. The boy squashed against me looks anxiously out like a trapped animal. The woman continues talking, quite oblivious of the problem.

The driver speaks to the youth beside him and then opens the door. As he gets out, the youth slides quickly across to place his foot on the brake pedal, just arresting the car as it starts to run backwards. Clearly there is no hand brake. Over his shoulder I notice the car has done over half a million kilometres!

After wedging a rock behind the back wheel, the driver raises the bonnet and disappears from view in a cloud of steam.

'We can get out?' I ask the prosperous one. He calls to the driver, who answers in Berber.

'He will be ready in a minute,' says my interpreter. I resign myself to remaining wedged between the old man and boy. We are halted in a small valley with a dry stream below on our right and rolling barren hills all round. No cultivation, no buildings, just rock and shale supporting the odd tree and cactus. The perfect ambush spot in a western movie.

The old man slams the bonnet, kicks away the rock and climbs back in. An anxious moment follows as the car starts to slide backwards until he is able to take over responsibility for the foot brake. I gather from the conversation that we are to return to the last village for assistance.

By then he has reversed the car across the road, so that its rear is on the edge of a drop of perhaps a hundred metres into the rocky valley. He revs the engine for a hill start. In an idle moment, I wonder how fast the reaction of his wizened, sandled foot will be when the delicate moment comes to transfer it from the brake pedal, which is keeping us from certain death, to the accelerator, which will hopefully propel us out of trouble. The interior is by now silent, even the woman having sensed a drama. The engine clatters, steam issues, the car jumps forward, necessitating a mad grappling with the wheel to prevent overshooting into the opposite ditch. Miraculously all is accomplished and within moments we are back on the road heading in what for all of us is completely the wrong direction.

On arrival at the village we transfer into another taxi and proceed once again on our way, reaching Tiznit just after sunset. I pay the driver, pick up my backpack and head towards the main gate, its silhouette in the dark now dominating the huge town wall.

'*Monsieur, Monsieur...*' I force my way through the crowd towards the buses. As luck has it, I soon find one going to Agadir, so buy a ticket and climb aboard. Before doing so, I check with the conductor that the bus goes to the centre of Agadir and does not end at Inezgane, the suburb to the south described at the start of this chapter.

'*Oui, oui, ça va.*' Thank goodness; I should be back in two hours.

The bus travels fast. No one gets on or off and I begin to advance my prediction as to when we will be back in Agadir. In what seems exceptionally good time we hit the outskirts, soon to find ourselves swinging into a parking bay next to several other buses in Inezgane.

🌴 🌴 🌴

Most people get off. Not sure how long we will be there, I stay in my seat, watching firstly a fight between a youth and old man, either drunk or deranged, on the pavement, then the general mass of humanity seething below my window.

New passengers are followed by a mass of boys selling goods – bananas, watches, mineral water, fans, ices, jewellery – all offered by kids streetwise beyond their years. Some are aggressive, some high, some flirtatious. All display, in their clothes and expressions, poverty which one longs to ease. I buy several items for which I have no use, just to pass on a few coins.

When on earth is this bus going to leave? We have now been stationary for about half an hour. Surely we should be moving? I am not too worried because the scene on the pavement is so enthralling that I am relatively happy peering out from the safety of my seat. Equally the evening is rapidly passing and I want to get the journey over.

It eventually comes to light that this bus only goes from Tiznit to Inezgane. After a pause it then becomes a completely different bus from Inezgane to Marrakech, making as its first stop my destination in the centre of Agadir. In other words when I had asked in Tiznit if the bus went to the centre of Agadir, the affirmative answer was technically correct even though my informer failed to tell me that there would be an hour's delay in Inezgane. A not untypical occurrence for the foreign traveller.

This fact is just dawning on me when the first beggar comes on board and starts his story from the front of the bus. Two in succession give us a yarn followed by prayers, but having no change I ignore their outstretched palms.

Next comes an oldish man who walks down the bus regaling us with his misfortunes. His wheedling tone slightly annoys me so I decide he too will be unlucky. However, instead of passing, to my horror he stops beside me and tugs at my arm. This I cannot ignore, so I turn my gaze towards him. By now almost sobbing, he pulls up his shirt to reveal hanging from the pale skin of his stomach, a colostomy bag, half full. Revulsion and sympathy sweep over me at equal speed and in equal measure. His beseeching eyes have a look of resignation. I dig in my wallet for a note. His misfortune is impossible to dismiss.

19

Atlas Cedars

We are ever and always slaves of these,
  Of the suns that scorch and the winds that freeze,
Of the faint sweet scents of the sultry air,
  Of the half-heard howl from the far off lair.

Laurence Hope

The contrast between the lonely grandeur of the Atlas and the fertile plain to the north is considerable, not only because of the physical difference, but also in the amount of people in evidence and the bustle of towns and villages. The main road from Marrakech to Fez has none of the wildness of roads further south, but the greater population provides endless opportunity to watch local farmers and traders going about their daily business.

I had been to Fez once for two days and had seen enough to realise it was very special – probably the most interesting city in Morocco. On this occasion it is now only half a day away so, with time in hand, I decide to return and explore it more thoroughly. En route, the map shows some of the largest cedar forests in the country. A cousin of the cedar of Lebanon and now seen throughout Europe, the Atlas cedar, or more correctly *Cedarus atlantica*, originates in Morocco, where it grows in its natural state at between 1,200 and 1,800 metres. Over a cup of coffee I plan a stop-over to see them, choosing as a base the village of Azrou, some 80 kilometres south of Fez.

🌴🌴   🌴🌴   🌴🌴

From the moment I leave the bus I can tell I have made a lucky choice. With only three hotels, the village has none of the hallmarks of a tourist trap. For once no one lurks at the bus stop to ensnare the unwary, although I do lose several minutes while an argument develops between the conductor and a wild-eyed youth. Onlookers intervene to hold back the one from the other as a punch-up threatens – annoying for me, as I am anxious to use the remaining daylight to explore the cedar forests. When the row subsides, the gathering of onlookers disperses and I find myself walking towards the centre of the village on the lookout for somewhere to stay.

The recommended cheap hotel is full. There are two others, both equally down at heel, so I choose the aptly named Hotel Ziz. A quick check-in and dumping of luggage and I head out of the village on foot, following on the map a minor road which leads up into the hills to the area of the cedars. It is by now after three so I know I cannot delay.

Soon after leaving the houses I pass a cemetery. Burial grounds vary in appearance depending on the affluence of the population. Some have a proper stone wall and handsome carved gravestones. Others are nothing more than a roughly marked field with uncut stones stuck on end to mark the graves. It is only some order to the protruding stones which shows that this particular piece of ground should be treated with reverence, and more than once I have realised when it was too late. Moslems are always buried, never cremated, and though sometimes carried to the graveyard in a casket, they are laid to rest wrapped only in a winding sheet or shroud.

The road climbs through rough pasture showing brown at the end of summer, then on through a wood of twisted oaks, with leaves and acorns similar to but smaller than their English cousins. Away from the village the trees come right to the edge of the road, hedging me in and muffling all sound. Being low in the sky, the sun blinds with its brightness. The day is still and golden. I choose a verge which allows me to walk in shade and at the same time discover thickets of brambles covered with small sweet blackberries.

Gradually green oaks give way to holm-oaks on both sides of the road, tall, mature trees covered so thickly with leaves that the forest floor lies dark and cool beneath. Although patches of sunlight filter through, the impression is one of mysterious half-light. Of cedars there is no sign even though my map puts me in the centre of a cedar forest.

I am hot and thirsty and this inaccurate cartography annoys me. In my mind I start composing a complaint to Mr Michelin, but soon decide that the forest of holm-oak has a charm of its own. Indeed I even contemplate stopping where I am to enjoy the stillness and silence, returning tomorrow with a guide to find the cedars. It is

142

while this idea is developing that I suddenly notice high above, the unmistakable outline of a magnificent Atlas cedar rising out of the lesser trees around it.

Further on, more appear, but by now I am beginning to feel tired. The cedars are a kilometre above me and to reach them will require a stiff climb through the holm-oaks. I am not too worried about navigating without landmarks nor do I expect hazards in the woods, nevertheless I stand for some time in the sun, trying to decide whether to head into the forest or return the next day. Eventually I strike out in the direction of the most prominent cedar.

Unaccountably I soon find myself on a small track leading in roughly the right direction with a climb that varies from steep to relatively easy. Beneath the trees my shoes shuffle through many seasons of dead leaves, cracking dry twigs as they go. The forest feels dry and dusty. Thin particles hang in the air, caught every so often in sunbeams penetrating the canopy like shafts of light onto a cathedral floor. Gaining height, the path becomes suddenly steeper before opening at last onto a scree of rock. Just above I can see what I am after – a thick trunk with elegant branches covered in needles, the wood showing alternately red and grey in the evening sunlight.

Disregarding warning signs of a headache, I press on to the crest of the hill, beyond which I am rewarded with the sight for which I have been searching – an untidy forest of cedars stretching as far as the eye can see. Not the neatly trimmed versions beloved of British tree surgeons, nor the carefully ordered lines of conifers found in Europe, mixed in with other species, these magnificent cedars are wild and unkempt, dead branches at their feet, split stubs protruding from their trunks. Most have not just one trunk, but several main limbs separating near the base and tapering upwards like giant candelabra. Despite the haphazard way they grow and the damage, the trees look healthy, vigorous even, which is a relief as someone told me that large areas of Moroccan cedars are dying off. These ones are flourishing.

After pausing to absorb the sight, I leave the path to walk amongst them, soon penetrating depths where thick grass lines the floor and a strong scent of resin hangs in the air. I do not think it is just their association with English country houses that gives these trees such grandeur. Their age and rarity must be part of it, combined with the size and elegance of outstretched limbs. Certainly, standing alone amongst them I feel myself in the presence of personages august and venerable.

I sit for a cigarette. The sun is now low in the sky with only the tops of the trees still caught in its light. Down at my level the mass of branches is rapidly transforming the dappled shade of daylight into a mysterious world of gloom and shadow. Several times I hear a strange cry, sharp and wild, unlike any other I know. I put it down to some kind of buzzard but am far from certain. Otherwise the trees stand still and silent.

I have no idea whether local people come up here or if I am a rare intruder. The path I followed must have been made by someone; equally, no other evidence exists of humans, like the litter which finds its way so easily everywhere else in Morocco. And I am now miles from any houses. Not for the first time do I get the feeling of being somewhere magical. The haunt of spirits. Is it possible I am being watched? Gradually I become conscious of the hairs standing up on the back of my neck. My senses are alert to every sound. It would be wrong to say I am afraid but something about the forest is making me faintly uneasy.

Anyway, it will be dark in half an hour and I am some way from the road. When I stand up I instinctively listen to see if anyone else moves, but nothing stirs. One last look at the cedars, a final inhalation of their resinous scent, then back towards the crest and down the other side. Where I can see through the trees, the view from the hill-top is impressive. In the short climb earlier on I had gained surprising height and can now look miles out beyond Azrou to the escarpment in the direction of the royal city of Meknes. The line of hills opposite must be a good 30 kilometres away and is still in sunlight as I start for home.

A couple of times I look over my shoulder as I walk down the track. I am a long way from civilisation so do not expect to see people, but one never knows. Also, as I have said, there must be someone using this little path. After the scree I again enter the holm-oaks, which, being on a north-facing slope, are now dusky. Then, just as I spy the road some way below, I hear footsteps rustling the leaves to my front.

I stop and stand still, straining to see who is there. Not afraid, just curious. Suddenly my eye catches a movement and I turn my head. My heart jumps as I see about 50 metres to my front two baboons the size of large dogs moving through the trees towards me. As I watch I notice three more, fanned out, line abreast. Stopping every so often to pick at food, they walk on all fours but stand sometimes to examine up the trunks of trees.

I have no idea if they are dangerous but their size and number gives some concern. I saw baboons many times when working in Zimbabwe, and heard stories about the injuries their fangs can inflict. These in Morocco are not of course the same type of baboon, being Barbary apes from the land of the Berbers, but that knowledge is not prominent in my mind right now. While I watch, one of them makes the wild cry I had heard earlier among the cedars and was unable to recognise. So perhaps I was right after all. Perhaps pairs of eyes had been watching when I had such a strange feeling deep in the forest an hour ago.

As with all animals, I decide they will be less friendly if surprised, so I shuffle my feet and move enough to be noticed, hopefully without alarming them. The leading one soon sees me. He stops and stares and then crouches. I continue, moving slowly so he can get used to me before I have to move through them. Equally it is getting darker by the minute and I have no intention of being out here at night. By now the others, too, are stationary, staring in my direction, their senses alert. I curse my heart for pounding so hard. Can they sense fear in a quarry? Are they pack-hunters like wolves, afraid to attack singly but prepared to do so in the safety of numbers?

I stop, as I am otherwise going to head straight into them. Six of us watch and wait. For several agonising minutes a stalemate occurs. Then, just as I am wondering what to do next, the leading baboon stands, turns, drops onto all fours and walks stiffly off. The others follow, moving slowly as if uncertain whether they are doing the right thing. Gradually the way through becomes clear. I move cautiously, quickening pace as the road gets nearer, hoping no others are hidden in the trees ahead. When behind them, I break into a run towards what for some reason I assume to be safety. Dry leaves cascade, twigs snap, cobwebs brush my face. Finally I reach the reassuring familiarity of tarmac, turning breathless to see if I have been followed. But I am in luck. The trees stand silent. No sound follows me and from outside, the forest path appears already to have been swallowed by the night.

All that remains is to walk back in the dark along the 8 kilometres of forest road to the village and the doubtful pleasures of the Hotel Ziz. On the way occasional unidentified sounds in the verge cause me to pause, pulse racing, ears straining, trying to distinguish between impending danger and the normal sounds of the night. Once I hear that wild cry far above me from the area of the cedars, but only once. Down at this level all seems safe. I make good time, and as the trees recede am able to savour lungfuls of cool night air. Even so, it is with a sense of relief that I reach the familiarity of buildings and light and people going about their business.

145

As a result of these tribulations, the headache which has lurked threateningly in the back of my head all afternoon intensifies, necessitating a short rest and a couple of aspirin at the hotel. While lying on the bed I am annoyed to notice only one sheet beneath the blanket. A mistake or a deliberate economy measure? Either way I am not happy. It is one thing to share a dirty old blanket with someone you know slightly, but much less bearable when you have no idea whose face or feet have been in contact with it the night before. I find a youth at the desk and explain the shortcoming.

'No problem,' he smiles obligingly, causing my heart to sink. He does not of course take my word for it. We have to return to the room and undertake an elaborate inspection of the bed, after which he informs me, as if it is his own discovery, that there is only one sheet. I nod encouragingly. He goes out, leaving me under the mistaken impression that he will do something to rectify this simple omission. Once more I slip off my shoes and lie down, falling almost immediately into a deep sleep which lasts until conversation in the street outside brings me to my senses. My watch shows I have slept for over an hour. It does not matter, but I imagined the concierge might by now have put in an appearance with the other sheet. Reluctantly I put on shoes and wander down to the desk.

'You have found me a sheet?' The same youth is on duty.

'No,' he replies. 'There is no sheet.'

'Oh. Why not?' It annoys me to be charged the going rate for a room without the basic services. Instead of answering, he smiles and beckons me to follow him along a passage and up narrow stairs with no lighting. As we reach the top he pushes open a door and steps out onto the roof. A wonderful view is revealed over the town, but right now that is of secondary importance to a clean sheet for my bed. We walk across the dark roof, past chimneys and skylights, to pause in front of a washing-line whose contents sway in the breeze.

'This is for your bed,' he says, pulling the corner of a ringing-wet sheet towards me. 'But you cannot have it tonight because it is wet.'

'There must be other sheets,' I say, already aware that I am not going to win this one.

'There are no other sheets tonight, but tomorrow *inch'Allah.*' He shrugs a look of optimism. He is unaware that I am only staying one night. Resigning myself to this unsatisfactory and unhygienic state of affairs, I go back to my room, collect a pullover and money, and head out into the street to find solace in something to eat.

146

20

Sulphur Springs and a Massage

Oh threats of Hell and Hopes of Paradise!
One thing at least is certain – *This* Life flies;
One thing is certain and the rest is Lies;
The Flower that once has blown for ever dies.

Edward Fitzgerald

By now it is after nine. I know from experience that a village like this will have one or two tourist restaurants selling alcohol, but they will already be closed. The only places open will be the pavement cafés and fast-food stalls used by locals. The popular ones usually have a television inside, which acts like a magnet, leaving outside tables virtually empty.

At this hour, proprietors are anxious to pick up their last customers so at every few paces one is subjected to entreaties by those still touting for business. The noise from televisions; packed rooms full of faces staring at the screen; groups of men in djellabas and turbans sitting round pavement tables sipping mint tea; the smell of animal fat on charcoal rising into the haze of cigarette smoke, all make the evening quest for food a microcosm of Moroccan village life and something which never fails to fascinate me.

I select a café and sit down. Just as I order a sandwich of pitta bread filled with small *merguez* sausages, a loud upper-class English voice pierces the air as unmistakably as a Chelsea car alarm in the silent hours. More than a little surprised, I trace the voice to a figure sitting half inside the café. Looking for a while, I make out two Europeans in deep conversation over supper. Having not spoken English for two weeks this is an opportunity too good to miss.

'A little less noise over here please.' I have walked over and am standing beside their table. The two young men turn open-mouthed for a second before gaining their composure. We introduce our-

147

selves. They are Christopher and Anthony, both mid-twenties, on a two-week holiday from the City of London. A celebration is called for, so more Coke is ordered while I move to their table. They have been in the country for five days, during which they have packed in half a volume of typically Moroccan experiences. They are clearly sympathetic characters, already, like me, smitten by the romance of it all. We become instant friends in so far as we agree to travel together next day in their hire car.

The plan is vague, based on a picnic lunch at one of the largest cedars in the country, named after the popular French administrator General Gouraud. This passes off successfully, including the bartering of various items of our luggage for trinkets from stall-holders in the car park. By early afternoon we are heading towards Fez, having avoided the newly created ski resort of Mishliffen, in which none of us escapists from Europe can raise the slightest interest.

'I see there are sulphur springs near Fez,' I say. I have been regaling my companions about my last visit, when the pleasure of watching the sun set over Fez was spoilt by my guide doing his utmost to persuade me to have sex with his younger brother in a nearby cemetery.

'It's normal,' he kept saying with a knowing smile. My 'not for me it isn't' seemed to fall on deaf ears.

I am now reading *Rogerson* as Anthony drives the rather dull road towards Fez. 'I'd like to try the hot springs.'

'Well, if you would, we might as well do so this evening before we look for somewhere for the night,' says my driver. An hour later we are in Moulay Youseph searching for space amongst dung and refuse to park the car.

Rogerson tells us, and I know anyway, that Moroccans are modest bathers. Although those with a different mission have no compunction about displaying their wares, the average man in the street is quite the opposite. In other words some form of covering of the nether regions is mandatory in public baths or even showers. Picture then these three Englishmen abroad, wandering in the general direction of the crowd, their swimming things and towels beneath their arms and positively no idea what they are letting themselves in for.

The first problem is to know exactly where we are heading. *Rogerson* is not specific. The village is famous for hot springs, but quite how one takes advantage of them, none of us knows. Eventually it falls to Anthony to do the spadework. When the next opulent Moroccan heaves into sight he is intercepted.

'*Bonjour, Monsieur...*'

148

It seems there are two possibilities. Either we turn left at this juncture and enter a building for an individual bath and massage, or we continue along the path to the communal *piscine* or swimming pool. We opt for the latter. Many years ago I bathed in the hot springs at Banff in Canada, swimming round in steaming hot water while around the edge of the pool snow lay crisp and even. Obviously there is no snow here but the idea of a plunge in a steaming swimming pool within a stone's throw of the desert seems a good one. We walk on, eventually finding the entrance to the *piscine* in the shape of a large building, presumably the changing room.

We pay and enter. The first impression is the smell. Not pleasant but could be worse. Is it the cumulative odour of many men's bodies and underclothes? No, probably not. Almost certainly sulphurous smells from the springs. The changing room is full of men in underpants of every description. Middle-aged men mainly, some gross, others like the proverbial butcher's pencil. We each select a cubicle and undress, handing in our bundles at a desk. The attendant points to a doorway which leads to a tiled passage with several bends. Suddenly turning a corner, we come upon the most extraordinary sight. Oh my goodness. Not the balmy outdoor pool I had expected, but an indoor one packed to the gunwales with bare bodies.

One side of the pool goes right up to the wall, with the other three solid with semi-naked men sitting four tiers high, sweating and watching. Steam rises from thick green water. The skylight is misted, shrouding the whole area in a sickly half-light. The smell, again unattributable, hits the nostrils, causing my eyes to smart. Everything and everyone drips or glistens. The background burble of conversation is punctuated by frequent shouts from the many bodies in the pool.

The entrance is crammed with more naked flesh than the ceiling of the Sistine Chapel, so we have little option but to jump in. Feeling like a parachutist beyond the point of no return, I do so, taking care to avoid fellow bathers wallowing in the shallows. The water is hotter and the pool shallower than I have anticipated, so my body suffers a double shock as my feet hit the bottom. Looking round for the others, I see them both watching my lead.

'What's it like?' calls Anthony.

'Fine. Come on in.' My attention has been distracted by a voice in my ear. I turn to see an emaciated man with a cast in one eye and a drooping moustache standing beside me in the water.

'You like massage?' he asks with an inane leer.

'No thanks, mate, I'm OK.' In fact the man is most unattractive and I feel far from OK. I stride through the water to distance myself, avoiding eye contact with anyone else. But as I look round, most people are savouring the springs without any thought for their neighbour. The drill is to spend a certain length of time submerged and then sit out on the edge to cool down.

Suddenly one voice breaks into song, the refrain being picked up by several hundred men in the most extraordinary way. I ask for an explanation and am told the bathers are thanking Allah for his kindness in giving them the springs. So wonderful!

For some time I debate whether to put my head under or not. These springs are said to cure everything from psoriasis to syphilis. Having so far managed to avoid both, I do, however, suffer from recurring ear problems dating from skinny-dipping in the Thames years ago. It is hard to be sure whether the effect of submerging will do them good or harm, but because of the heat I am by now getting desperate. The water tastes strongly of salt so I clamp my mouth and try to avoid licking my lips. Enough of this indecision! Without further ado, I bend my knees and go under.

Despite my misgivings, the sensation is exquisite. I can almost feel the sulphur doing good, and the water is most refreshing even at that temperature. I wallow for several minutes before deciding a rest is in order, and swim over to steps festooned with naked flesh.

When a hand grips my arm I am not altogether surprised but I do turn to see the owner. This is a youngish man of the butcher's pencil variety. Saying nothing, he holds on, directing me up the ladder and round the side of the pool. Ignorant of what I should be doing and anxious not to offend, I allow him this licence. When we have cleared the crowded gangway he touches the ground by the pool with urgent gestures which can only mean I must sit. I am not sure of his status. Is he an official of the pool or a gifted amateur? In sagging underpants with no identification, all men are equal and I am none the wiser. It seems safest to play along.

When I sit on the mosaic floor he indicates me to lie. He then places both hands underneath and turns me over so that I end up on my front at the foot of a row of well-fed individuals watching proceedings from a cooling-off bench.

Without any pre-warning I spend the next ten minutes being submitted to an elaborate and undignified massage whilst observed by six or eight benign and overweight Moroccans. God knows if my masseur has had any training. He is in fact a mixture of masseur and osteopath. He starts by rubbing most of my body with a ribbed

150

'Each village is dominated by a kasbah, some still in use, but most derelict'

Berber girls in the high Atlas show their henna'd hands

'My attention is drawn by spiky leaves, huge clusters of yellow dates sagging beneath them'

The derelict Glouai kasbah on the dirt road north of Agdz.

'...the Draa river sustains a vast oasis of date-palms and cultivation.'

Zagora. '...where the first real sands of the Sahara begin.'

Auberge Repos-Sable. 'A nearby group of camels... reinforces my decision that this is indeed the place to spend the night.'

The Anti-Atlas. '...a typical Berber - thick dark hair over a fine young face.'

glove. This brings up an embarrassing amount of dirt and dead skin, which is periodically removed by a bucket of hot water, passed to him by a friend. The shaming amount of dirt is not unexpected after so long on the road, but I am sorry to see my suntan visibly disintegrate.

After the rubbing, he starts work on each limb and then the trunk. The technique is engaging. Having selected the area for attention, he slaps it once, quite hard, then pummels with his palm before working it with his hands. At the same time, to prevent me slipping into a false sense of security, he periodically, and without warning, gives random slaps to other parts of my anatomy. The whole process happens in silence except for a kind of stage kiss or exaggerated sucking sound which accompanies each slap.

What is perhaps more alarming, if anything can be, is the time when he suddenly bends one arm behind my back and twists it with a cracking of joints and some pain. After this, legs and ankles are subjected to the same torture. He clearly takes his duties seriously.

Soon I am turned over for further treatment, including more twisting of the legs, my torso being lifted and crunched and my head jerked from one side to the other with frightening force.

Two incidents I will not forget are the moment when I am lying on my back being rubbed or jerked or whatever and three large Moroccans walk almost over the top of me due to the narrowness of the sidewalk. I look up at stretched stomachs and sagging breasts while they peer down. Suddenly drops of salty liquid arrive on my lips. Has it run down my face, or is it bath-water from their hair. Even worse, can it be sweat dripping off their bodies? I will never know, nor do I wish to.

The other incident is when, while I am still lying on my front, the man trusses me up like a turkey with arms and legs collected behind my back. Clearly the final *coup de grâce* is imminent. Whether through nerves or genuine amusement at the improbability of the situation, I suddenly get the most terrible giggles and have to unwrap myself to lie in a heap while tears run down my face. Luckily my man is replenishing the bucket. When he returns I am still laughing, having caught the eye of one of my companions. With a look of contempt the masseur watches for a second and then throws the bucket over me. It does the trick enough to enable him to do his final party piece – namely to wind his own legs round mine and then, squatting to bend forward, pick me up from behind by the shoulders until I am clear of the ground. One final powerful and hideous crunch of everything is accompanied by a cacophony of kisses, before I am tossed like a used rag onto the mosaic floor.

Next it is Christopher's turn. While I regain my breath and self-respect, I watch as he undergoes the same routine. With the benefit of having seen the treatment meted out to me, he is better prepared mentally, if not physically. I am ordered back into the pool so I miss the rest of their ordeal but it is no doubt similar to mine.

Having recovered my composure, I climb out and follow the cat-walk towards the exit. Some way round I meet a man with one of those ribbed gloves, giving himself a thorough workout and swabbing the soap, dirt and dead skin back into the pool in which we have just been swimming. Charming after the event, but I am glad I had not seen him before I went under.

21

A Garden of Eden

Smells are surer than sounds or sights
To make your heart strings crack

Rudyard Kipling

The old medina of Marrakech must be one of the most picturesque
places in Africa. Seemingly unchanged since the Middle Ages, it is
a mind-blowing kaleidoscope of ancient, medieval-looking buildings
jostling together above narrow streets and twisting passages. Grand
stone houses built around courtyards cram next to mosques, doss
houses, cafés and lesser dwellings of mud. Bags of merchandise
spill from shop fronts into the street, while artisans work outside in
wood, metal, leather or anything else you can think of. Pottery and
brassware compete for space with carpets, hides, sacks of herbs,
even live chickens and rabbits. Butchers' shops display fly-blown
sheep's carcasses, unskinned goats' feet, camel tripe. Everyone is
on the move, either on foot, donkey or moped. Colours, noise and
bustle are augmented by a pervading smell of hot cooking oil, charcoal, dung, exotic spices. During my first visit in the winter it
rained, turning the streets into mud and causing a thin shroud of
smoke to hang in the air, the product of a thousand anvils, ovens
and cooking fires.

Most postcards show part of the town in the foreground, including the magnificent ochre walls, with snow-capped peaks of the
High Atlas hanging like clouds along the horizon. Dark green palms
and citrus trees contrast strikingly with the ethereal pallor of distant
icy wastes.

Marrakech sits on a plateau of rich farmland, with orange groves
running up to the town walls and a huge palmerie to the north. To
the west is a residential area of smart hotels and further out a
modern but scruffy industrial suburb. One road runs due west some

170 kilometres to the coast and the charming port of Essaouira. In the other direction the same road continues north-east along the northern edge of the Middle Atlas towards Fez. The huge natural barrier of the High Atlas begins some 60 kilometres to the south. To cross it three roads lead from Marrakech, each one of which I used on various occasions. Apart from these, only one other metal road crosses the High Atlas in Morocco, some 300 kilometres to the east, running from Fez almost due south to the oasis valley of Tafilalt down near the Algerian border.

No doubt a number of caravan routes and pathways still wind their way over the mountains, but a detailed study of the map shows only one other proper crossing. It is an unmetalled track about 200 kilometres east of Marrakech which from the south follows the gorges of the Dades and Todra rivers up to the village of Imilchil in the middle of the mountains and then winds northwards across the Middle Atlas to rejoin the road to Fez. From start to finish the track is 150 kilometres long, not counting the inevitable twists and turns made traversing passes. On my next leave I decide to make this crossing in order to have a proper look at the mountains.

🌴🌴   🌴🌴   🌴🌴

To save time, I fly from Marrakech to Ouarzazate, spying down onto rocky heights and deserted valleys similar to those I will soon be crossing. The plane arrives at a small airstrip in the fierce heat of late morning.

I collect my bags and go to look for a taxi to take me to the bus station in town. The Negro driver has his radio at full-blast, making conversation impossible. The obligatory meter is nowhere to be seen so I am not surprised when, ten minutes later, he helps me out with my luggage and demands £4 for the 2-kilometre journey.

'Look, my friend,' I say, 'I have been living in this country for some time. Don't try to fool me.'

An expression of injured innocence. 'How much will you give me?'

'Here,' I say, handing him £1, which I consider more in line. With an angry grunt he turns on his heel and soon shoots out of the yard in a cloud of dust and reggae, leaving me to discover which of the various old buses loading at this time goes to the Dades gorge. Luckily one is about to leave, so, having been conned out of another few coins by the man loading luggage, I buy a ticket. Soon I am sitting in a corner seat, peering out from behind sun blinds as we leave town.

The bus contains an assortment of men with a few well-wrapped women sitting at the back; poor people returning to villages after visiting the souk. Usually the seat next to an infidel is the last to be filled so I am accustomed to being left on my own. However, extra passengers come on board as we pull clear of the town and I am soon wedged in by an old man in full regalia.

With no schedule, I have only the vaguest plan of where I will get off. The road follows the course of the Dades river even though it is seldom visible. The country is undulating and parched, with signs of cultivation but nothing growing, presumably as a result of the drought which has run in this area for several years.

The valley of the Dades is famous for its *ksour* (singular, *ksar*), large fortified houses sheltering several families built near each other to afford protection from neighbouring tribes. Because of the colour of rock in this part of the country, the buildings have a distinctive pink hue which gives the area the name '*vallée des roses*'. As if to reinforce this, huge fields of roses grow nearby, used in rose water, a mild cologne sold locally and exported. Passing by in the autumn, I do not see any roses but the water is on sale everywhere so I have no reason to doubt their existence. Indeed I would dearly like to see them as the sight and smell must be spectacular in such an arid land.

As the bus grinds past groups of *ksour* and small villages, I look out, trying to decide whether to pause and explore or push on towards my destination where the Dades swings north into the mountains. My ability to move on an impulse is somewhat hampered by my companion, whose bulk and clothes have trapped me securely in the corner. The decision is slightly influenced anyway by the fact that I know that Imilchil, the village in the mountains, is the venue once a year for a Berber marriage-market between local boys and girls. I have vaguely arranged to meet the British Defence Attaché and his wife there next weekend when the fête occurs. I am therefore inclined against losing time exploring the *vallée des roses*.

When eventually we approach the village of Boulmane Dades, where my route turns north, I strain to identify the turn-off from inside the bus in order to call it to a halt. As luck has it I am able to spot the junction ahead of us. With some difficulty I extract myself from the folds of my companion's robes in time to jump down and reclaim my luggage. Within seconds I am standing alone on the side of the road as the bus disappears in a swirl of dust and diesel.

Intending to hang around until local transport passes, I find a suitable place to await developments. Soon two boys appear on bikes. They eye me shyly then approach and ask where I am heading. I tell them I am waiting for a bus up the valley.

155

'There is no bus up this valley, *Monsieur*,' says the older of the two. It seems the only option is to hitch a lift but I am saved further contemplation when a car screeches to a halt beside me.

'*Bonjour, Monsieur...*' The usual yarn from a shifty-looking individual in the passenger seat of a battered Mercedes. What am I doing? Where am I going? No there is no bus. They will take me up the valley. His cousin has a small hotel just by the famous gorge. We will go there. It is a pleasure to meet me. German?

'How much to take me up to the gorge?' I ask, still not convinced by the speaker and his companion, who sits irritatingly revving the engine.

'Sixteen pounds,' he replies. I am at a disadvantage, not knowing how far up the valley the gorge starts. Neither do I know if several hotels are to be found or if it will be easy to find a room in someone's house.

'That's too much,' I venture. He speaks to the driver and then says,

'Twelve pounds. It's a long way. Twelve pounds very fair.'

It is one of those occasions when an instant decision is needed. I do not much like the look of them – both in their thirties and obvious hustlers. Equally the sun has passed its zenith. If I have to wait too long for another lift I risk finishing the trip in the dark.

'OK, twelve pounds then.' The man gets out to put my luggage in the boot. He opens the back door from inside as the outside handle is missing, and indicates to me to get in. As soon as we are ready, the driver lets in the clutch and the car shoots off on the start of one of my worst drives in Morocco.

There are two problems. The first is simply one of speed. The road is hewn into rock, with the river below on the right and a steep escarpment on the left. It climbs gradually, hugging the side of the valley and snaking round blind bends and narrow bridges. The surface is adequate but not good, scattered with potholes and lumps of debris fallen from the cliff above. Our driver seems to know most of these as he pursues a weaving course at a speed perhaps twice as fast as I would choose. With one hand on the wheel and the radio blaring, he nods his head to the beat. Every so often he turns to speak to his companion, seemingly unaware of the approaching corner or the alarming drop on our right.

The other trait which does not endear him to me is that he is clearly the local 'Jack the Lad'. No group of houses, gathering of labourers, or donkey carrying man or woman can be passed without a furious tooting of the horn and a wave from his window. This greeting is as often as not followed by a backward glance to

156

check on the effect while the car speeds blindly towards the next hazard.

'I think your friend is driving too fast,' I shout after a particularly anxious moment when my stomach has moved somewhere into my chest.

'*Oui, oui,*' the other roars with laughter, shaking the console to his front. I should have kept quiet. My remark spurs the driver to even greater efforts to test the car and its passenger to the limit.

Luckily traffic is light. As we climb, the valley narrows. Beside the river lies a patchwork of rich green fields and orchards, divided by hedges and impeccably tended. On either side of the valley, at the same height as the road, is a precise line where cultivation ends and pure red rock begins, with no vestige of plant life on it. Looking higher, the surface takes on a weird and extraordinary appearance. At this stage of the late afternoon strange formations are distorted by low sun into something even more curious than the normal moonscapes. The contrast between the rich valley floor and the violet rock-face higher up is remarkable. A plan is forming in my head as I determine to explore the area more fully and at my own speed.

We pass various collections of houses grouped, usually, round the foot of a magnificent *ksar*. Built in a square, they mostly have ornamental castellations and intricate wrought-iron work across narrow windows.

Eventually, just where a bridge crosses the river at the start of the gorge, we swing into the car park of a small *auberge*. Standing among fig trees, it is set slightly apart from a village further up the road. Far better than anything I have expected, it looks perfect provided the price is right. I climb out while my original guide disappears into the hotel and returns with a ring of keys.

'You like to see room?' he asks.

'Yes please.'

I follow him into the shade of a courtyard with passages and doors leading off it. A mulberry tree grows in the centre, with rough rose bushes around its base. We climb stairs to a door, which he unlocks, ushering me into a simple room with double bed and adjoining bathroom. More importantly the window looks out over the river and the deep green cultivation of the valley to bare red peaks beyond.

'How much?' I have been stung once by the cost of the lift and am certainly not going to be stung again.

'Twelve pounds for the night,' he replies.

Returning to the desk, I confirm the price with the concierge. It seems fair. The *auberge* is far better than I dared expect and a per-

157

fect base for exploring the valley. I take my luggage up to the room and then find the driver and his companion.

'Look, since I have paid you so much I would like you to take me down the valley again for five or six kilometres so I can walk back on my own.'

I am taking a risk travelling again in the crazy car, but it seems such a good way to explore the valley without covering the same ground twice on foot. Before leaving the hotel I take the precaution of booking in for dinner. Soon, without further mishap I find myself set down at the side of the road with two hours' daylight remaining and the valley stretching away to my front. The noise of the car is replaced by silence.

🌴 🌴　　🌴 🌴　　🌴 🌴

I take a general look at what is laid out on my right below the level of the road. The river itself is about 20 metres wide and flowing fast. It is probably not deep, but here and there stepping stones or a rough bridge show that the locals do not fancy wading. Branching from the main river is a mass of canals and viaducts constructed from packed mud, taking water to the fields. These main arteries sub-split into smaller channels, which peter out where the water dissipates amongst trees or crops. I see small open fields of maize, potatoes and deep green lucerne. Also orchards of what look like peaches and other fruit. In some places, particularly along the edge of the river, the dense foliage of wild fig trees overspills into neighbouring fields. The atmosphere is one of remarkable serenity, punctuated only by the sound of women's voices and the twittering of innumerable tiny birds.

I am uncertain whether I should walk in these fields, which presumably belong to someone, but, deciding it is unlikely to do any harm, pick my way down from the road towards the river. A bonfire attended by two children smokes nearby, so I walk over, being indicated the path in exchange for an old Biro from my trouser pocket.

For some time I wander among the fields and trees in this Garden of Eden. Groups of women work among the crops, sometimes seen, more often heard. If surprised, they call softly to each other and cover their faces with colourful cotton scarves. But before they do so, I am able to glimpse the handsome features and dark flashing eyes so typical of the Berbers.

Anxious that they do not form the idea that I am spying on them, I go to some trouble to advertise my presence at a distance and avoid passing too close. Once disturbed, work stops and they gaze after me, whispering coyly until I am out of sight.

A strong smell of figs pervades. Wild fig trees grow along the hedgerows and beside the river, the fruit smaller and rounder than our own Turkish variety, some dark purple and ready to eat but most still green. Other species quickly identified include almonds, which have already been harvested, as well as walnuts, whose fruit hangs heavy among green and brown leaves. Peach trees grow in little orchards, their fruit also smaller than those in England. Many are laden with ripe peaches, others have been harvested, the fruit laid out to dry on rocks above the cultivated area. In several places I come across women and children stoning or turning them. Eventually they will find their way to the souk as dried fruit – a Moroccan speciality.

Clumps of bamboo grow along the banks of the river, to be used as lathes in the ceilings of mud houses. Also orchards of quince, for flavouring tagine stews, and most common vegetables like potatoes and carrots as well as thick bushes of mint. Lucerne and clover too are growing as fodder for livestock. Rose bushes form an unkempt tangle in some corners, their flowers turned to hips by now. I smile to myself when coming across the common-or-garden bramble such as I have spent many hours wrestling with at home. Blackberries are always our best crop but I am surprised to find they have even established a foothold here in North Africa.

The paths are not easy to follow. Some start out clearly and then shrink to nothing. Others go a few yards then split with no single one looking more important than the next. Once or twice I walk along the edge of an aqueduct where life-giving water whispers beneath overhanging fronds. Every now and then a distinct plop comes from ahead as a Jeremy Fisher, reclining in long grass on the bank, senses my arrival and springs for cover. Several times I pause to absorb the atmosphere of well-being and tranquillity. It is such a contrast to the parched landscape of this morning and also to the effort of having to keep my wits when travelling among avaricious strangers.

'*Salut.*'

I am mistaken if I think I will be able to walk back up the valley unaided. The speaker is another Lahcen, a tall pleasant-looking schoolboy of about 15 who has spotted me from the road and come to volunteer his services. I do not argue as I know he is unlikely to take no for an answer, and anyway by now I have a number of questions. Besides, he is personable and I can soon tell his French is good. We set off along secret tracks, crossing the river now and then and discussing everything under the sinking sun.

159

'Would you like some fruit?' he asks as we pause in a grove of fig trees. Despite misgivings I feel compelled to say yes, so he tells me to wait while he goes foraging. After a few minutes he is back with a handful of figs and peaches, their juices running between his fingers. Somewhere deep in my subconscious I hear the voice of my old nanny warning me never to eat raw fruit, particularly if it is still green. Particularly too, I can hear her say, when offered to you from the unwashed hand of an Arab schoolboy. But I cannot disappoint my new friend after the trouble he has gone to.

'Thanks,' say I, taking the handful and casting caution to the wind. In fact they are delicious and I am pleased to report no unseemly *bouleversement* later.

By now the sun is off the valley, catching only certain peaks high on one side. We decide to make our way back to the road. On reaching it I thank him with a tip and say goodbye. He is a rare example of someone who comes to my assistance not for financial gain but simply out of curiosity.

My wanderings in the sun have made me thirsty so I decide to walk back along the road on the lookout for a shop selling bottled water. As soon as the sun leaves the peaks the valley darkens. Ahead is a village and I can just make out a number of figures on the road. With school over, everyone is out of doors enjoying the last light before returning to candlelit interiors. Gangs of children play and call to each other. Groups of women stand chatting in doorways. Older men sit along walls, watching the world go by or discussing the business of the day. Everyone wears robes.

As they recognise a stranger, and a European on foot no less, the children call out a shrill, *Bonjour Monsieur; un stylo, s'il vous plaît.'*

'*Monsieur, cinque dirham, s'il vous plaît.'*

I do not think anyone really expects me to stop and fish in my pocket for a Biro or money, but it is worth a try, even if only to show their friends they are up to conversing in French with a stranger. I walk on.

For some reason no shop appears. I cannot believe there is none, so when I see a man standing on his own in a doorway I go over to seek directions.

'There is no shop,' he tells me. 'What is it you want?'

'I am after some water.'

'*Monsieur*, you are welcome for tea in my house. Come in

160

please.' He pushes open the door, indicating a dark interior. I thank him and agree to pause – it seems rude not to.

His house consists of one room, with a second, into which the door opens, where he keeps a gas cooker, vegetables in wooden storage boxes and a number of plastic water containers. Lighting a candle, he shows me into the main room. The only item of furniture is a low bed covered in blankets. Rugs cover the floor beneath a line of shelves of clothes. Piles of books and a transistor radio lie scattered untidily about the place as in any room not expecting visitors.

My host's name is Aly. He works in the village school, teaching maths and Arabic to seven- to twelve-year-olds. Probably everything else too, I imagine, as in these rural villages there will only be one or two teachers in the whole school. He must be about 30, with a gentle face, but, as I later discover, a precise almost argumentative manner. He is predictably polite, insisting that I sit on the bed while he goes next door to make tea. Soon he returns and we talk in candlelight about the village and the Arab-Israeli accord which is currently being negotiated.

'Why don't you stay the night here?' he asks. 'It is not much but I have food and some blankets. I don't ask for anything.' It is a kind offer which would undoubtedly lead to interesting conversation. But I am so taken by the room awaiting me in the *auberge* that I am reluctant to sacrifice it. Also Aly is very intense and I feel that a little of him could go quite a long way.

From the outer room he returns with a handful of walnuts, which we crack on the stone floor and eat in semi-darkness with our mint tea. I discover that Aly is an Arab from Casablanca – the only Arab in this village of Berbers, he tells me. I ask if that causes any problems but he says no. I find myself wondering whether it is just co-incidence that one of the few times I am given something at no charge in Berber country is in the company of an Arab.

Not forgetting that I still have some walking to do, and mindful of the early hour at which country hotels wind down, I eventually stand to leave. On the way out I notice a large sack propped against the wall with English letters on the side.

'*Qu'est ce que c'est?*' I ask. It turns out to be flour from Canada, part of an aid programme run by the Canadian government for school-children in the Maghreb. Well done Canada, I think, as I thank Aly and bid him goodbye.

Coming out into the dark, it takes me a few moments to regain my vision. Here and there gas or candlelight suffuses doorways and windows. A scooter passes, its headlights picking out the road and knots of figures still standing outside. I walk on, clear the edge of the village and then have a kilometre or two of country lane before turning a corner and seeing across the valley the distant lights of the *auberge*. A sickle moon has appeared, lying on her elbow, benignly observing this tranquil scene. Away from the village the only sound is the distant calls of children and the gentle swish of the breeze in the almonds below the road. The smell of fig and other well-watered vegetation lingers strongly on the warm night air.

Suddenly something flies close to my head. I stop and peer into the gloom. Yes, there it is again. I strain to catch a glimpse of whatever it is, eventually kneeling to silhouette it against the sky. It turns out to be a pair of bats, skimming and diving above the road. Small ones, about the size of those in England. I cannot examine them, but enjoy for a moment their unfettered wheels and dives before continuing on my way.

It is with some relief that I collect my key from the desk at the *auberge* and cross the darkened courtyard to my room. I have just undressed for a shower when someone knocks at the door. Outside stands a barefoot boy in loose white kaftan, wanting to know when and where I would like dinner. I tell him I will be ready in half an hour and will have it outside on the terrace looking down the valley.

'The other visitors are eating inside,' he says with a worried look. Not wishing to share such a picturesque spot with two French couples, I say that I still prefer to sit outside on my own.

'*D'accord, Monsieur.*' He leaves me to shower, inevitably in cold water.

My apparently unusual request to eat outside and alone must have struck a chord with the boy, another Mohammed. He is most attentive throughout the evening and stands for ages talking to me when not wanted inside. He speaks good French and is also, needless to say, a highly efficient waiter. Although only 14, he has fine features and a serious expression softened occasionally by a charming smile.

After supper, the concierge appears, shoos Mohammed away, and asks what I want to do the following day. During a long discussion he tells me that the only practical way to cross the Atlas is in a hired car with a guide. I agree that he should find both for the day after tomorrow. The time factor becomes less critical since he also says that the brides fair at Imilchil has been cancelled by the police as a result of fighting last year. I can therefore forget meeting up with my British friends.

I tell him that the following day I would like to climb the mountain

162

up behind the village, one of the major peaks in this part of the Atlas and the highest one visible from here. He says that the best plan would be to climb that peak, spend the night out on the mountain, and then return via a dry gorge to where the Dades river emerges a few kilometres above the village. I can then spend another night at the *auberge* and set out the following day to cross the Atlas. We agree terms and all is satisfactorily settled except the question of a guide.

His first suggestion is that I should go up the mountain with the man who originally brought me to the hotel in his friend's taxi. I decline on the grounds that he annoyed me by overcharging. When I reveal the amount the concierge sucks his teeth in well-practised horror and agrees that perhaps that is not the right person after all. He says that Sayid, one I have already met in the hotel, is the most experienced person to drive me over the Atlas, but he will have to go to Ouarzazate to hire a car. Eventually he comes back and asks if I mind taking the young Mohammed up the mountain as my guide.

I am not sure what to say. Mohammed is an engaging young man whose company I feel sure would be agreeable. However, his age is a cause for concern as, if I am going to be out all night, I want someone who not only knows the way, but can also deal with emergencies such as a broken leg. The concierge assures me that Mohammed is good, so I agree to take him, confirming it with the boy amidst many nods and smiles, on my way to bed.

22

A Night in a Cave

Unless you carry the gypsy eyes
    That see but seldom weep
Keep your head from the naked skies,
    Or the stars'll trouble your sleep.

            Rudyard Kipling

It is some time before I sleep. For several minutes I lie looking down the darkened valley. From below the window, the sound of running water tinkles upwards from the river. A bright moon is silhouetting the line of mountains to the west but no lights mark the villages past which I walked that afternoon. I imagine my young guide Lahcen, asleep with his brothers in a small room somewhere down the valley, his head uncluttered by thoughts beyond his village and school. By contrast I can picture the teacher Aly, striving desperately to keep abreast of world affairs, crouching by the radio in the *chambre* where I drank tea. The lack of electricity makes everyone retire early. The valley and fields are left to brood in silence, appreciated only by those like myself who can compare them to another less tranquil world so very far from these mountains.

Next morning I am having a cup of coffee on the veranda when the concierge approaches. It seems that he has changed his mind about my guide, and the young Mohammed is to be replaced by an older Mohammed. I ask to meet him and am soon talking to a youth of about 18 wearing jeans, leather jacket and black turban. First appearances are encouraging so I agree the change and an hour later he and I set off with rucksacks containing sleeping bags, food and water.

After crossing the river, we walk through more fields and groves before taking a rough track leading up the side of the valley. The going is steep and the track too narrow to walk side by side so I follow him in silence. In a surprisingly short time we have left the rich green of cultivation and are walking across red rock and shale with nothing growing either side.

When we stop for a smoke, I am able to learn a bit about my guide. It seems that he was brought up in the valley, but worked for a year in a shop in Casablanca. He did not enjoy city life so returned here to pick up whatever guiding jobs he can from passing tourists. Some apparently come in pairs, others in groups, normally from France and Germany. I notice he is wearing rather smart walking shoes, which he says were given him by a German at the end of his holiday. He goes on to tell me that most tourists only want to do a day trip up the Dades gorge, but that sometimes groups trek for a week or more in the mountains. On those trips donkeys carry the stores and tents.

We continue on our way. Next time I look, the green fields are barely discernible, snaking along the valley floor below and behind us. Ahead lie a number of crests leading upwards towards the summit of the main mountain which is our target at the head of the valley. It looks austere and a lot higher than I had originally realised. Despite a nasty belt of cloud, the walking is hot work. Mohammed removes his leather jacket but to my surprise keeps on the black turban, which seems to me picturesque but a little inappropriate for such strenuous exercise.

The path peters out as we gain height, so we walk over rock and bare earth. With the increase in altitude have come tufts of scrub, covered in dust but presumably green when it rains. We are now able to walk side by side and talk. Mohammed tells me we may come across *les nomades*, families who move up to the high grazing in summer and then retreat back into the valleys when the snows come. He says they are very poor but might ask us into their tent for tea. I find it hard to imagine anyone living so far from the source of food and water. True, they probably live off goat meat and camel milk but there is no sign whatever of water in any of the dried-up streams.

Every so often I catch the suspicion of a strange and rather delicious smell. In the absence of anything else to think about I puzzle for some time over its source. It is strongest when I walk behind Mohammed so I begin to think it might be something in his rucksack which has spilt. Precisely what, though, I cannot imagine. Then I start to wonder whether it is possible that my guide is wearing scent. Rather unlikely, I feel, that he should anoint himself prior to a trek in the mountains, but then with Moroccans one can never be quite certain. I have not come across it before but perhaps he has slapped on rose water to humour the European. I walk on in his fragrant slipstream, intrigued but none the wiser.

Our objective, the summit, resolutely refuses to come any closer even though we have walked several kilometres and the valley below has long since disappeared. With the exception of scrub, the landscape is totally barren and very dry, the surface sometimes earth, more often shale or pure rock. The going is not difficult although constant climbing is tiring. I have to assume Mohammed knows where we are heading, not so much now when the summit is obvious above and ahead of us, but for the return journey. His French is not brilliant but by now we have struck up a good relationship so that our halts include some light-hearted moments and several photo calls. It seems extraordinary in a way to be totally alone with, and dependent upon, a complete stranger quite so far from any other living soul.

Suddenly my guide stops and holds up his hand. I stand behind him, catching my breath, and then hear what it is that has alerted him. Floating intermittently on the wind is the faraway sound of a human voice. Mohammed turns,

'*Les nomades*,' he says, peering over to our left. '*Voilà.*'

He points towards a distant fold in the face of the mountain. I stare for some time but can see nothing, although I can now clearly hear the faint sound of a man calling, almost chanting, the cadence of his voice echoing off the rock-face.

'Can you see him?' I ask. Mohammed walks back to me and points. Still I can see nothing amongst the outcrops and crags. He puts an arm round my shoulder and raises his other hand in front of my face to point. He is not wearing scent. After much searching I eventually identify the tiny figure of a man in djellaba walking slowly among the rocks right over the far side of where we are looking.

'What's he doing?' I ask.

'He's calling his goats,' he replies. 'Do you want to go over to him?' We do a quick calculation and decide there is not really time for such a diversion if we want to get to the summit and back to a cave before dark. A pity as I would like to have learned something of *les nomades*. However, not only will it put us behind schedule, but also I am starving and in dire need of a break for something to eat.

Before moving on, we stand for some time watching the distant figure and listening to the strange sound of his voice. He could almost be Moses going up the mountain to collect the tablets of stone.

A feeling of elation and relief hits us when we finally reach the

166

peak. Mohammed lets out a whoop and runs the last few metres ahead of me, turning, laughing, to shake my hand and praise Allah for His greatness. The sense of achievement makes a strong bond. What I have not realised is that beyond the summit is a sheer drop to a dry gorge which must be more than 2 kilometres below.

For several minutes we stand looking one way across the tops of neighbouring mountains towards where a thin sun fights a losing battle with incoming rain clouds. The other direction reveals a quite extraordinary formation of volcanic rock, folded like a row of collapsed dominoes and stretching away from our feet into the distance in a spectacular mix of colour and shadow. Peering down into the gorge, I can just see the tent and goats of another nomad although they look like specks among the rock and I only notice them when Mohammed points them out. Like so many young Moroccans, his eyesight is superb.

With the coming of rain clouds the wind has risen. In such an exposed place it soon chills the sweat on our backs. Mohammed climbs down onto a ledge just below the edge, and with some trepidation I follow. It gives protection from the wind but leaves us perched none too safely on the edge of the highest cliff I have ever seen in my life. He gets out unleavened bread and tomatoes for sandwiches while I find my water. Both are especially good after our climb and we spend some time enjoying them while taking in the view.

Mohammed's plan is to spend the night in a cave which the nomads use with their flocks. We leave the top of the mountain at about half past three and start walking down and across so as to be sure to hit the Dades gorge tomorrow. He tells me he knows of a good cave on the way. Moving downhill requires less effort, but the angle of descent makes it uncomfortable, particularly for those of us without the benefit of a smart pair of German walking shoes.

At one halt he says we should gather material for a fire. I watch him pull up bits of scrub, concentrating on those with large amounts of root showing above the surface. When I do the same, the mystery of the scent is solved. As I crush the tiny leaves in my hand they give off that delicious and unusual smell which I had attributed to Mohammed earlier on in the day.

'What is the name of this stuff?' I ask.

'Thyme,' he replies, only in French, of course, it is pronounced 'teem'. So the mountainside is covered in wild thyme. As we walk we gather armfuls of thyme roots so that when the cave is eventually reached we have with us the makings of a good fire.

The cave is in fact one of six in a line which appear suddenly in a fold in the ground. A stone wall has been built across the front of the five smaller ones, closer inspection showing these to be for live-stock. The sixth one, at the end of the line, is to be our hotel. Not knowing quite who or what to expect in the way of other guests, I allow my guide to go inside first. Ideas of snakes, wild cats or even other humans are soon dispelled when he reappears to call me in.

Inside, the first thing I notice is the dryness. Not all that surprising, I suppose, but I half imagine that the moisture of winter snows might linger for ever where the sun never shines. The cave is about 6 metres deep by 2.5 wide. A ledge runs along one side, with a hollowed-out oven at the far end. The sides are partly rock, partly packed earth, and everywhere except the floor is black from the soot of earlier fires. I am also struck by the cleanliness. Mohammed says he does not imagine anyone has been here since nomads used it on their way up in the spring. Even so, there is no sign inside or out of rubbish, bones or human waste that I have come to accept as part of the Moroccan way of life.

About half an hour of light remains, but the thick cloud which now covers the sky means that the interior of the cave is already gloomy. Dumping the thyme in a pile, we unpack rucksacks while still able to see. I am a little puzzled when Mohammed produces water and then instead of drinking, uses it to wash his hands, passing me the bottle when he has finished. Still in his turban, he then takes off his jeans, and replaces them with baggy cotton trousers to sleep in. We have brought a couple of candles so I position them in hollows in the side of the cave and then light a cigarette and settle near the entrance to watch night fall. Mohammed goes outside, presumably to pee.

After sitting alone for about ten minutes, I begin to wonder what has happened to my friend. I poke my head out of the entrance and peer around. To my great surprise he is up behind the cave praying, standing and kneeling and bending towards Mecca as is the custom. I notice he has placed a small cloth on the ground as a prayer mat.

I say great surprise. It is of course a tenet of Islam that all believers pray five times a day, one of the most important being just after sunset. On other occasions when I have asked friends whether they pray, I have got a mixed response, varying from yes to never. Certainly I have not noticed it playing much of a part in the lives of the many young people I have met during my travels. I get the general impression that, as with Christianity, praying is something people grow into with the responsibility of middle age and marriage. Anyway, I am delighted to see Mohammed praying. He strikes me as a bit of a tearaway and not the type who would do so. I go back inside lest I distract him, realising why he washed his hands. Islam demands clean hands before praying.

By then it is almost dark outside and black within. On Mohammed's return I light the candles and we select a fireplace, putting a small pile of thyme onto it. He strikes a match. The dry leaves flare into a bundle of crackling flame while the roots contract and twist as the heat devours them. Burning thyme makes an exotic smell which soon fills our cave. This is followed by thick smoke that initially draws straight up to the roof and out of the entrance, but after a few minutes begins to seep across the inside at head height, causing a momentary stinging of the eyes and a rush outside to escape.

How strange it is to stand gulping in lungfuls of cool night air, and then to look up at the outline of mountains all around in the silence of total emptiness. Although the moon is hidden, enough light shows to silhouette a bank of rain clouds scudding across from the west. The only sign of life is the glow of firelight behind me, reflecting outwards from the mouth of the cave. I reckon we must be at least 12 kilometres from the nearest other human.

The fire is of more visual than practical use, the dry thyme burning too quickly to form a decent base. To make it work properly one would need to be more selective in the thickness of root. Nevertheless, when the burning herb settles we enjoy several minutes warming ourselves while gazing into the flames and smelling the sweet aroma. As it dies to a pile of glowing embers Mohammed makes sandwiches and we sit in the candlelight, eating and talking. We then lay out sleeping bags, have a last cigarette and turn in.

The cave is not cold so I take off jeans and pullover to use as a pillow. I spend some time moving around on the hard ground trying to get comfortable. When eventually I lie still I can hear the even breathing of my companion already asleep beside me, still in his turban. My mind starts to turn on the events of the day and then to think of some of the strangest places I have ever spent the night. A snow-hole in Norway and on the banks of the Zambezi spring to mind, but in any future list a cave half-way up the side of a mountain in Morocco will probably get a mention.

It is not a good night. Even with the padding of a sleeping bag I doze only fitfully, constantly shifting position. Several times my mind returns to the pleasant little room in the *auberge*, and I ask myself what moment of madness persuaded me to sacrifice that for this far from cushy billet. It is not until the first thin light of dawn shows in the mouth of the cave, that I finally fall properly asleep.

Mohammed, despite an apparently deep sleep from the moment we bid each other goodnight, seems in no hurry to get up, so it is not until about eight o'clock that I am woken by the sound of him moving about. Knowing it will be more comfortable standing, for once I need no prompting to unzip my bag and pull on clothes. Outside, the cloud of last night has been replaced by an orange glow in the east where the sun is about to start its journey across a violet sky. Utter silence prevails.

We rinse our hands as before. I do not plan to shave and, like many Moroccans of his age, Mohammed does not need to. He prepares another sandwich while I pack my rucksack.

The return to the *auberge* is uneventful but takes us sharply down the side of the mountain into the most extraordinary narrow gorge. Carved by torrents of water gushing off the mountain after the snows each year, it is not more than 10 metres across at the widest but has sheer walls perhaps as high as a four-storey building. At this time it is completely dry, the floor covered in gravel, the lower sides worn smooth by the passage of a thousand tons of rock and debris. Indeed, in some places huge boulders almost block our way where they have found temporary rest against an obstruction in their path.

Once again I find myself somewhere hidden and mysterious, known only to guides like mine from the village and a few nomads who might use this route for access to the mountains. No sign exists of regular traffic on foot or donkey.

The gorge is about 1.5 kilometres long, reminding me very much of the entrance to the hidden city of Petra in Jordan. An ideal place, in times of tribal feuds, to conceal troops. More recently, a perfect spot for brigands on horses to hide until news reached them of a caravan heading up the main route ahead of us. With secret valleys like this it is no wonder the French took so long to subdue the Atlas tribes, and then only with the assistance of Berbers bribed to help. Indeed, *Rogerson* tells us that as recently as the 1950s the Foreign Legion picketed heights in this region to discourage snipers from interfering with tourists.

Perhaps because the end of our walk is in sight, Mohammed is full of chat as we work our way downwards. The gorge ends abruptly where it meets the Dades, and we come out into a wider valley carrying both river and road. Soon we are in the domesticity of cultivation. We arrive back at the hotel in time for me to have a shower and join a group of French tourists for lunch on the veranda.

23

Across the High Atlas

Had I the heavens' embroidered cloths,
    Enwrought with golden and silver light,
The blue and the dim and the dark cloths
    Of night and light and half light...

W.B. Yeats

Sayid, my guide for the drive across the mountains, is older than those I usually acquire, being 28 and married with children. He is a full-time guide and his age and the fact that he can drive gives him a somewhat superior air. At my expense he has hired a Renault *quatre chevaux*, the basic model which has exhausted its shelf-life in Europe but is still much in evidence in North Africa. The type with the gear change on the dashboard.

The car is certainly not new, but I am reasonably reassured of Sayid's competence when I see him loading jerrycans of extra petrol. We also take sleeping bags, food and bottled water, setting off at lunchtime the following day with a rousing send-off from the staff of the *auberge*.

As the village disappears, the road climbs while the river slices into the side of the mountain, leaving no space for road or track beside it. The gradient is steep, with many hairpin bends, but extra height makes the view down into the gorge increasingly spectacular. In many ways similar to the dry gorge we walked through the previous day, this one is larger and of course has the deep green river in its bottom, sparkling up in the noonday sun. Getting higher, I am reminded more than once of the Grand Canyon even though the scale is very much smaller. I have not yet got to know Sayid but he seems amenable enough, happy to stop whenever I ask to get out and survey the scene unfolding before us.

By now the road has turned from tarmac to gravel. Of necessity it clings to the side of the mountain, with hewn rock on one side and an infinite drop on the other. Practically no traffic moves in either direction, the only other vehicles being the occasional lorry grinding along in a cloud of dust, usually with men swaying precariously in the back. Our car motors in fine style, with Sayid proving to be a competent driver. After my experience in the Mercedes, this discovery comes as something of a relief.

Eventually the gorge falls behind as we cross areas of empty barren rock, or open plateau where the river meanders through fields of maize and lucerne. The surface remains fair, and with so little traffic we are able to make good time. In the distance I notice the castellated roof of a kasbah dominating fertile cultivation. I can tell a village is tucked around it.

'There's a village along here,' says Sayid. 'If we are stopped, say you are hitching a lift with me.'

'Stopped by whom?'

'The police.'

'Why can't I say that I am a tourist and you are my guide?'

'Because you should not be here with me,' he answers, lighting a cigarette. Oh dear, here we go.

'Surely we are doing nothing wrong.' I cannot see the difference between being a hitchhiker or a tourist who has hired him for the day. Either I am being dense or he is keeping something from me.

'The thing is, I am not registered with the police as an official guide, so you should not be paying me,' he explains.

'Well, that's not a bad idea,' say I – not perhaps the most subtle joke to make to a Berber. Driving on, I ponder the significance, if any, of his remark.

Sure enough, on approaching the village we are waved into a siding by two *gendarmes*, immaculate in grey uniforms with red trimmings. After many '*Bonjours*' and handshakes through the windows our papers are inspected, mine receiving a cursory look while Sayid's are examined in some detail. The conversation lapses into Berber, the general tone apparently friendly, although at some stage Sayid gets out and continues the discussion behind the car. For once I do not get the feeling of guilt normally associated with interviews of this type. I sit for what seems an incredibly long time, every now and then looking in the mirror to see them still in deep conversation.

At long last Sayid comes back to his door, shakes hands and climbs in. We start up and drive off towards the village.

'Pigs,' he says almost to himself.

'What was all that about?'

'They accused me of acting as an unlawful guide. I had to give them thirty dirhams to forget it.' Unable to see where the crime lies, I put the episode down to local custom.

Not for the first time, one of my problems stems from not having a proper map. Since the small villages on this isolated road have no name-signs I have very little idea where we are, and more particularly how far we have gone. Eventually we start climbing again into a desolate landscape with no fields or signs of human habitation. The surface of the road has deteriorated and our poor Renault crashes and bounces across jagged rock like a small toy pulled carelessly by a child who has long since outgrown it.

By now the sun is sinking. Some time ago I took the time when we passed a lorry, discovering that no other vehicle appeared in either direction for two hours. I am not too worried about punctures as we carry a spare, but I am about breaking a wheel-bearing. The strain must be tremendous. I remember too *Rogerson*'s advice that the drive can be done in summer in a two-wheel drive vehicle, but 'at some risk to your sump'. How right he is, but no consolation in October as the bottom hits yet another rock with an agonising metallic twang.

The next valley is inhabited and shows signs of rain. Potholes brim and water lies beside the track. People and donkeys work in fields of lucerne which our route skirts on its way to yet another *tizi*, as the mountain passes are rather charmingly called. Rounding a corner, we suddenly come face to face with a considerable landslide of rock and mud which must have fallen across the track last night and is now blocking our way.

'*Merde*,' says my companion. The road is impassable so we walk down into the field below and then along to where a scree of rock runs beside a stream. It seems just possible that we might be able to take this route to work our way round below the obstruction. I walk on to find a suitable place to rejoin the track while Sayid returns to the car. He may not be a registered guide but he does know how to drive. Very expertly he manoeuvres off the track and down into the field.

With the recent rain I am worried the ground might be sticky, and indeed it is. For an agonising moment as he reaches the grass the wheels spin and the car stands still. I start to run back to push but he tries again and this time the Renault slides crabwise and then slowly forward towards me. So far so good. At the start of the scree Sayid gets out again for a further look. Then he starts forward. After several anxious minutes while I walk ahead indicating major obstacles and Sayid bumps over a mixture of pebbles and small boulders, we miraculously reach the final rise back onto the track. I rest my shoulder against the rear of the car.

When he lets in the clutch the engine roars. The car lurches forward, jerrycans bounce in the back, wheels whine on mud. But no joy. Sayid stops to engage a higher gear. I heave with all my might and gradually the faithful old buggy inches its way up the slope, juddering and spinning until, after an age, the front wheels gain the track. With great relief I watch Sayid nurse her the last few metres up onto the piste and turn in the direction we are going. We are past the landslide but have lost half an hour.

The worry now is whether we will meet other rain damage further on. Had we been benighted down in the valley, we had at least seen people who would offer shelter. But now, as we climb once more into the mountains, we leave all signs of people and cultivation behind. The sun has about half an hour left in it. I know from my map that somewhere ahead lies the village of Agoudal, but before that, one more *tizi*, namely Tizi-n-Ouano. I guess we are climbing towards it now.

A final anxious moment awaits me. In the middle of nowhere we come to a crosstracks with two ways of equal-looking importance ahead of us. Sayid stops, puzzled.

'Which one is it?' I ask, not certain why he has stopped.

'I am not sure.'

'I thought you had done this route often.' I had assumed it was a regular trip for him.

'I have only been this far twice,' says my unofficial guide, 'and the last time was in the spring. It looked different then.'

Now he tells me!

'We'll take the right one. I am pretty sure that's the way.'

My faint '*Inch'Allah*' passes without comment as we set off again into the setting sun.

I begin to think there is little pleasure in travelling these really rough routes. To me the excitement of getting off the beaten track and enjoying solitary mountains is dulled by constant fear of being benighted in the middle of nowhere and then spending a worthless day trying to get help – if such a thing is to be had at all. I long for a sign that we are somewhere near Agoudal.

After further agonising clangs, we stop to top up and admire a spectacular view back across the mountains we have just crossed. Apart from the track, no mark of man is to be seen anywhere. To our left a huge dry valley stretches away beneath a rounded peak in the full orange glare of evening sun. To our front lie roll on roll of mountains, their north sides already in shade, smooth backs silhouetted like a school of giant porpoises swimming in an inky sea. Behind us jagged peaks show a patina of pink, orange and gray as sun and shadows play slowly across them. Ahead the track at last seems to drop. We have reached what I later discover to be the highest navigable pass in North Africa.

Although the track then inclines downhill, it is not possible to hasten as treacherous potholes and lumps of rock litter the surface. Nevertheless it is good for my bruised morale. As we pick up the headwaters of a new stream, the valley begins to flatten with green patches of grass showing between the rock. A herd of goats appears over on our left, the first living creatures for perhaps an hour. Goats mean people and it is not long before Sayid says, '*Les nomades*,' and points into the shadow up the side of a hill where I can just make out a large black tent.

A small figure is already running at full speed down towards the track. We stop the car and get out just as a girl of about ten reaches us and stands breathless nearby. We bid her hello, or rather Sayid does in Berber as I know she will not speak French. She points to her mouth with the universal sign for food. Her rough white woollen coat is frayed and dirty, but a charming little elfin face peers from beneath a red and black scarf knotted over her hair. Typical Moroccan elegance. Digging in my pocket for coins, I tell Sayid to ask if I can take her picture. She stands while I snap and then runs back towards the tent, her mission accomplished.

I would like to visit the tent but it is already in shadow, the light no good for a picture. Also I am anxious to reach Agoudal before dark. We both agree this is not the moment for a proper halt. Before leaving, I take a look at what the nomad camp consists of. The tent is long and low and, as already mentioned, black. Until recent times, black tents were made from goat hair and white ones from sheep's wool but nowadays most are canvas. Around it stand more goats and donkeys as well as at least three camels. It is surprising to see them so high as I am sure they feel the cold. No doubt they are essential for moving the tent, not to mention supplying daily milk.

I would dearly love to spend time seeing what the family consists of and their way of life. Instead I unpack a sweater and once more we set off.

Maybe it is my imagination, but the track seems to improve as the terrain flattens onto a high plateau. In the gathering twilight we pass a couple more herds of goats, which is a good sign, returning the picturesque waves of shepherd-boys wrapped in djellabas as we speed by. At about the time we put on headlights, the first signs of Agoudal appear ahead of us.

175

As it turns out, we do not spend the night in Agoudal. Sayid is keen to go a bit further and assures me the road improves beyond the village. I would prefer to stop but am not prepared to argue, once again being at the disadvantage of not knowing how long the whole journey will take.

When we pause to buy matches I notice a sight I shall long remember. Because of the cold at this height, practically all the inhabitants are going about their business wearing burnouses with the hoods up. Not a motor vehicle is in sight to spoil the effect. It feels uncannily as if we have arrived at some great medieval monastery, and the figures walking in the dusk amongst rambling castellated buildings are monks from some ancient order.

Agoudal gives the impression of a remote and fascinating village which I would like to have savoured had we had more time.

On leaving we get lost in a maze of buildings and narrow streets barely wide enough for the car. Sayid annoys me by driving faster than necessary, rudely scattering humans, donkeys and chickens in his wake and then having to turn round when we end up in a cul-de-sac. Before long, though we are back on course for Imilchil, our headlights picking out the track, stone walls marking nearby fields.

I already feel cold. Inevitably the car has no heater, and the further we drive the more my legs complain. The sky is clear and dark, with the first stars looking small and reluctant above us. I even wonder if there will be a frost. Ahead the lights of a slow-moving lorry appear, contorting shapes of trees and rocks beside the road. When we eventually catch up I can see men standing in the back, enveloped in dust, turbans hiding faces, eyes strange and wild in our headlights. We press on, with me now more keen than ever to stop for the night but not very hopeful of a bed.

We have been driving for about seven hours and I think Sayid too has had enough. When at last our headlights show houses at the foot of a mountain, I suggest we look for a room. Thank goodness he agrees, stopping for directions and being indicated a building at the far end of the village. I wait in the comparative warmth of the car while my guide goes in search of the owner. Gusts from a strong wind, which I had not previously noticed, buffet the car as I sit there. The visiting moon is now fully up, lighting the scene and casting long shadows down the track where it passes between low buildings. Tiny dots on a huge landscape.

After a couple of minutes Sayid appears, accompanied by an old man carrying a lamp. They walk to a door at the far end of the house. A quick look inside and my guide comes back for the car.

Two large poplars stand at one end of the building. When I step out the wind is rattling through the dry leaves as it rushes down the valley, the sound making me feel twice as cold as perhaps I am. Very quickly we unload, find a torch and hurry over to the room. It turns out to be small and white-washed, with only two items of furniture – a table and one huge bed covered in rugs and goatskins. Sayid follows me in and surveys it for a second before asking if I want anything to eat.

'Yes please.' By this stage I do not care what it might be. Our trip has not been unduly special but we have done a considerable mileage across difficult terrain in an unsuitable vehicle. We have climbed the highest navigable track into the heart of the High Atlas, seeing scenery of grandeur and solitude which could not fail to move any sensitive soul. We have only narrowly avoided being benighted by a landslide. Perhaps of more immediate significance to me is the fact that I have shared this arduous journey with someone, apparently unqualified, about whom I know absolutely nothing. The effect of these different demands on my emotions, coupled with the physical discomfort of cold and apprehension, have used up more than enough spirit for one day. I feel drained and ready for bed.

I follow Sayid along to the main door. This part of the building doubles as a café with a counter and small table for eating. The room is lit by a gas lamp hissing from a beam. Behind the counter stands an elderly man with a tweed jacket over his white robe and a cream woollen turban round his head. After a short discussion in Berber, Sayid asks if an omelette will be all right. I nod, thankful at last to be in the warm, with the imminent prospect of that huge bed down the passage.

Against all odds the next half-hour turns out to be one of great pleasure, entirely due to our host. He does not speak more than a smattering of French, but asks politely, through Sayid, where I come from, what I am doing. I in return talk about the village, and about whether he sees many tourists. He is a handsome man with all the pride and independence of the Berbers in his features. The cream wool of the turban makes fine contrast with a deep brown complexion. Despite living in the extreme climate of these mountains, his skin is flawless, looking almost soft over his cheeks. It could be my imagination but I feel his eyes too have a hooded benevolence as they sparkle in the candlelight.

I wonder how old he is. Since the life expectancy of country people is less than 50 he is probably not much older than me, but there is something noble, almost venerable, about his appearance and the way he conducts himself in such modest surroundings.

The others soon lapse into Berber but I enjoy listening and watching their faces in the soft light. The omelette our host produces is every bit as good as I have anticipated, being cooked as usual in raw olive oil with various herbs thrown in for good measure. When I finish he asks if it was all right.

'Very good, thank you. Just what I needed.' He nods politely and collects up the dishes.

Two weeks earlier I had been back in London and attended a dinner given by the Moroccan Ambassador in honour of Prince Sidi Mohammed, Crown Prince and now King of Morocco. The dinner was ten courses, more or less the complete gamut of Moroccan food. Afterwards the British Ambassador and I had to walk for an hour round the streets of Belgravia to settle our stomachs. I cannot resist savouring the contrast of this evening's simple supper even though my thoughts are impossible to share with my companions in that small room high in the Atlas.

I am not sure how long the others will talk. Still suffering from lack of sleep earlier in the week, I decide to call it a day. I stand up and tell them I am off to bed.

'Is there a bathroom anywhere?' I ask.

Sayid translates. With a wry expression and Gallic shrug the old man indicates the great outdoors. Smiling comprehension, I leave, having a pee in the village street en route to our room. The stars are now fully out, gloriously sharp in the thin mountain air, but it is too cold to linger. Once back inside I take a slug from my bottle of whisky, then lay out the sleeping bag, covering it with goatskins to revive my frozen legs.

The bed proves to be marvellously comfortable. Lying there in the candlelight, feeling the warmth seeping back into my body and listening to the wind sighing and rattling outside, I have an overwhelming feeling of relief and well-being. By the time Sayid turns in I am dead to the world.

I sleep the sleep of the just, waking next morning to hear my guide snoring quietly beside me. Through the gap round the door I can tell it is daylight. The wind has dropped. I get up and go along to the shop for hot water. By the time I am dressed and shaved Sayid is up and our host has coffee and bread ready. A quick breakfast then we load the car, pay him £15 for everything, and set off again towards Imilchil.

'Was that man married?' I ask as we climb a minor *tizi*.

'Of course,' replies my guide.

178

'Then why didn't his wife help with the cooking last night?' I imagine that any similar café in Europe would be a joint effort.

'She was in the home,' he answers. 'That was not woman's work.' Once again I am reminded of the great gulf between Islamic culture and our own.

Apart from its fame as the venue for the auction of brides, Imilchil has no special significance except that it sits in the centre of the High Atlas. As such, it is roughly the half-way point of our journey. The track skirts the town and we decide not to deviate as there is insufficient time to explore properly. We stop for coffee at a hovel on the outskirts and then press on, following the stream along a wide valley with the best grazing I have seen for ages.

In half an hour we reach a lake of several hundred hectares, le lac de Tislit. Working in the desert and spending most of my free time in the south of the country, this is, I think, the first lake I have come across in Morocco. With no wind, the surface is completely flat, reflecting like a picture postcard the surrounding mountains in the morning light. It is a scene of total calm, the only sounds coming from several duck feeding along the shoreline.

We stop the car and walk down to the water, which picks up deep blue from the sky as we approach. Lighting the first cigarettes of the day, we sit on rocks by the shore to wonder at this marvel of nature and absorb the tranquillity of such a pastoral scene. The lake and hills seem so gentle compared to the harshness of the mountains behind us. Through half-closed eyes, we could easily be in the north of Scotland.

The rest of the morning is spent working our way downhill through north-facing valleys of pine and cedar. Being over half-way, the sense of urgency has gone and we can linger as the spirit moves us. The route is picturesque and ideal for picnics. Still no traffic to speak of, so we have the country to ourselves, stopping every so often to sit in the sun and admire the view, or make a sandwich and lie by the stream.

The surface of the track is better than that of the previous day over the *tizis*, although sometimes it almost disappears, even on occasions following the same course as the river-bed. Our little Renault does valiant work, bumping and banging along without complaint like a busy donkey on its way to market.

179

The terrain starts to spread as we cross into the Middle Atlas. Though high peaks remain, they are further apart, the track being able to take a more leisurely path through fields of rough grazing. We pass several boys selling apples, big dark-red ones like in a Walt Disney cartoon. I wonder if they taste as good as they look.

'Shall we stop for apples?' I suggest.

'Yes, but not here.' Sayid waits until we see a youth working in an orchard by the road and then buys some off the tree for a few coins. They turn out to be delicious, hard and sweet and full of refreshing juice. We drive on, chewing away until the bag is empty.

One change which becomes increasingly noticeable is the huge vistas that unfold now that the landscape is more open. It is not exceptional to be able to look 30 or 50 kilometres across rolling tree-covered hills until the distance merges into a haze of heat and dust. I find myself wondering if the Middle Atlas, while less spectacular and wild than the High Atlas, are not more restful to gaze upon. They still have the untouched secret valleys but the whole picture is painted on an altogether more benevolent canvas.

Just as the wheel of fortune seems to have turned in our favour, the Renault develops a fuel blockage causing agonising jerks leading to a gradual loss of power. We could stop and spend another night by the road, but being constrained by financial and time penalties decide to push on, each praying to his respective God that the car will carry us the last 50 or so kilometres to the main road to Fez. Our prayers are grudgingly answered and as the sun sinks from view we limp into Kasba Tadla, where we plan to part company.

The bustle of humanity seems extraordinary after two days of solitude. A hotel is soon found near the bus station in preparation for my departure tomorrow. The original plan was for Sayid to head straight back to Ouarzazate to hand in the car, but the fuel problem and consequent lateness of the hour make him think twice. He helps me to my room and cannot be blamed for yielding to temptation when he sees the spare bed and adjoining bathroom. I go downstairs to tell the concierge of our change of plan, my head reeling from the unfamiliar sound of wailing Arab music from a radio at full throttle in the foyer.

The young man looks up as I appear. He fumbles among the papers in front of him and picks one up.

'Where is this address?' he asks, holding up the form I have filled in with my details.

'What do you mean?' I say shortly. It is a stiff drink I need, not petty bureaucracy.

180

'This address in London, is it a house or apartment?'

I have given all the information required and am not going to be harassed.

'Why do you want to know?'

'Because I want to write to you when you back in Great Britain.' A huge warm smile. 'Here my address. You write to me too.' He offers a neatly written card. I relent and give details in as friendly a way as I can manage. I have his card to this day, but have as yet received no communication from Mr Driss Rbaba.

24

The Tangerines

...He who defines his conduct by ethics imprisons his song-bird in a cage.

Kahlil Gilbran

I suspect that to many who have never been there, the word Morocco probably conjures up thoughts of Casablanca and Rick's Bar, or of Tangier and louche living before the war.

I had to pass through Casablanca on a number of occasions but it was not somewhere of enormous appeal. It is the industrial capital of the country and also the biggest port. With a population of over 4 million it has all the glamour and squalor of any metropolis, but most of its original charm seems to have been elbowed out by commercial expediency. I was, though, fortunate enough to be shown privately round King Hassan's new mosque in its final stages of completion. Built by the sea from public subscription, it has been officially opened since I was there. Whatever anyone may think about the cost or indeed need for such a place of worship, reputedly over three times the size of St Paul's Cathedral, to me it was a building of breathtaking scale and beauty, and worth a special visit for anyone.

I was much more interested to see Tangier, Morocco's oldest city, which for the first half of this century enjoyed international status outside the protection, and therefore laws, of either Spain or France. Although most people agreed it was but a shadow of its former self, the very name, for me, still held a kind of fascination. Rumours of an old guard clinging on to a pre-war lifestyle made me all the more curious. And anyway its situation, facing Spain at the entrance to the Mediterranean, was an added attraction. I also wanted to see the Rif Mountains, which lie some miles to the east. On another of my leaves I decided to explore this part of Morocco.

Having been given the name of an old-established member of the British community in Tangier, I call him from Rabat and accept his invitation of a bed for a couple of nights (very kind since he has never met me). After an interesting bus ride through country altogether more green than further south, I arrive at the drop-off point in the centre of town.

Like anywhere of a certain size, the centre is a mass of humans and vehicles. The shouting of excited voices, hooting of car horns, bustle of people on narrow pavements, all give a feeling of urgency and life. Most of the buildings are old and substantial. As in Casablanca they are mainly white, although without exception in need of a good coat of paint. Modern architecture is little in evidence, a fact that reinforces my preconception of a town of fading splendour. Conversely I see no one in djellaba or other traditional dress.

It takes only a matter of seconds after getting off the bus for a man to try to interest me in hash. He seems to know instinctively that I am English. I tell him where to go, but even as I queue to telephone my host, he pursues his sales pitch. When the subject is finally exhausted he offers to be my guide. Mercifully the telephone at last comes free and I am able to turn my back.

My host, Patrick, is out but has left instructions for his man, Hamid, to collect me. I am therefore left with a quarter of an hour in the centre of Tangier to fend off both my original assailant and several others. Finally an old car comes cruising along the boulevard with a middle-aged Moroccan peering out of the window. Our eyes meet and we both know we are right. Hamid places my case in the boot and heads off into the jostle of traffic, out through the Grand Socco in the centre of town towards the overlooking hills.

Once clear of the traffic, the density of buildings decreases and large white-washed walls appear on either side, hiding opulent properties from which huge eucalyptus and plane trees overhang the road. The way then dips and climbs further towards an expensive residential suburb where palms and cedars indicate mature estates whose houses cannot be seen. Every so often the sea comes into view, its azure blue contrasting strongly with the green foliage in the gardens. I can clearly make out the coast of Spain reflecting in sun along the horizon.

Patrick Thursfield's house is exactly as I had imagined: white-washed walls, good English mahogany furniture, decent pictures and a mass of books. Elegant and comfortable, with a certain style. Beyond the windows an untidy garden stretches seductively into the distance. I am introduced to the cook, a middle-aged woman whose welcoming smile makes up for her lack of French, and to a youth sitting in the kitchen. He too shakes hands with many smiles and is introduced as the under-gardener. It seems that Patrick, who is unmarried, has a staff of four looking after him.

The young man gives me a drink and shows me into the drawing room to await the return of my mystery host. After a quick look at the titles of his books, I wander out onto a large veranda which leads into the garden itself. It is a glorious time of day, the sun still showing but low in the sky, its rays dissipated by branches of cypress and cedar.

The garden harbours a mass of foliage of an exotic and unfamiliar kind, interspersed with geraniums and lilies and other blooms whose scent hangs strongly in the air. Glass in hand, I wander round discovering a swimming pool as well as various secret walkways. New scents hover enticingly at every turn. Pockets of warmth linger even in areas now in shade. Birds which have no doubt dozed silently during the heat of day now sing tunefully from verdurous glooms and winding mossy ways.

After half an hour on my own, I hear the sound of voices and on entering the house meet my host. Patrick is an author and critic who first came to Tangier in the late fifties. He turns out to have owned properties of various sizes, and is clearly someone who lives well. He shows me into a charming bedroom styled in a subtle mixture of English and Moorish. A comfortable bathroom adjoins, with old-fashioned basin and bath of a size seldom found in England nowadays. After a bath and change we head back into town for dinner.

My arrival in Tangier seems to coincide with a flurry of social activity. The next day I punctuate local sight-seeing with a lunch party in the dappled shade of Patrick's veranda, and then a large cocktail party that evening. In between times I am able to enjoy talking to my host and hearing something of the way of life of the expatriate community.

The community is not British so much as English-speaking, with Americans, Danes and others as well as some of the original 'Tangerines' from pre-war days. The attractions seem to be the climate, the cost of living and, for some, the long tradition of sexual tolerance.

There are, of course, a number of women in evidence, both single and married, and also several couples who divide their year between Europe and Tangier. But the majority of those I meet are single men of a certain age who have retired there for the reasons mentioned. Most, it seems, either live with a companion not usually brought out for public scrutiny, or have access to one or more as required. They are old enough to be quite frank in what they say and to make light of having apparently found there a lifestyle which might be difficult at home.

I am pleased for them but not convinced. Patrick once says that the worst thing a European can do is to fall in love with a Moroccan since it is unlikely to be requited. But having spent some time in the country, I feel that those inclined in that direction might find it difficult not to lose their hearts and suffer the consequences.

🌴 🌴 🌴

The cocktail party to which Patrick has had me invited is given by a gentleman retired from the fine-art world in England and America. It turns out to be a big event in the social calendar. He lives in a magnificent house right down in the town but within its own high wall and luxurious garden. The party itself is outside on a veranda, but it is necessary to walk through the house to get there. This allows a tantalising glimpse of an interior of Chinese screens, old masters and gilded mirrors offset by marble and bronze statues and heavy ormolu furniture. Waiters in smart local dress hand round sustenance. The guests, mainly male, include those I have met at lunch plus a large number of new and interesting faces.

Despite grand surroundings, the atmosphere is relaxed and friendly. Introductions are not needed, with most people happy to approach a stranger unannounced. Kisses are standard for those men who know each other – both cheeks, usually accompanied by a hug. Indeed I think the British Ambassador and myself are the only two offered hands to shake. As the evening wears on I notice kaftans, earrings, make-up and more kisses; all quite uncontrived and carried off with good taste and restraint. I also notice that apart from the Ambassador's daughter and one man's Moroccan boyfriend, I am about the youngest person in the room.

We arrive at seven and the party is still going strong at nine. The waiters keep coming; the volume of noise, conversation and exaggerated shrieks of emphasis grows louder; an inky night sky-watches, clear and silent through the palms. As I look around the half-light I find myself wondering how many of these people have found in Tangier the contentment that has evaded them at home.

How many of these buoyant smiling faces are but a mask for darker secrets?

Dinner is arranged in a restaurant, full for the main part of prosperous Moroccans – what my friends in the Atlas would consider *capitalistes*. Their opinion of us is not clear but I imagine in this cosmopolitan and ancient city they must accept such invasions as part of everyday life.

When the evening is over and the last goodbyes have been said on the pavement, Patrick and I drive through deserted streets out of town to the wooded hills and sweet night air of his home.

🌴🌴　　　🌴🌴　　　🌴🌴

Over several days I meet many of the best-known Tangerines. I also visit a number of their houses, either on the hills behind the town or down in the old medina. The artistic bent, which is something of a common thread, has resulted in many fascinating interiors where Moorish fabrics, rugs and artefacts lie comfortably beside traditional European furnishings. Indeed, those with a sense of style have created very wonderful houses and gardens. Plentiful cheap liquor and servants have also played their necessary part in developing a lifestyle which suits a certain temperament.

If Tangier has recently had a social fulcrum more popularly accessible than the drawing rooms of David Herbert or Patrick Thursfield, then it is probably the lawn or dining room of Guitta's. This dilapidated house behind a wall a few blocks from the Grand Socco has been the mecca of the expat community for years. The owner, Mercedes, of English and Argentinian background and unspecified years, presides over a moderate kitchen and ancient staff, but her personal attention and charming manner have ensured a faithful clientele. I am taken there on a Sunday and enjoy lunch beneath swaying palms while others sit in the sun reading the papers or dissecting the party of the night before.

As in any small community, the business of minute post-mortems on every social encounter is an almost daily ritual, bringing out the worst in all concerned. Slights and petty jealousies assume an importance second only to the price of gin in the Gibraltar supermarkets.

🌴🌴　　　🌴🌴　　　🌴🌴

On one occasion I am taken by Patrick for a drive along the coast to Cap Spartel and then down to a restaurant on the Atlantic just where the sea is perpetually agitated by tides flowing in and out of the Straits. How different is the sight looking south, of dead-straight Atlantic coastline and angry surf, to the restful swell of the Mediterranean just round the corner. It is not until going there that I discover that Gibraltar is not at the mouth of the Mediterranean at all, being several kilometres along the Spanish coast from the narrowest part. Even so, one can easily appreciate its strategic value in the days before an attack aircraft could be overhead from Oxfordshire in less than two hours' flying time.

I spend one afternoon battling my way along the streets of the old town. On Patrick's advice I start at the Anglican church, for years a famous rendezvous. The place is deserted, the cemetery, tended but overgrown in parts, an oasis of sweet smells and quiet shade. The gravestones give an intriguing record of previous generations of Britons who found contentment in this Islamic country. For me the highlight is the grave of *The Times* correspondent Walter Harris. In *Morocco That Was*, required reading for anyone interested in Morocco, he has given us a definitive evocation of this country a hundred years ago.

Walter was an adventurer and sportsman, wild and unconventional. His grave is immaculate. Standing alone in the sun, I get an unexplained feeling of sadness when I read the inscription which he must have chosen:

'He Loved The Moorish People And Was Their Friend'.

My sober frame of mind disappears as soon as I am back in the street. No time for sadness here. A mass of humanity shouts and jostles its way in every direction. Car horns blare, scooters appear under my arm, everyone seems absorbed in frantic activity. I feel sure Walter would approve.

As usual I enjoy looking, sometimes at individuals, sometimes at incidents, sometimes even at the grand buildings along the way. I have a map but tend to wander. I discover the site of the fort built by the British in the seventeenth century. On *Rogerson*'s advice I visit the Pasha's palace overlooking the Straits, but for some reason miss the club once famous for its staff of pretty Moroccan boys dressed in Scottish kilts!

On another occasion I get a lift eastwards along the coast of the Mediterranean and am dropped off at Cap Malabata, about 15 kilometres from Tangier. I spend an enjoyable half-day walking back along unspoilt cliffs and bathing on a deserted beach. I am glad I choose that particular beach because a bit further on, where the outskirts of town begin, I come across one of the largest and nastiest open sewers I have ever seen. A river of effluent gushes down a channel across the sand into Tangier bay, leaving a huge dark slick to float around on the tide. Even the locals, not renowned for their squeamishness on such matters, make wide detours to avoid it.

Approached from the east, the skyline of Tangier impresses with many modern high-rise buildings glinting in the sun. Closer inspection is not universally favourable but the town does have a dynamic feeling of expansion and commercial bustle. Shortly after leaping the sewer, I come to the beach made famous by the sexual peccadillos of the colourful Joe Orton. Were he alive today, though, I doubt he would still rate Tangier. The licentiousness he found so irresistible seems to have gone. Male prostitutes have been replaced by windsurfing instructors. If depravity remains, it is successfully hidden under the boring mask of Euro-respectability.

And that seems to me to be the trouble with Tangier. To say it is too civilised would miss the point. Too much the product of outside influences might be more accurate. I have set out on my travels in search of Morocco, but find in Tangier on the one hand a mélange of races and cultures which owes as much to Europe as Africa; on the other a group of incredibly hospitable expatriates whose siren voices of alcohol and sophistication could, after months in the desert, easily deflect me from my aim. I decide to move on before easy living brings my travels to an end.

25

Arcadian Interlude

For I know of a sun and a wind,
    And some plains and a mountain behind
Where there's neither a road or a tree
    But only my maker an' me.

Rudyard Kipling

Most of my time in Morocco was spent in the Atlas and along the Atlantic. However, when daydreaming at the map in my office, my eye often fell on the Mediterranean coast and the Rif mountains. I wondered how that part would compare with what I had already seen. Would European ways have infiltrated across the Straits of Gibraltar? Would the people be any different in an area more influenced by Spain than France? Would the distance from the wilderness of the Atlas and Sahara have tamed them? They were after all descendants of the famous corsairs of the Barbary coast.

I had particularly noticed on the map a small road which leaves Tetouan and follows the coast eastward to El Jebha and then on to Al Hoceima. I decided to hire a car and explore this road, at the same time looking at the Rif mountains. Car hire in Morocco is not easy and is also expensive but, after some help from Patrick and much bargaining, I found myself at the wheel of a Fiat Uno, negotiating my way through the Tangier traffic on the road to Tetouan.

Inland from Tangier the country is relatively flat but the start of the Rif mountains can be seen in the distance. Even if they were not visible, the lie of the land has just enough relief to suggest mountains somewhere in the vicinity. I am reminded alternately of Devon, the Welsh Marches and Northumberland. The first hour of driving

takes me across rolling fields of barley, wheat and pasture –
marginal country in British farming terms, but a lot greener than
most of Morocco and restful to the eye.

Today the sky is clear except for isolated puffs of thick white
cloud hanging over the distant mountains. The satisfaction of escap-
ing the bustle of Tangier and getting onto the open road is tremendous. Straight away I start seeing drifts of wild flowers. A short stop
shows nine varieties jumbled together, their brightness creating a
startling carpet along the verge. With the greenery and water comes
a softening of colours, imparting a much more gentle feel to this
part of the country than the areas of my earlier travels.

It does not take me long to discover that the driver's window of
my little car will not fully wind up. No problem at the moment as
all windows are open, but it will make the car impossible to secure
at night. I also notice a hairline crack across the windscreen. I am
not intending to drive cross-country, but neither have I ruled it out,
so a crack which might open up if the vehicle comes under stress is
not ideal. Other than that, she works fine and my spirits are high.

Near Tetouan I find the turn for the coast road and strike east, soon
reaching sand dunes behind the beach. By now mountains have
appeared ahead of me, running straight into the sea in the direction
in which I am heading. Before reaching the coast the road climbs,
following the edge of the hills from there on, sometimes high up,
sometimes dipping and running parallel to the beach. Wherever the
land is flat enough to plough, a patchwork of small fields shows.
These are not only in the valleys, but also across the backs of hills
and even way up above the road. Slopes too steep to cultivate are
covered in a mass of scrub, the richness of leaves and tangle of herbs
and flowers not unlike the *maquis* in Corsica. A detectable herby
smell too fills the air, though not as strong as that of the real *maquis*.

Soon after climbing into the mountains it dawns on me how few
people are about: hardly any of the usual donkeys and children
going to and from the fields; only occasional figures bending among
crops; practically no traffic. I cannot account for this emptiness,
which seems almost sinister. Further along, in the bigger valleys,
plenty of people are in evidence, but for the first few kilometres I
have the place more or less to myself. What I do see is a network of
military lookouts within view of each other all along the coast. The
soldiers' attention is directed out to sea and they never do anything
more than wave as I pass. I hear later that their role is to prevent
traffic in Spanish goods coming into Morocco, or drugs and people
heading outwards for the greener grasses of Europe.

Sadly the cloud which I noticed earlier sitting picturesquely on the mountains expands and closes around me, darkening the land-scape and threatening rain. Interestingly, it follows very exactly the contour of the mountains. Out to sea waves sparkle happily, and where the road dips into a wide valley a break in the cloud allows the fields the full glare of the sun. But mostly the scene has a dull, dank look to it.

I am disappointed by the coastline, but this may be partly due to the weather. With very few exceptions the beaches are either pebble or have a thin strip of grey sand at the foot of considerable cliffs. Indeed, unless one was prepared for a major hike it would be impossible to get to the sea anywhere except in the few open val-leys. At the start of the drive I buy the usual sandwiches, intending to stop for a swim and food along the way. As it is, I remain fully clothed, including a sweater. I eat my lunch in a bed of wild flowers, watching waves breaking along a grey and deserted beach hundreds of metres below.

My spirits revive when I reach the village of Targa; nothing special in itself, but sitting in a valley wide enough to create a gap in the cloud. Indeed, the area around the village is charming in the sunshine, a mass of small fields, interspersed with hedges of thorn and prickly pear and dotted with wild figs and walnuts. Always too the graceful palm to remind one that the desert is not a million miles away.

Here at last are signs of people at work – women in brightly coloured clothes doing their washing in the river, garments laid out on stones or draped over bushes to dry; donkeys hobbled at the roadside, their owners labouring in lines in the fields; old carts pulled by mules taking lucerne back to feed stock. All the panoply of a rural community.

The chief task at this time of year is the harvesting of wheat. Done here by hand, it seems to involve the whole family, men and women working together in lines, gathering the sheaves in their arms then slicing the stalks with a sickle. Normally the older women sit in groups minding young children while anyone big enough to do so is co-opted into some form of work. Always too the attendant donkeys standing patiently in the shade until their turn arrives.

One aspect of life all over Morocco which never fails to impress me is the young age at which children start taking their turn at daily chores. Almost as soon as they can walk, boys and girls are entrusted with grazing one or two old sheep. By the time they are six they will be riding alone by donkey to the well to fill water cans. Not long after that they will be off in the fields with small flocks, some-times accompanied by grandparents but soon on their own. Frequently one sees tiny girls of perhaps seven or eight almost hidden beneath huge bundles of maize or lucerne. Moroccans may work their donkeys hard, but they do not spare their children either. On this drive I see countless examples of whole families in the fields, everyone contributing something.

It is a pleasure to see most people in traditional dress. The clothes here are quite different from those in the Atlas, as a result, I suspect, of Spanish influence. Practically all the women wear plain or patterned pantaloons beneath long skirts of red and white or red and blue, the red an attractive mulberry colour. A pullover or smock of faded dark blue or white makes up the top half. On their heads, both men and women wear wide-brimmed straw hats, often decorated with coloured strands of straw or cotton. Beneath these some women also wear headscarves – the overall effect being most colourful in the fresh green of harvested fields.

To start with I am puzzled by the appearance of straw hats. If the aim is to protect heads from sun, why do the Atlas Berbers, whose sun is hotter than here, seldom wear them? The answer is of course obvious. Here in the Rif where there is a reasonable rainfall and therefore no desert, there may be winds, but no dry sand to pick up and drive into people's faces. The straw hat is therefore a convenient way of protecting from the sun. But down in the Atlas, less rainfall means more desert. The turban, which can be wrapped round the whole face to protect from sand as well as sun, becomes essential.

In the late afternoon I arrive at the village of El Jebha. This is as far as I intend going along the coast and anyway the road turns inland. The village itself is disappointing, smaller than I expect and lacking any noticeable architectural or scenic charm. After parking the car I head for the entrance to the fishing harbour, where, to my surprise, an armed soldier stands on duty. I walk straight past but am soon called back and asked my business. I explain that I am a tourist and that I want to look at the fishing boats.

'*C'est impossible,*' he says, with a foolish smile.

'Why?' I really do feel such needless bureaucracy deserves at least a token challenge. Indicating for me to wait, he disappears into a hut, soon to reappear with another soldier who asks various questions and then demands my passport. When I hand it over I cannot know that he will spend nearly half an hour checking every stamp, telephoning his superior and generally wasting my time. Eventually I leave it with him and walk back to the village to a pavement café and a most excellent glass of coffee.

192

When all is said and done I am, of course, allowed into the harbour, although it is disappointing and certainly not worth the wait. All the time I am becoming a little anxious because with so much cloud I know it will get dark earlier than usual and I still have some way to go. I study the map. Two routes lead out of the village. One retraces for a few kilometres the road I came in on, and then turns inland. The other climbs out of the village and across the mountains to a town called Ketama.

I know only two things about Ketama. The first is that the town is situated near famous and beautiful cedar forests. The second is that it lies at the heart of the main kif-growing region and is widely held to be the centre of the Moroccan drug trade. The combination of these two means I have to go there.

26

Kif in the Rif

Life is a short trip,
The music's for the sad men.

Alphaville

The road to Ketama winds steeply up from El Jebha, Quite soon I am able to stop and look down a great distance to the tiny outline of the village on the shore below. Further to the east lies a deserted stretch of coast which would have been fun to explore on foot had there been more time. But as a result of the delay at the port, the day is deteriorating fast, assisted by dark clouds now hanging ominously over the direction in which I am travelling. For a second it crosses my mind that I might be heading for trouble. I get back into the car and start off again up the side of the mountain.

Once more a complete absence of traffic. Apart from one open pick-up full of men coming towards me, the hillside is deserted, which is probably just as well. The road is only wide enough for a single vehicle in most places, with a precipitous drop on one side. It is comforting to know that competition is unlikely from the opposite direction.

Although darkness is fast approaching, little can be done to hasten my journey. A warning bell sounds in my head when every so often the surface of the road changes from tarmac to rock. This is not on account of roadworks, but rather, as far as I can see, through neglect and lack of use. It seems not impossible that the road may peter out altogether high up in the mountains and I will have to retrace my steps in the dark, which is not a pleasant prospect. All I have to go by is a map of too large a scale to give any detail of the route. The drive looks reasonably short *à vol d'oiseau*, but that does not account for the twists and turns taking it over the mountains.

The other worry playing on my mind is that the higher I climb, the closer I am getting to where thick cloud is closing in. For a few moments things improve when, from behind me, the sun suddenly struggles through, illuminating everything in a bright orange glow. But only briefly. Soon it sinks back into haze along the horizon and, as the last rays filter away, the first drops of rain land on the windscreen.

The temperature is none too good either and of course the window that will not wind up now comes into its own. Never mind, think I, lights and heater will sort that out. But this is not to be. The lights are just adequate but the heater blows only cold air, which neither demists the windscreen nor warms the interior. The sparkling sea and bright fields of the afternoon seem ages away in conditions that are speedily becoming wintry.

One dramatic moment occurs when I come round a corner and there on the road in the misty gloom are two horses with a boy on one, his face hidden in a white turban. As usual he is riding bareback, leading the other on a halter. The horses, alarmed by my sudden appearance, stand nervously on their toes. I know a huge drop lies beyond them. Very expertly he guides his own horse to the edge and coaxes the other beside him. As I drive past he unaccountably finds a spare hand to give a slow and elegant salute.

It is something of a relief to see another human after half an hour without anyone. By now it is almost dark and the mist has turned into a pea soup fog such as I never expected to see outside England. My legs are cold because of the open window; the lights and windscreen wiper are barely adequate; the tarmac peters out for several metres at a time, and I have no idea how much further I have to go. I can safely say that these conditions and uncertainties are making this one of my least amusing experiences in Morocco.

Battling on, wondering what on earth I am doing, I suddenly see headlights approaching through the fog from the opposite direction. Because the road is so narrow I find a passing place and halt. To my surprise a police car pulls alongside.

'Bonsoir, Monsieur.' The driver winds down his window and talks across to me, his companion watching with a stern expression. They ask what I am doing, where I am going, where I have come from etc. Twice he asks if I am alone. Not all that surprising, I suppose, as I must seem an odd one to find half-way up the mountain at night. When I ask if I am all right for Ketama, I learn to my horror that it is still 50 kilometres away. I expect them to search the car for hash but with a pleasant smile and a 'Bon chance,' they wish me goodnight. I can only presume that my harassed demeanour has

195

none of the hallmarks of the professional drug-dealer.

One aspect not already mentioned is the fact that in addition to petering out every so often, the road is littered with frequent vicious potholes. These obstacles lie in ambush whenever the fog parts enough for me to get up speed, and then shake the car mercilessly, causing worries both about the crack in the windscreen, and more particularly whether the chassis or wheel-bearings might give up the unequal struggle. The thought of being benighted up in these mountains is not a good one. Years ago I spent a morning looking after Signor Agnelli, head of the Fiat empire. Now I say a silent prayer that he has caused his cars, and this one in particular, to be properly put together.

Another facet of this journey is the length of time the road continues climbing. It is clear that Ketama will be in a valley as it stands on a stream, so some way before getting there the road will have to level and then start losing height. On the several occasions it does suddenly begin to drop, I foolishly think that perhaps this is the start of the descent, but always after a few hundred metres it climbs again. I have no means of telling how far I have gone as the indicator is broken. Eventually I start willing the journey to end even though, as it turns out, I still have some way to go.

After more anxious kilometres, covered cautiously as I slow right down to identify the edge of the road, stationary lights appear in the fog to my front. As I pass I am waved down by the driver.

'*Buenas noches.*' He comes to the window with a broad smile. I answer in French but he soon realises I am English.

'Where you going, *amigo*?'

'I'm going to Ketama,' say I, mustering as much confidence as I can.

'No, no, Ketama no good,' he smiles. 'You come stay at my farm. I have everything. You come with me. We have food, maybe a little whisky. Anything you want. You smoke?'

'No, that's very kind, but I have to get to Ketama.' I am not sure why, but I am quite certain I do not want to go to this friendly man's farm. After a relatively good-natured exchange I tell him that I really must go, and goodbye.

One of the most worrying aspects of the drive, apart from the depressingly long time spent climbing, is the fact that I see not a single light from any building. Perhaps none exist in these mountains. Or, and this I feel to be more likely, the moment the locals see clouds descend they go inside, light fires, roll themselves joints, and are now away with the fairies. Who knows? But it would be comforting to see signs of life somewhere.

196

Another car is halted at the side of the road. Again I must slow down to pass. This one has three men sitting across the front seat. The usual pleasantries from the chief, followed by 'Don't go to Ketama, come to my house, I have everything you want. You stay the night. All very friendly' etc., etc. Oh dear. I go through the same routine, but this one refuses to be so easily deflected. Not for the first time that evening do I feel a nagging fear in the back of my mind. Twice I try to excuse myself and leave, and twice he becomes almost aggressive in asking me to stay. Eventually I insist that I am going anyway and goodbye. I leave with a roar of engine and the sound of his shout in my ear.

Drawing away, the lights of his car turn to follow, but of course there is no escape. I do not know the road and the fog is so dense that it is impossible to hurry. In the mirror I can see him closing behind me. For a short while he follows until I pull in to a passing place and let him by. The car speeds past into the cloud, leaving me wondering what will happen next. I have 500 dollars in the seam of my trousers. I pull the notes out and slip them under the matting on the floor. The rest of my luggage is that of a poor tourist, not a dealer in hashish. If it is money they are after they will hopefully realise their mistake and leave me alone.

I am not totally surprised when on rounding a corner I come to the same car again, this time stationary but in such a way that I cannot pass. I have to stop. The man is already out. He comes over and says something in Spanish before starting the same old routine in English. Why do I want to go to Ketama? What do I smoke? How much do I want to buy? He is not blessed with tremendous charm and I find myself both annoyed and wary. I know very little about dope but it seems that half the worst crimes in Britain are committed by people under its influence, so I am cautious lest his actions are not those of a rational man.

I stay in the car. When he eventually walks back to his, I move slowly forward. His friend, thank goodness, backs to let me by. No harm done except perhaps to my nerves, which are by now a little frayed. I suppose it is the same as on the beach. No one can believe that a single European could possibly find his way there except in search of one of two commodities so readily available in Morocco.

And still the road winds on. Thank God I have plenty of petrol as one thing I know will not be found up here is a garage. A stop through either lack of fuel or mechanical failure would make it impossible to avoid a trip to one of these magical farms.

Eventually, to my immense relief, the fog begins to thin. Pressing on, the impenetrable denseness turns to wisps and then at long last we burst out into clear black night. Incredibly the faintest light still lingers in the western sky, indicating it is still only about nine o'clock. It feels more like midnight. My eyes soon adjust to looking further afield instead of peering into mist 5 metres ahead. The road runs high above valleys filled with the fluffy white cotton-wool from which I have just escaped. I stop the car and get out. Thin cold air fills my lungs. Silhouettes of mountains stretch into the distance, dark and mysterious. A slight breeze brushes my face, otherwise complete silence and great beauty.

In the cold mountain air it is easy to forget one is in Africa. If someone had taken me there blindfold and asked, I might have said Bavaria. I have to remind myself that if and when I find a village it will have a mosque; the people will speak a language of which I know nothing; no red-faced German will pour me a glass of pils. There will be none of the familiarity which this landscape and temperature call to mind in the dark.

Having long since given up on the map, I decide to press on, hoping for a signpost. When one duly appears I find myself on a larger road about 10 kilometres from my destination, and at last in traffic, something noticeably absent all evening. Near Ketama, the headlights start to pick out cedars either side of the road. These are nothing like the stunted, twisted cedars up near the snow-line of the Atlas; more like the large trees round Azrou, with straight trunks and flat boughs sloping to the ground. I judge them to be easily a hundred years old, well spaced out with what looks like grass beneath.

On reaching the '*Bienvenu à Ketama*' sign, I am surprised to find no lights either above the sign or in houses along the way. I slow down, my one idea in life being to find a hotel for dinner and a hot bath. Just as I am contemplating this the headlights pick out a sign saying 'Tourist Hotel'. Thank goodness.

But still no lights. I can tell I am in the village from parked cars and people on foot. Every now and then a glow seeps into the street indicating gas or candlelight, but no sign of electricity. Surprising for a town of this size. As a result of the blackout I soon find I have driven right through the village, completely missing the hotel. At the same moment a gang of ten or so youths comes into sight spread across the road. I have to slow to avoid them and immediately know I am in Morocco.

'*Monsieur, Monsieur,* what do you want? Are you looking for a hotel? My father has very good hotel.' Etc., etc. They run after the car, waving and shouting.

After a rather forceful 'no thank you' I am then faced with the embarrassment of having to turn and drive through them once more to get back to the centre of town. The same shouting again and a cheer when I am finally past. Needless to say the hotel is only a matter of metres further on, and by the time I have spotted it, found somewhere to park and got out, I am almost literally mobbed by the same youths all grabbing my arm, pushing each other away, trying to sell me anything and everything all at once. It is at this stage that the window problem once again rears its head. The moment comes when I must abandon the gallant little car, window open and surrounded by strangers, to go into the hotel.

As far as I can tell, some of the mob remain outside but most of them, all talking at once and jostling each other to attract my attention, follow in. There is clearly an acute shortage of tourists at this time of year.

The first thing I notice is the gloom of the interior, caused by the fact that gas lanterns provide the only source of light. As my eyes take in this ominous sign, I realise from the noise that on the other side of the building is a large room full of people. Coming from it loud and clear is quite my least favourite type of Arab music, wailing furiously, with all the signs of a party getting under way. After the traumas of the preceding three hours, a non-alcoholic party with Arab music is all I need.

The concierge does his best to disperse my entourage while I explain what I want.

'Do you have a room please?'

'Certainly, *Monsieur*. For how long?'

'One night, please.'

'Certainly, that will be twenty pounds.'

'With bathroom etc.?'

'The room has a bathroom, *Monsieur*, but I am afraid there is no hot water as we have not turned on the generator.'

'Oh! Why ever not?' My irritation rises in inverse proportion to the prospect of a hot bath.

'Unfortunately you are only person staying and we cannot afford to turn on the electricity supply for whole hotel for just one bathroom.' Fair enough, I suppose, but damned annoying.

I ask for a porter and am accompanied to my room by a youth with gas lamp. The room is all right but rather too close to the party. I cannot have a bath, neither can I warm up any other way, nor can I go to bed because of the terrible noise permeating down the corridor. Oh dear. The youth lingers in the doorway.

'Is there any food please?'

'Certainly, *Monsieur*, no problem.' That fatal phrase.

'All right, I'll be along in a minute. Please alert the chef.' The boy leaves. I collect my thoughts and then pick up the lamp and head back towards the music. The chief aspect of the hotel which worries me is the way rowdy youths from the street seem to have free access to the inside. The concierge appears to have no authority, so the safety of one's belongings, not to mention one's person, is in danger of falling prey to their attentions.

Nearing the hallway, I am spotted and surrounded once more by youths offering everything imaginable. In the absence of any guidance I follow the general movement of bodies into the main room towards the sound of music, finding to my surprise a huge bar along one side. Everyone is drinking alcohol – mainly large quantities of beer. Thick cigarette smoke combines with the smell of hashish and beer to create a powerful atmosphere. The room is pleasantly warm from so many bodies, the band at one end playing so loudly that conversation, particularly in French, is virtually impossible. I order a drink for myself and several companions who are by now studying my every move. After talking for a bit, I stand against the bar to watch the dancing.

I have mentioned before that Moroccans love dancing. Their strong sense of rhythm, added to a complete lack of inhibition, makes a scene like the one in front of me marvellous entertainment. A few women dance either with men or together. Many men also dance alone, just moving in time to the beat with no thought for anyone else. The music swells and drops. Figures twirl and shake, legs describe meaningless but intricate rhythms across the floor, faces rapt and content. Since conversation is limited, those around me sing along or stand watching and smoking in silence. A few turn their backs on the band and prop up the bar, shouting to their companions and ordering rounds of drinks which soon disappear.

I am disturbed by someone pulling my arm. The man next to me nods in the direction of the bartender, who signals me towards the door. Supper perhaps? I start to extract myself from the crowd, surprised at the interest this causes until it dawns on me that I am the only European in the building.

Supper is adequate; I sit alone in a large darkened dining room, chairs upended on most of the tables, a gas light hissing in the centre of mine. The background sound of music and conversation is interrupted periodically by various of my earlier companions coming to check my progress. Some stand for a few moments until my calculated lack of response sends them wandering back to the action. One annoying young man sits himself down, launching into

200

a long plan involving me leaving the hotel and coming to his family farm for the night. He proudly tells me that his father is the biggest drug baron in Ketama and that all my problems will be solved if I avail myself of his hospitality.

My own view is quite the reverse. Other than a sneaking interest to know exactly what goes on at these farms, I can think of nothing more tedious than going home with him. Various hints that I would like to be left alone fall on empty ears and he is still with me when I stand to leave.

'*Monsieur*, you drink with me. Come.' Once again it is more of an order than a question. I follow him back along the dark passage to the dance-hall, where the number of people has increased and the atmosphere thickened. He pushes a way, sometimes rudely, sometimes with a friendly slap on the back, through youths watching the dancers, glasses and smokes in hands. He is clearly someone of significance as everyone seems to know him. We, or rather I, order drinks and stand with our backs to the bar while a roomful of men under one influence or another sway and shuffle to the excruciating din.

🌴🍸   🌴🍸   🌴🍸

Luckily the volume, as I have already said, is such that conversation is impossible. We have been standing there for about ten minutes when I realise from the direction of people's gaze that a commotion is coming from the far end of the bar. Two youths in heated argument are surrounded by others shouting the odds, some trying to intervene, others drawing up battle-lines opposite each other. Before long the inevitable scuffle breaks out, hands grabbing collars, voices raised, faces thrust forward with aggression. Pushing and prodding leads to the first slaps to the head, delivered with unexpected ferocity. Elsewhere, some choose to ignore developments, others are too stoned to notice; the barman continues serving drinks, and the band plays on...

Within no time the group of those fighting rather than watching has grown, spilling onto the dance floor, pushing tables and chairs into a jumble against the wall. I have no idea of the cause of the row but it appears to give rise to strong views. Luckily the density of bodies is such that scope for a real punch-up is limited, hostility being for the main part confined to one group crushing against the other, with just those in front causing aggravation. My companion, he of the drug-baron father, seems to have forgotten me, watching proceedings intently and shouting instructions in an unpleasantly hostile tone.

And then things change. Someone from the hotel makes an announcement by loudspeaker. Hangers-on drift away, inadvertently giving the assailants more room. The original hard core suddenly find themselves with the opportunity to swing a punch, and a proper fight ensues.

As far as I can tell, one particular youth is at the centre of the dispute. Two others needle him, slapping him round the head and pushing him back towards the bar. Blood runs from nose and lips. His supporters are shouting, preventing his retreat but taking care not to draw the fire of his assailants, although other scuffles are developing nicely in the wings.

After minutes of painful punishment the youth makes a break for it, lunging sideways and running towards the door and, more worryingly, me. A roar goes up as the attackers chase and grab him almost at my feet, struggling and punching him and those who have by now decided to join in.

I back away, trying to make myself inconspicuous, which is not easy being probably the tallest person in the room. My erstwhile companion, whose verbal contribution has grown by the moment, weighs in, pushing and slapping with the best of them while the whole group seem in danger of enveloping me.

It is time to go. No one has done anything to threaten me, but the general atmosphere is taut and many of those involved are clearly either drunk or high.

Taking care not to knock into anyone in a way which could be misinterpreted, I ease my way along the front of the bar towards the door, hastening nonchalantly when a gap appears. At the reception a further row is in progress between the concierge and a knot of youths. Without stopping, I take the darkened passage to my room, locking the door behind me with a feeling of relief at having escaped what has all the ingredients of a high-class brawl.

Ketama has exceeded my expectations as a frontier town. I realise as I stand listening for further developments along the passage that the rush of adrenalin has made a bath unnecessary. My body burns with excitement, my pulse racing until well after the hotel falls silent.

The next day comes hot and clear and the hotel is back to normal by the time I appear for breakfast. I pay the bill and drive off towards Fez without staying to explore. I never discover the cause of the fight, neither am I fussed. I have seen enough to form the impression that Ketama will reveal a side of Morocco I prefer not to know.

27

Agadir to Ouarzazate

For a thousand years, 'neath a thousand skies,
  Night has brought men love;
Therefore the old, old longings rise
  As the light grows dim above.

Laurence Hope

Perversely, I rather like Agadir. As the main tourist city in Morocco it in many ways stands for all that I spent my days trying to avoid. But, because of its airport, I have been there so often that I have developed an accommodation for the town in my affections. However hard one may try, it is difficult from memory to conjure up the actual feel of a country, but from the moment of arrival in Agadir the essence of Morocco and its people flood back into the conscious as if one has never been away.

To the east of the main tourist area is the Place de l'Espérance. A short walk beyond that lies Talborjt district caught somewhat awkwardly between the new town and more native streets. It is to this area in particular that my mind turns because it is here that I have often stayed awaiting buses to take me on my travels inland: an area of pavement cafes, street stalls and seedy hotels among clothes and jewellery shops of a reasonable standard. Nothing of any great age as Agadir was reduced to rubble by a shock earthquake in 1960.

The bus terminal opens the eyes of the newcomer to what lies ahead. Buses from everywhere arrive with country folk unspoiled by city ways. Hanging around, they form a weird and wonderful mix of dress, traditional or modern, denoting their place of origin: bright colours from the Atlas, blue turbans from the desert, wrapped faces from the north. There are always also young European backpackers, confused by the vagaries of timetables, the fairness of their skin distinctive despite weeks in the sun.

203

I adopted two contrasting formats for supper in Agadir. One was to go to the area of the bus terminal and sit at a pavement café with a cheap supper of fish or meat cooked over charcoal. The point of this was certainly not the food. It was the opportunity to observe the comings and goings of the fellow travellers, beggars, glue-sniffers and old European queens wintering cheaply who gravitate to this quarter.

The alternative was to walk the length of the town to the port, where the Restaurant du Port has one of the best fish menus I have found anywhere. Several are the nights I have wandered back through deserted streets, well satisfied by oysters, bouillabaisse, shrimps in mayonnaise, *calamar*, or whatever else had been brought in that afternoon, my steps perhaps a little unsteady as a result of overcompensating for many days without alcohol.

One night I decide to change this routine and eat at a tourist rest-aurant near the sea-front. Soon I am sitting on a patio a stone's throw from the beach, surrounded by German, French and Moroccan families. Between the patio and the beach runs a wide pathway, used apparently by everyone out this evening. A mass of people of all types and ages stroll past taking the night air. From next door a canned Bonnie Tyler tells all who care to listen, the story of her 'heartache'.

A sudden movement causes me to look down. A mangy cat is ingratiating itself against my leg. Anglo-Saxon expletives go unrecognised so I use my shoe to direct it to another table, where its purrs and wheedling are better received. But peace is short-lived. The empty space is quickly occupied by two dogs of indeterminate type who begin a programme of mutual sniffing. They are too absorbed in each other to bother me so I decide to leave them for the moment.

My order is taken by a charming waiter just as a man starts singing in Arabic from the depths of the restaurant. For several minutes he and Bonnie Tyler battle it out, until he prevails and she is switched off. Secure in victory, he moves on to John Denver, singing most beautifully words he cannot possibly understand. With a high, clear voice and accent that makes even dull words seductive, he is backed by an infectious rhythm which soon distracts me from the usual people-watching. I find myself wondering what pictures 'Blue Ridge Mountains' or, more particularly, 'Shenandoa River' can conjure up for him, but then I realise they do not mean a huge amount to me either and I still enjoy the songs.

My food comes and goes. The people on the sea-front wander by. The dogs beneath my table are now locked in most satisfactory copulation. I am happy enough with my choice of restaurant when I hear, not for the first time, a clap somewhere behind me. Turning, I find a boy of ten or twelve performing acrobatics for the next-door table. Two quick somersaults are followed by him bending backwards and flicking his feet into the air to walk around on his hands. A flick back onto his feet, an enchanting clap of the hands and he is onto the next trick.

I am instantly captivated, not only by his dress of black trousers, white shirt and red waistcoat, and the delightful expression on his face, but also the incredible control exercised over his body. The whole is a fascinating package as far as I am concerned. Another clap; this time he pulls out a chair, on the arms of which he raises himself into a slow handstand, lowering his legs down and through the back until he is able to extend them outwards and wrap his arms round them, with his body woven into the back of the chair. After a round of applause he carries out the same exercise in reverse, ending up by springing lightly back onto his feet with another little clap. I need hardly add that when he passes round a plate I grossly overtip him, making up for the German couple next door. Having gazed with rapt attention throughout the performance, they wave his plate away without contribution.

He moves to other tables while I watch from a distance, pleased to see that for the most part he is suitably rewarded. Having eventually covered the whole restaurant, he pulls on an old anorak and saunters off, giving me a last unexpected and dear little smile from some distance. Soon he is in the crowd, indistinguishable but a great deal richer, I fancy, than most of the other youngsters aimlessly wandering the front.

I am on another week's leave, overnighting in Agadir in order to pick up a hire car the next morning. That having been done, the car stocked with essentials and filled with petrol, I am off to visit the Draa valley, one of two oasis valleys running south from the Atlas into the Sahara.

By midday I have turned off the main road to Ouarzazate at a village called Aoulouz and taken a dirt track into the Atlas in the area of the Jebel Siroua. This drive, which is strongly recommended by *Rogerson*, proves a superb choice even though the going is alarmingly rough and no signposts exist to guide the unwary.

205

To start with, the track follows a series of valleys, rich with olive trees of great age overhanging the road and providing respite from the sun. Few people are about, just the odd man or boy on a donkey heading from fields spread across the valley floor. A couple of villages are soon behind me as the track leaves the greenery and starts to climb. This is just the sort of adventure I like – an unknown route, no clue as to what lies ahead and no idea where I will spend the night.

The High Atlas, of course, stretch from the Atlantic coast across Morocco and Algeria into Tunisia. The highest summit, Jebel Toubkal, at just over 4,000 metres, is higher than anything in Spain or the Pyrenees but 800 metres lower than Mont Blanc. It is roughly three times the height of Ben Nevis. I have never climbed it, although it is easily enough done with the aid of a guide and, so I am told, a donkey to carry one's things!

As shadows lengthen I have gained considerable height. The air is distinctly fresh, cool even. From the enclosed topography of the valleys, the track edges its way up the side of mountains, gradually revealing great tracts of country beyond the tops of lesser hills. The late afternoon is the best time to see such views because of the changing pattern of light and shade and the definition afforded by shadow. The atmosphere is anyway clearer than on the dusty plain. The total lack of traffic, too, is welcome, despite the vague worry as to who will provide assistance in a crisis. In the end I drive for the rest of the afternoon without seeing a single other vehicle.

The direction in which I am heading is west to east, with the irregular volcanic tops of the Jebel Siroua on my right. To the left, mountains of the High Atlas form an intriguing series of ridges, climbing gradually but separated by vast deserted plateaux which stretch into emptiness; rock and shale and bare earth sprinkled with scrub turned brown by dust. In the distance certain peaks stand out against the sky but I am too far south to be able to see the snows of the Jebel Toubkal.

Several times I stop to enjoy the utter solitude of such grand territory. Anyone who has read so far will already know my love of this type of scenery, where nothing is in sight to hint at the existence of man. Nothing on the ground, no vapour trails in the sky, just brooding consuming loneliness and silence that rings in the ears.

At one stop I find myself reminded of a conversation I had with the Master of my college at Cambridge. A woman friend, whose husband was terminally ill, had asked where she could take him to prepare for his final journey. An impossible question, but my friend had suggested the church on Torcello, an island in the lagoon of

Venice. That small church, he said, was the one place on earth where in his life he had felt nearest to his Maker. Standing in the evening sun among these savage, solitary mountains, I find my senses lifted in a curiously religious way as if I too can almost feel His presence.

I have only recently read the beautiful words of Khalil Gibran's *The Prophet*, which seem to say it all:

> For what is it to die but to stand naked in the wind and to melt into the sun?...
> Only when you drink from the river of silence shall you indeed sing.
> And when you have reached the mountain top, then shall you begin to climb.
> And when the earth shall claim your limbs, then shall you truly dance.

In these surroundings I do not think it would be difficult to let slip one's hold on life.

From such lofty heights my thoughts quickly descend to the more immediate consideration of where to spend the night. Somewhere ahead lies the village of Askoun, but it is difficult to be sure how far. I push on in the twilight until a herd of goats appears, ranged across the road and barring my way but also indicating habitation. A shepherd-boy in indigo blue djellaba appears from nowhere and nods encouragingly when I attempt my best Berber pronunciation. At the next rise I can see the roofs and walls of the village. The track soon leads me among them and I head for a large flag, which turns out to mark a military compound.

Rogerson says that in the mountains few people speak anything but Berber. Luckily the two men at the gate speak French.

'I'm looking for somewhere to spend the night,' say I after the usual greeting.

'There is no hotel here, *Monsieur*.'

'What about a room in someone's house?'

'It's possible. Come, I will show you.'

So saying, one of them climbs into the passenger seat and directs me through houses until we stop outside a door in what passes for the village square. Without speaking, he goes inside. Soon he is back with a man whose features are hidden in the dark. While waiting I have seen no one at all, so conclude that I will accept whatever this man has to offer more or less regardless. He says I can have a room for about £3 – way over the going rate, but driving across the

207

mountains at night is out of the question, and the lack of other people, plus the language problem, does not encourage looking for different lodgings.

I thank the guide.

'Watch out for the dogs. They are very savage,' he says as he turns back into the darkened square.

Soon I find myself being led by gas-light along a stone-floored passage and down steps towards where I can hear and smell goats. We turn left before entering a small room with two palliasses, a low table and a picture of King Mohammed V, grandfather of the present King and still much revered for gaining Morocco's independence from the French. Two young girls and a boy appear from the inner recesses and stand staring at me. I wonder when and if his wife will come to inspect.

Placing the hissing gas-light on the table, my host goes to a pile of blankets, from which he pulls a couple and shakes them out. For the first time I can take a look at him. With bad teeth in an otherwise unremarkable middle-aged face, he wears a white scarf over his head and a plain dark burnous. While working he talks away quite happily in Berber, not apparently expecting an answer but nevertheless determined to say his little bit. His monologue is interrupted every now and then by the bleating of goats the other side of the window at the end of the room. The smell of goat flavours the air and I can hear the staccato sound of their feet moving on a hard surface next door. One look by torchlight at the loo causes a rapid withdrawal with the hope that it will not be needed. I notice the older girl has a nasty cough.

But still things could be worse.

What could hardly be worse is the food my host produces. Uncooked omelette is a charitable description of the runny mess set proudly before me on a dirty metal plate. To go with it is a lump of stale bread and a mug of pretty revolting tea. I suspect the girl has cooked it, preferring not to think about her cough or other matters of hygiene for that matter. I am hungry so there is not much I can do but get it down as quickly as possible. No adult woman ever appears, indicating my host may be a widower or divorced.

Before going to bed I wander out into the square. In contrast to my small gas-lit room, the air is thin and cold, making a pullover essential. Outside, no lights show and the small mountain village appears deserted. The stars are their usual brilliant selves. I am about to walk away from the buildings to have a proper look at them when a distinctly unfriendly growl followed by vicious barking comes from several dogs at the far end of the square. A horror

of wild dogs quickly overcomes my interest in astrology. After pee-
ing hurriedly beside my car, the only one in the village, I return by
torchlight to the safety of my room.

There is little to say about the night except that straw-filled palliasses are not as comfortable as perhaps they sound. While I doze,
the dogs begin barking, turning the deserted village into an amphi-
theatre for their nocturnal rituals. Calls from those I have detected in
the square are answered by others scavenging beyond the houses
and even away in the nearby hills. I wonder how locals who might
have to be about at night keep them at bay. Do the dogs leave
Berbers alone and only challenge the infidel? Whether they make
the goats uneasy I do not know, but my companions punctuate the
night with occasional bleats, while somewhere deep down the passage the girl coughs herself fitfully to sleep.

By the middle of the following morning I am still on a dirt track but
well on my way to the main road to Ouarzazate. I woke early, staying just long enough for a shave and tea. Near to midday I walk to
a village and buy bread, stopping a few kilometres on to have lunch
looking out over a vast empty tract of land.

As I sit, my eye is caught by a man with two asses laden with
panniers making his way slowly towards me up the side of the
mountain. Some way off he stops and empties manure from the panniers, leaving mounds to be broadcast later on. He spots me and
waves. His task accomplished, he abandons the two beasts and
laboriously climbs up to where I am sitting.

'*Bonjour, Monsieur.*' He speaks reasonable French and tells me
he lives in a village in the lee of the mountain.

'Would you like tea?' I say yes, simply to get the chance to talk
to him. What I have not realised is that he must go back to the village to collect it. 'I will be about an hour,' he says.

Having accepted his offer, I feel it rude not to wait, so I take off
my shirt and sit in the sun. The biblical group of man and asses pick
their way down the side of the mountain, and many minutes later
reappear, panniers full, the man clutching a small rush basket. The
same routine follows until at long last he reappears at my side,
radiating pleasure. We choose somewhere to sit before the bag is
opened to reveal a metal teapot and two cups as well as a bag of
almonds still in their shells.

I am glad I have waited. He is a dear man who tells me he
worked in the Sahara for several years and now farms a few fields

here in the mountains. He has a wife and six children in the village. Life is hard, he says on several occasions, and I cannot argue. He pours the tea in the usual way. Then, using a pebble, cracks nuts for me without taking any for himself. Luckily I remember a melon in the boot of the car. When the time comes to go I give it to him, sending him on his way praising Allah and full of smiles. I only record this incident as it is so wonderfully spontaneous. A example of what can be found away from the tourist trail.

🌴 🌴 🌴

I do not really like Ouarzazate. Like several other medium-sized towns, what charm it may have had has been subsumed by tourism. Perhaps the greatest thing in its favour is a shop selling alcohol, the only one I know of south of the High Atlas outside Agadir. Having regained the tarmac, I soon find myself in this shop filling my arms with tins of beer.

I would have got here earlier, but my attention was distracted by a striking European girl standing on the pavement, having her clothes adjusted by a friend. In the middle of nowhere she had decided to dress in an amazing denim ensemble whose trousers parted down the seams, held nearly together by thongs but showing a significant amount of elegant leg. The main function of the top seemed to be to display her breasts and naked stomach. I watched her, not so much for what she had to offer, which was undeniably enticing, but to try to fathom out the thought process she must be going through to wish to parade herself in an Islamic country like this. Does she know nothing of Moslem customs? Has she not read any guidebooks? Who anyway does she expect to impress in Ouarzazate?

In the street the girl had annoyed me. But when, a few minutes later, she appears on her own in the shop, my irritation melts away. There is nothing like her where I work.

'*Allemagne?*' I ask. We have already made eye contact several times wandering round the shop. It would have been difficult not to!

'*Oui.*

'You speak English?' I ask.

'Yes. You are English? Oh, I thought you were French.'

It turns out she is part of a film crew working on a documentary in the desert. Ouarzazate has been the venue for the shooting of several famous films including much of David Lean's *Lawrence of Arabia*, perfect light and an inexhaustible supply of cheap extras being the main incentives. Several old sets still stand forlornly

210

between town and desert – absurd, but considered by locals to be of great interest to visitors.

We separate, she to look at rugs and me to join a brisk trade in beer and pastis. Inevitably we meet again at the check-out.

'Do you know a good place here to stay?' I ask.

One of the advantages of my sort of wandering is that plans can be changed in seconds. The best part of the day is over and, after several months in the desert, I feel this girl is too elegant to be over-looked for the sake of a few hours' travelling time.

She and the rest of the crew are staying at an hotel on the edge of town. I am encouraged when she suggests I try it.

'It's almost empty,' she says.

I walk to her car. The companion I saw before is waiting behind the wheel – not a woman, as I thought, but an androgynous Asian male. I forget his name but he is apparently the cameraman, and a good one too. I follow their hired Toyota back to the hotel and sud-denly, there I am, booked in quite unexpectedly to spend the night in Ouarzazate.

Ingrid, for that is her name, is in a team of four, the others being a highly intelligent and pushy German of about 30, and a Brit who seldom says anything. The German is odd but fun, the Asian also very bright, and the Brit, as I say, something of a bystander. A stylish girl, Ingrid seems strangely cast with them. Perhaps that is why she latches on to me about as hard as I do to her.

Dinner goes well, mainly thanks to Nicky, the noisy German, who talks incessantly. Although at some stage I tell them of my job in the Sahara, and also about this and other visits to Morocco, I avoid giving details of the last two days. It is just that in a brightly lit din-ing room full of alcohol, good food and largely superfluous waiters, the solitude of the mountains seems such a very different world. I want to keep its magic to myself – to protect it somehow from being trivialised in small talk.

Afterwards, either through discretion or tiredness, the others go straight to their rooms, leaving Ingrid and me to find our way out to the pool. In semi-darkness we sit talking with no difficulty. She is bright but with a degree of naïvety which makes a nice combination. A waiter brings drinks and then hovers until dismissed by Ingrid in perfect French.

If you are half-way attracted to someone, the edge of the Sahara is as good a place as any to make up the difference. Sitting out by the pool after a good dinner, fanned by desert breezes and over-watched by a million stars, I have to pinch myself more than once at my good fortune. Ingrid is most people's idea of a typical

211

German: tall and angular, with short blonde hair and piercing blue eyes, I put her at about 30. Her conversation in fluent English is serious but animated. Despite provocative clothes, her manner is natural and attractive although a determined character lies barely concealed.

When we eventually stand to leave I have done no more than touch her arm once or twice in conversation.

'Well. You can kiss me goodnight,' she says, sounding incredibly German. It is impossible to imagine an English woman saying such a thing – I am not even sure if it is a statement or a question. She stands just to my front, eyes level with mine, small, pearly teeth catching the light.

'Of course.' I lean towards her.

'Not here. Inside.'

One more hard pinch.

I relate this incident only because of its scarcity value in the depths of Maroc. For me, at any rate.

28

Kasbah Camping

I thought we slept on the desert sands
Where the old date gardens lie,
And a golden mist of quivering stars
Was scattered across the sky.

Laurence Hope

Ingrid takes her work seriously. She has already told me they will
leave before dawn to catch the early light and there is no question
of her opting out. They will be back around midday. I could say this
leaves me in a dilemma, but in fact it does not. I decide to await her
return.

By the time I have made this decision she has gone, this time
wearing leather trousers against the early chill. It is too late to sleep
again. The hotel is waking, maids' sandals slapping along the passage outside our room. I decide on a quick breakfast then a walk
round the large kasbah in the centre of town, the first opportunity I
have had to see inside one.

Several things strike me about the kasbah, which I later discover
to be common to most. The first is the labyrinthine nature of the
layout. Endless small rooms lead into each other with low-beamed
ceilings and narrow passages; but every so often are grand rooms
decorated with fine mosaics, usually greens, blues and whites –
far more elegant than the shabby exterior might suggest. Also
marvellous wrought iron across most of the windows. Intricate
patterns through which to gaze from shaded interiors into dazzling
sunlight outside. Upstairs a barely perceptible breeze stirs each
room, carefully funnelled by ventilation holes at strategic points in
the walls.

The art of harnessing the breeze is something desert-dwellers
have perfected. Most mosques have holes in the upper walls similar

to the kasbah. In the Sahara I once attended a gathering of elders of the Saharawi tribes, called by the Polisario leadership. The General and I flew by helicopter right down to the Algerian border where temperatures over 140 degrees Fahrenheit are common. That particular day was hot and still, so it was in some discomfort that we rode by jeep to the tented camp. Apart from the distinguished deportment of the old tribal chiefs, my abiding memory is of the coolness inside their tents. This was the result of shade, but also because by raising the right amount of awning in precisely the right place, a breeze had been conjured out of nowhere to caress the interior and all those in it.

Constructed out of mud bricks, a kasbah like the one in Ouarzazate would be less than two hundred years old, otherwise it would have collapsed. But the inside feels as old as time. Anyway, with the violent events of early last century, its sturdy walls and silent courtyards must surely harbour secrets. I enjoy going round it even though not a stick of furniture is to be seen and anyway my mind is somewhat preoccupied elsewhere.

By the time the others return I am having a swim. Ingrid confirms the wisdom of my decision to stay by appearing at the pool in a stunning bikini. We lunch together outside, the others preferring the air-conditioned interior. Eventually the midday sun gives us an excuse to retire, which results in my final departure being much later than intended.

It is about five o'clock when I am once again on my own, south of Ouarzazate, winding my way up the last tizi before the start of the Draa oases. Near the top, passengers from a broken down taxi wave wildly as I pass, and through some vague sense of desert chivalry I stop. Soon I find myself lifting two pleasant young schoolmasters towards my destination, the unpronounceable village of Agdz.

One of them speaks good English. Behind dark glasses lurks a wide-boy who starts singing 'An Englishman in New York'.

'You like this song?' he asks.

'Yes.'

'Who is the singer?'

'Sting, isn't it?'

'Oh, very good, very good. Sting very good too.'

(Several months later I happen to be introduced to Sting at a party in London. I enjoy being able to report that he is much admired in the Draa valley!)

We reach Agdz at dusk. I hope the teachers will give me a bed, but in the absence of any offers, drop them and set off on my own to see what can be found. Two local hotels look uninspiring, so on an impulse I follow a sign to 'Kasbah Camping', taking a dirt track a couple of kilometres north of the village. I have no tent but feel something may turn up. It is a lucky hunch.

The campsite consists of an area of grass beneath huge palms divided from the main palmerie by a low earth wall. On one side a small plunge-pool is overlooked by a terrace and open-air dining area. To the left the high mud wall of a village affords some privacy. Beyond the camping area sits a large kasbah, its four squat towers protected by a perimeter wall. The site is romantic and empty except for two cars parked by tents beneath the palms.

I am contemplating this scene from the car when a teenager in sleeveless grey shift saunters over. He tells me I can either sleep 'on the terrace' for £2 a night, or in the kasbah for £4. I choose the latter, never having expected such an opportunity.

This kasbah and a derelict one on the dirt road into Agdz once belonged to the Glouai family, made famous by Gavin Maxwell in his haunting book *Lords of the Atlas*. The Glouai dominated much of the High Atlas for the first half of this century, owing their position to the French whom they supported against the Sultan. Not surprisingly they fell sharply from favour on the restoration of King Mohammed V and I have read a macabre account of Thami el Glouai, old and ugly, grovelling for pardon at a private audience with the new King, unaware of a hidden camera which later broadcast his undignified performance to the world.

The main Glouai kasbah at Telouet is a must for anyone crossing the High Atlas from Marrakech to Ouarzazate. Situated about five miles from the main road it has a silhouette comparable in size to that of Windsor Castle and even close inspection is impressive despite the fact that the buildings are derelict. Sometimes a soldier can be found to take you round the empty courtyards, dusty rooms and darkened harem where the mountain sun never shines. Early last century, if Maxwell is to be believed, great cruelty occurred in this remote fortress and to me, notwithstanding its ruined state, Telouet has a compelling feeling of melancholy.

Back outside the smaller kasbah, the youth, Salim, picks up my bag and a torch and leads me under the palms to the entrance. The large wooden door is open, revealing wide flagstones leading through to a courtyard. It is by now too dark to see much, but I can tell the centre is filled with bushes while a cloistered passage skirts the edge. Following this, we come to a gap into a second courtyard, similar in size to the first. The place looks and feels deserted. At the far side he pushes open a door. With a match he lights a candle and as the flame settles I find myself in a room empty except for a double mattress and blankets on the floor at one end. A nice contrast to the room in Ingrid's hotel.

The next thing I notice is that the white-washed walls and ceiling are covered with wonderful designs – not mosaics, which I almost expect, but extravagant swirls and patterns of Moorish origin in faded reds and blues.

'You would like some food?' he asks. I nod.

He hands over a key, leaving me to sort myself out. Candle in hand, I wander into the cloister to locate the loo. It is nearby, nothing luxurious just the usual earthenware hole, but reasonably clean. For a moment I pause in the courtyard, looking up at the silhouette of square towers and beyond them a black sky studded with stars. The kasbah stands solid and still, the only sound being that of a light breeze whispering through the shrubs.

I shall not dwell on supper, which is unremarkable. The pleasure lies in sitting out by the plunge-pool beneath the palms. The Draa valley borders the Sahara, so the temperature is noticeably hotter than at Ouarzazate or anything I have met so far this trip. I sit in shirt-sleeves enjoying the same warm wind that rustles leaves and causes elegant trunks to wave gently across the stars.

I am not alone for long, being joined by two couples from the campsite; the first, a charming and attractive Frenchman and girl on vacation from Paris, the second, another equally pleasant Frenchman with his Irish girl-friend. Enjoying the company of such people reminds me how lucky I am with fellow travellers in Morocco. People who crave the same adventures as I, and who are therefore prepared to put up with discomfort and uncertainty, are generally sympathetic characters.

Towards the end of the evening, when he has cleared the dishes, Salim joins us. I would not describe him as a brilliant cook, but he is enthusiastic and friendly and has looked after us well. He has very dark skin but typically delicate Berber features and amazingly white teeth, which flash in the half-light when he smiles. For most of the evening his attention has centred on one of the French students, but she has eyes only for her companion. He is unlikely to score there. Eventually he must reach the same conclusion as he comes and sits down. I give him a beer and we are soon in easy conversation.

When the party finally ends, the others return to their tents while Salim guides me back through the palms to the kasbah. Without a torch we negotiate the two courtyards. There is something strangely conspiratorial about following his silhouette and slapping sandals into the heart of the empty building. At the door of my room, he lights a candle, bringing the small chamber to life.

I am ready for bed but Salim seems in no hurry to go. I offer him a cigarette. For some time we smoke in silence, him drawing deeply and exhaling towards the patterned ceiling. Gradually it dawns on me that he is charged with nervous excitement, so to encourage him to leave I excuse myself for a pee. But when I return he is still there. In my absence he has moved the candle across the room. Now he is lying on the mattress studying my map.

'Can you understand that?' I ask. 'Can you find where we are?' He smiles over his shoulder and shrugs.

'Come.' He beckons. 'Show me.'

I cross the room. The map is upside down. I kneel and turn it and together we search for Agdz.

Poring over a small map with a stranger is an intimate affair. If the map is on the floor of a deserted castle, the degree of intimacy can intensify. A warning bell rings in my head. It is time this young chancer was on his way or at least on his feet! At that moment the candle gutters towards extinction, bringing the geography lesson to an end and offering an excuse to break the spell which seems anxious to ensnare us.

When he finally goes I sleep, but wake unaccountably in the night. For a long time I lie sensing the stillness of the thick walls and empty building around me. Eventually I wander out into the courtyard. The immediate impression is one of silence, although as I listen a dog barks fitfully in the direction of the village. I can also hear, but not see, the clacking of dry palm leaves, ruffled by night breezes beyond the kasbah wall.

I try to imagine what the scene would have been like when Kaid Glouai was in residence. I can almost picture sentries wrapped in burnouses keeping watch from the towers and manning the main gate in that state of half wake, half sleep which passes for vigilance. Would they have fires to ward off the chill of dawn? Probably. To me it is still pleasantly warm, but the locals will feel the cold more than I.

And what about flocks? Would the courtyard be cultivated as now, or would it be the domain of goats, sheep or camels? I suspect it would, with attendant noises, and fragrance. These kasbahs were built to guard the palms but also to exercise control over the caravan route up from West Africa. They had military value which took priority over the creation of verdant gardens.

217

I stand for a long time lost in thought until a cock crows from the outer courtyard. Almost imperceptibly the sky has begun to change colour.

29

From Palliasse to Palais

> My kingdom is a burnt-up land
> Half buried by the drifting sand.

James Elroy Flecker

It does not take me long next day to see enough of the *palmerie* to decide to spend a second night. Besides, the accommodation is cheap and the obliging Salim will take care of my needs. At breakfast, I book in again before spending half an hour in the plunge-pool. Sometime later I set off through the oasis.

I am not certain where precisely the Draa rises, its water coming from the melted snows of the Atlas. From the map the river appears to flow from the huge lake of the El Mansour Dam, east of Ouarzazate, cutting through the Jebel Sarhro before winding its way nearly 200 kilometres south to beyond Zagora, where it finally squanders in the sands of the Sahara. The dried-up Oued Draa then curves westward, eventually meeting the coast near Tan Tan. Down there many years can pass without sign of water. In the hundred kilometres from Agdz to the last dwellings at Tinfou, the river sustains a vast oasis of date palms and cultivation supporting habitation either side of the valley. Each village is dominated by one or more kasbahs, some still in use, but most derelict, the *pise* walls having long since decayed.

There is something hugely restful about these palms. To a certain extent it must be the deep green of their leaves in contrast to the barren red rock above the watercourse. Also the welcoming shade. Also too, their elegance. More than 30 varieties of date-palm exist, but to me they look much the same. Each tree or group of trees is owned by a family and jealously passed down through the generations so they seldom come onto the market. Ownership is known by everyone but, despite that, the oasis is dissected by endless low mud

219

walls, hundreds of years old. My abiding memory is a sense of prosperity and utter peace enhanced by the gentle swishing of the breeze.

Fragments of palms over 8,000 years old have been found in Sumeria. Since earliest times the nutritional value of dates as a high-energy food was valued, particularly by the nomadic peoples of North Africa and the Middle East, where few other crops were so reliable. But dates do not keep well so elaborate steps were taken in the old days to construct storage areas of palm leaves in the upper storeys of houses, where the temperature remained reasonably constant. Under these conditions their shelf-life could be greatly extended.

The narrow paths through the palms are almost addictive. Each time I consider heading back to the kasbah my eye is drawn by yet another secret way disappearing beneath fronds of spiky leaves, huge clusters of brown or yellow dates sagging beneath them. As well as the walls the oasis is criss-crossed by a mass of water channels, scooped from the mud and mostly dry at this time although a programme exists to water the whole area at intervals. Where they contain water the banks are thick with grass. Scattered pomegranate trees provide refreshment for workers.

Considering I am there during the date harvest, the place is surprisingly empty although a few men and women are at work. Dates grow on stems from fruit-bearing branches beneath where the leaves begin. The method of harvest is simply to cut the branch off at the trunk. The dates are then lowered to the ground and, still attached to their stems, dumped in a donkey cart. Depending on water and the amount of care it receives, a good date-palm in this part of the world can yield 200 pounds of dates a year or more.

Later on, many leaves are also pruned, leaving small protruding stubs which gradually crumble into the elephant-hide texture of the main trunk. I notice that some of the men and boys climb to the top of the tall trees unaided, their knees straddling the trunk. Others use a leather strap passed round themselves and the trunk and moved upwards as they progress. The dates themselves are delicious, dryer than those bought in England and in my opinion none the worse for that.

My bearings I keep by the Jebel Kissane, a most handsome feature which dominates the first part of the valley. By late afternoon I have walked to the top of the oasis and come out into a small village where mud houses crowd together along narrow streets round a mosque. Almost immediately, I am spotted by a schoolboy, who accompanies me through the maze of alleys, passageways and derelict buildings whose walls are now unsafe. In some parts houses stand so close that the upper storeys meet, creating dark corridors never reached by the sun. In places like this it would be easy to lose one's sense of direction even though the village is small. The shade conveys a strong feeling of secrecy.

The walk back is longer than I expect, passing through perhaps five similar villages. At the boundary of each I lose one guide and am taken on by others either singly or in pairs. I enjoy this as they are without exception the most endearing kids, even though my reservoir of small change soon dries up. Some way from the 'Camping' I stop to listen to the evening prayer-call from the minaret of a nearby mosque. No sooner has this one started than so too do all the others up and down the valley, haunting voices echoing out over the palms and away into the hills beyond.

My mind turns suddenly to the forlorn figure of Gordon alone on the walls of Khartoum. He must have looked out over a similar dusky oasis while these same cries heralded the end of another day without hope.

By now individual trees are barely distinguishable, with just the highest fronds showing in the gathering gloom. When I look towards the village, few lights spill out into the streets. Robed individuals shuffle for home. The fever of life is hushed.

It is dark when I reach the 'Camping'. The tents of the two French couples have gone and the place looks deserted. Back in the kasbah I lie on my bed, hot and exhausted from all the walking. Sleep must overtake me because a few minutes later I open my eyes to find the candle lit and Salim standing nearby.

'Where have you been?' he asks. 'I have been waiting for you at the Camping.'

I explain that I had not seen anyone there earlier.

'You want to eat something?' At that moment I feel more like sleep but tell him I will be over in a minute.

After forcing myself awake I walk back through the palms. The camp is now deserted except for the distorted shadow of Salim moving about in the cooking area. I give him a beer and am well into my second when an urge to freshen up overtakes me. I borrow a towel and walk across to the pool.

The spotlight near the tables casts its light outward, catching the surface but leaving the depths dark and mysterious. Above the water a ball of tiny insects clusters, gossamer wings shimmering in the light. Crickets are calling frantically from the darkness. I undress, walk to the ladder and lower myself gently in.

Perhaps because I cannot see into it, the water feels almost viscous against my skin. I expect cold, but the initial shock is soon replaced by exquisite warmth. For a moment I touch the bottom. It seems strangely daring to stand alone and naked in the darkness, the unfamiliar freedom causing a shudder of sensual excitement. I go under and within seconds the dust and grime of the day are washed away. The water refreshes wonderfully. I wallow for several minutes before turning to peer up through palm leaves towards the stars.

With ears submerged I do not hear Salim approach. When eventually I climb out he is standing by my clothes, watching. I suspect he thinks I have been touched by the sun.

In a way of course he is right. Once out, the breeze soon makes me shiver. It does not seem to bother Salim despite his meagre shift, but he has been slaving over a hot stove. I borrow his torch and go back for a pullover and more beer. We sit for some time eating and chatting. As usual, I am amazed by the worldliness of someone who is unlikely to have ever left this valley; certainly he would not have travelled further afield than Ouarzazate. I find myself wondering, amongst other things, what on earth he would make of Ingrid.

The evening wears on. Gradually the effects of food and alcohol, as well as all the walking, take their toll. Although my body has recovered, the extremities are still cold and I begin to long for the warmth of my blanket.

As mentioned, the main town at the southern end of the Draa valley is Zagora. I am determined to go there both because by so doing I will see the whole of the oasis valley, and also, with the 'Gateway to the Sahara' soubriquet, its name holds a kind of magic.

For someone who thinks he knows a bit about Morocco this is more than naïve. As soon as I reach the main part of the town I can see it falls into the same category as Ouarzazate. In other words it has been taken over as the last place of opportunity to fleece the tourist. As a result I barely stop, taking instead the signs to Timbuktu. I do not, of course, intend making this crossing of the desert, but have noticed from the faithful *Rogerson* that there is a recommended *auberge* some 30 kilometres further south where the first real sands of the Sahara begin.

Initial impressions are good. Built in kasbah style and standing on its own with sand dunes beyond, the Auberge Repos-Sable has all the right ingredients. A nearby group of camels with deep blue saddle-cloths reinforces my decision that this is indeed the place to spend the night.

The change in temperature hits me as soon as I get out of the car. I am shown a room but opt instead to sleep on the roof, reckoning that in such heat, walls are unnecessary. I then recce a small plunge-pool, which is top priority after so long at the wheel. Not even a couple of monkeys sitting on the wall deter me and I am soon in the water. Then I set off in the car to explore the nearby village of Tinfou, the final outpost of this great oasis valley.

After a couple of kilometres of dirt road I park and walk towards the village. Almost immediately two children of about 12 tag along, asking if they can be my guide. I only want to get to the *oued* to see how much of the river remains, but as usual their sincerity and innocence is hard to resist.

Because it is late afternoon I only spend an hour in Tinfou, but in a curious way it leaves a lasting impression. The village is, as I have said, on the edge of the Sahara. Soon I see wattle fences of plaited palm leaves criss-crossing the sand in an attempt to stem its flow like breakwaters on a beach. Hollows have been scooped round outlying palms to prevent them being swallowed up. The houses, when we reach them, support dunes as high as the roofs on the windward side. The whole place is being encroached. With the assistance of wind the Sahara is on the move.

The boys point all of this out as we walk towards the river. At one point other school-children join us and I am sorry to see their heads completely shaven, presumably to discourage parasites. Their skin is rough with sores, their clothes threadbare. The village is one of real poverty.

My little friends, though, are winners in every way. Approaching the river, we walk between palms and small fields while they talk seriously in excellent French about the village and their lives. I ask one what he wants to do when he grows up. It upsets me when he says in all innocence,

'*Je travaillerai dans les champs* – I will work in the fields.'

My mind leaps forward 20 years. I have a vision of a stooped figure, weathered and aged before his time, with nothing to look forward to but an early grave. Silly of me really but made worse by the certainty of it and by his soft unblemished skin and carefree walk of childhood.

With some difficulty I privately tip my guides, knowing that if the older boys see they will demand the money when I have gone. Before leaving I ask if they will write their names and addresses in

French as I want to send photographs, which I know will mean a lot to them. They agree, so I give them pen and paper. By then the car is being besieged by a mass of scantily clad children. Eventually I manage to get clear although they chase after the car, waving and shouting until I am well out of earshot. After leaving my guides I am overcome by a feeling of sadness. Later when I look at the paper I find their squiggled names illegible.

The scene back at the *auberge* is a real contrast. Sitting in the courtyard awaiting dinner is a Dutch couple with an attractive daughter of about 30. Neither parent can speak English so she and I spend the evening comparing Moroccan notes and discussing all manner of things which I have barely thought about for several weeks. We agree that the *auberge* leaves quite a lot to be desired, but its site make up for most of them.

When the time eventually comes to go to bed, I climb stairs to the flat roof where a mattress and blankets have been laid out. The first thing I notice is the smell of camel borne on the warm desert breeze. Then the silence; then the stars. What more, I wonder, can an escapist from the real world possibly want?

There is something more, of course, asleep in a room downstairs.

In my job further south I often sleep out when on patrol in the desert. Invariably the pleasure is tempered by winds gusting with such strength that untroubled slumber is impossible.

On this night at the *auberge*, the breeze is gentle. I lie on my mattress in a benign mood, the sad memory of the boys in the village not forgotten but lodged in the recesses of my mind. A reasonable dinner, the second dose of female company in two days and the inevitable tin or two of beer have worked their corporate magic.

My knowledge of stars is woeful, it is their beauty that interests me. I shall not bore by describing them except to say that in the frame of mind I am in, on this empty rooftop on the edge of the great Sahara, they overwhelm. How long I lie looking at them I cannot say, but I do remember that each time I close my eyes I force them open again to memorise a sight which must last for ever.

I should not exaggerate. It is not just the stars. It is the overwhelming silence; the soft cool breeze on my skin; the feeling of being on the edge of infinity. God only knows how I finally get to sleep.

For some inexplicable reason I wake a short time later. From the direction of my feet, which is north, flickers of light play across the

224

horizon, sometimes furtive and barely noticeable, at other times flashes of real intensity. The weather is unchanged and I even wonder for a second if it can be distant car lights reflecting in the atmosphere. But there are no cars. I conclude it is an electric storm in the Atlas, although it must be far away as I can hear no sound of thunder.

Much more interesting to me is the fact that the moon has risen and is lying on her side about half full and totally serene. I can feel her illumination all around me. I get up, light a cigarette and look out across the desert.

Rather strangely I am suddenly back in England, driving into London along the M4. It is the end of a perfect summer's day. As the road climbs the first flyover, I catch sight of the moon above the rooftops to my front. Half full, she floats, strangely transparent against a black sky. Because my thoughts have been elsewhere, the sight of this nocturnal visitor comes as a surprise. I do not consciously disregard her, rather the opposite, but my concentration is directed towards traffic ebbing and flowing around me. If a moment of calm occurs I glance up at my silent companion, but before I can do more than check her whereabouts I am forced to abandon her in deference to some minor crisis on the tarmac.

When the road dips at Chiswick I am back at ground level and my friend becomes further screened by high buildings and the leaves of trees along the verge. For a while I try to maintain contact but in the end the task becomes too dangerous. She drifts to the back of my mind, to be marvelled at briefly as I walk from the car to the door of my flat. In London the sight of the moon is a momentary thrill. It stirs memories but they are soon obscured by more immediate demands of city life.

At night in the desert there are no distractions. It is possible to become totally absorbed by the moon, either looking in detail at its surface, or more likely falling under the general spell of its presence. Strangely detached it nevertheless dominates, imposing an eerie silence and suffusing everywhere in a veil of frosty light. Out here it cannot slip to the back of one's mind. It is the only feature. You can watch it for hours, or rather you can allow its presence to bewitch until the eyelids finally droop.

In the far distance the headlights of a car pick their way slowly across the desert towards Tinfou. One of the camels below me grumbles in his sleep. A meteorite slides across the sky. I lie back under my blanket, pulling it up against the night breeze.

🌴🌴 🌴🌴 🌴🌴

Next day I want to get to within easy striking distance of Agadir as the car is due back the following day. I decide to depart from my usual rule of avoiding smart hotels, and spend a night at one of my favourites, the Palais Salaam in Taroudant.

The Palais Salaam is built into the side of the huge ochre wall which surrounds the town. It, or part of it, was the Pasha's residence in former times. Taroudant anyway is a rather charming and unspoilt town in the centre of the rich orange groves of the Souss valley, about 30 kilometres south of the High Atlas.

What is special about the hotel is its layout. The rooms are built round a series of courtyards of different sizes on two levels, each courtyard containing either a swimming pool or an incredibly luxurious garden or, in some cases, both. The routes from one to another are not obvious and may take the form of a small door, a portico of Moorish design, or a passage overhung by bougainvillea or vines. In the larger courtyards, huge banana plants fight for space beneath palms swaying above the roof-tops.

Upstairs, groups of rooms may be connected by a narrow walk-way looking in one direction over the tops of trees and in the other through castellated walls onto the streets of the town. The scene at night is enhanced by well-placed floodlights which accentuate the foliage and cast mysterious shadows across the gardens. The rooms are of a good standard, mostly split-level – the bed on one and bath-room on the other. Of course some are more noisy than others and you may find the odd cockroach, but that is par for the course. On the whole they offer *tout confort*.

Coming out of your room at night you will walk along a passage gently illuminated by ornamental wall lights into one of the court-yards where the scent of lilies saturates the air. The impeccably clean pool will be floodlit, wisps of steam gliding off the surface. Downstairs you are momentarily lost in a thicket of banana leaves as you head for the outdoor bar. From a distant restaurant an Arab band wails its way through the evening programme. The Sahara seems a million miles away.

It is after dark when I finally reach Taroudant, the car caked in dust after many kilometres of dirt roads. I decide not to eat in the hotel. The walk into town follows the outside of the magnificent wall to the main gate, where a series of porticos are covered by castellated firing-points. Tall palms of great age survey the scene from gardens along the wall. Some traffic moves, while a mass of robed pedestrians head in both directions.

Previous experience has taught me that it is an easy town to get lost in, but I do not mind as every street reveals a new vista of

226

shops, stalls, cafés and humanity. I will go with the flow. To me, just being a fly on the wall as the locals go about their business is totally absorbing, the sights enhanced by snatches of music, exotic smells, close encounters with donkeys or mopeds. The main streets are lit, but either side lie dark alleys leading into a maze of back-streets which I feel might be better left till daylight. I sit for a while at a pavement café before returning to a side-street where I have noticed an array of food stalls.

This street is unlit, catering for the really poor: people in from the country with their produce, camel drivers, labourers. Along the wall, beggars crouch or rest on crutches, awaiting a charitable morsel. At the edge of the road stands a line of food stalls, each with a glow-ing brazier, the owners fanning the charcoal embers. Queues of cus-tomers wait in djellaba and sandals, their eyes missing nothing of the cooking food. Without street lights, just the occasional oil or gas lamp illuminates the wrapped figures. Everywhere among the shad-ows a mist of steam and smoke and the sweet smell of cooking.

I join a queue, receiving inquisitive looks from my fellow diners. A good thing, I feel, they do not know I am from Palais Salaam. An initial attempt to order in French is not understood. Eventually my gestures are rewarded by hollowed pitta bread filled with small circles of minced meat, probably the product of offal and those parts of whatever beast it is which cannot be sold intact. The slightly sweet taste indicates ass or donkey, but it is wiser not to contem-plate. Anyway, it was my choice to come here rather than eat in the hotel. I stand in the gloom, eating and watching the scene, wonder-ing just how long my stomach will put up with such provocation.

It is nearly midnight when I finally head back towards the hotel. Beneath the starry sky the streets are now empty, the shops all shut-tered. Beyond the wall an effeminate youth in white kaftan stops me by a grove of palms and is sent on his way satisfied, to a degree, by a couple of cigarettes. Back at the hotel the hall porter in full regalia smiles unctuously as I wander in. I rather wish he could know how his valued guest has spent the preceding hour.

30

Return to the Sahara

Close up the casement, draw the blind,
    Shut out that stealing moon,
She wares too much the guise she wore
    Before our lutes were strewn...

                    Thomas Hardy

For my last visit to Morocco I manage to borrow a car. The advantage of being able to move at will with no luggage problems is considerable. At the same time, though, it makes contact with locals less essential and reduces the chance of the sort of haphazard encounters at the mercy of buses and guides that I have come to so enjoy.

My penultimate night is spent in a smart hotel in Marrakech. For most of the morning I wander round the old town, savouring as usual the bustle, sounds and smells, and less so the inevitable gauntlet of '*Monsieur, Monsieur*' from begging children. The tide of humanity on the move never seems to diminish. To me, the vibrance has become addictive. People of every description pack the narrow streets and small squares. Where pavements exist, no one uses them, preferring to sprawl across the width of the road in a mob parted only occasionally by cars or donkeys.

I finally leave the hotel after lunch. It is spring. Outside the old city wall, branches of pale blue jacaranda brighten the streets, breaking the monopoly of dark green orange trees. In the foothills of the Atlas almonds blossom at every turn, delicate petals floating aimlessly about on the breeze like the gentlest of snow flakes. As the road climbs I look down at groups of mud houses, their occupants working in the fields, thin wisps of smoke seeping upwards from cooking-fires. The sun is out with not a cloud in the sky, although the height has put a nasty nip in the air. The locals, I notice, are well wrapped in burnouses and turbans.

Although the south-facing slopes of the High Atlas have little vegetation, the northern ones are covered in cedars. Not the grand elegant trees I explored near Azrou, these ones being twisted and stunted from the effects of wind and snow in winter and drought and sun in summer. Extraordinary, really, how trees can withstand such extremes. On this drive I climb above the snow-line and then stop at the highest *tizi* to admire the view. As soon as the car door opens, an icy wind makes me dive for my suitcase and a pullover. But borne on its cold freshness is the unmistakable fragrance of cedar.

Beyond the edge of the road a sheer drop of several hundred metres falls away. Far below, the roofs of a village can be seen, shoe-horned into a valley too narrow for proper access. From the houses a footpath winds its way up through the trees to where the glistening tarmac of my road snakes into haze down the mountain. The cedary smell hangs in the air, coming, I realise, from the fires of these houses and probably the fires of all other houses in all the other villages hiding in secret valleys throughout the Atlas.

Despite clear sky, a wintry feel pervades, tempering the sense of well-being brought by sunlight. In fact, the days are short. I am still in the mountains when the sun disappears, leaving the valleys sombre and bleak. I decide to stop for the night whenever the next suitable opportunity presents itself.

Chez Mimi is not the sort of name that inspires me with confidence in an *auberge*. Neither, mercifully, is it the sort of name that occurs very often in Morocco, a country which has firmly resisted the use of foreign words. It is therefore with a degree of trepidation that I draw up outside the *auberge*, my choice mainly influenced by the lack of other likely premises.

The style of the building too is unpromising, being an unusually poor imitation of old Moorish. The door opens into a bar selling coffee and tea and other non-alcoholic beverages. Gloom shrouds the interior, the only light being a gas lamp hanging from the wall. Three men stand at the counter, their orders being dealt with by a tall old man whose serene face catches the full glare of the lamp.

I ask if he has a room. Yes he does; would I like to see it? Leaving the others, he calls through the door behind him. A boy of about 14 appears and together they come round the counter and lead me by torchlight, through the building, past an empty dining room with chairs piled high on tables, out into a courtyard. I am immedi-

229

ately struck by a subtle but delicious smell whose source lurks somewhere in the darkness. We cross the court to a line of doors, the boy unlocking one with a large bunch of keys.

I have no idea what to expect beyond the door. To my pleasant surprise the old man's torch picks out first a large brass bed with proper linen and blankets, and then, even more amazing, a basin, shower and bidet behind a screen. I know from experience that it will be cold water only and that the shower is unlikely to work but the bidet is a new and unknown phenomenon. Even so, the room has a pleasant feel and, without further ado, I take it for the night.

'Where is the WC?' I ask, domestic trivia being never far from my thoughts. In a look somewhere between insouciance and resignation the old man nods towards the bidet.

'Is there another one?' say I resignedly, making a mental note to give the porcelain item a wide birth. But there is; the old man indicates a door as we cross the courtyard back to the main building. Once there, the deal having been agreed, he resumes his stance behind the bar, leaving his assistant to help with my luggage.

The boy carries my case to the room, lighting a candle when he has set it down. I try talking to him but soon realise he is dumb, my questions being understood but answered only by signs. A pleasant child, he does his best to make me comfortable and then asks through gestures if I want anything else. The answer, of course, is yes please, some food.

A lamp is placed in the empty dining room and a table quickly set. The boy sits me down and then disappears for what seems an inordinately long time. Sitting in the silent, empty and only partially lit room, my mind turns on a number of subjects, a recurring one of which is a drink, but of course there is none. I try not to be impatient but it is now many hours since I last ate and my tum is complaining bitterly.

Eventually the boy appears, closely followed by the old man. An omelette is set in front of me as well as bread and a Coke. Since serving in Morocco, I have become something of an expert on omelettes and this one, while not ranking amongst the really great, is perfectly acceptable. Once he is assured of my comfort the old man shuffles off, leaving the boy to study every move as I eat. His serious look and attentive manner is very dear but without conversation I can do little to communicate my appreciation except tip him generously when I get up. Sadly money does not really convey the message I want to give.

The secret of the delicious smell I noticed in the courtyard on my arrival is revealed as soon as I poke my head out of the door next morning. All along one side of the yard grows a line of lilac trees in full bloom, the scent even stronger in the morning sun.

As the boy helps me to the car, I wonder what life has in store for him. I do not know if he is related to the *patron*. If so, I feel sure his job is secure as the old man has a benevolent and dignified look which bodes well. If not, then I hope his pleasant appearance and willing manner will anyway keep him in employment somewhere. But beyond that it is hard to speculate. Will he ever marry and have a family of his own, or will the misfortune of being mute deny him so much of life that his friends take for granted? He has an endearing quality which keeps him on my mind long after the Atlas are left behind and I start on the long road to the desert.

The drive from the High Atlas to the Sahara is not hugely interesting, particularly once one is through the Anti-Atlas. The distance from Marrakech to where I work in Laayoune is 950 kilometres, roughly the same as from Brighton to John o' Groat's. What is unexpected is the quality of the road. With the exception of a few places south of Tan Tan where sand can blow right across and block it, the surface is excellent and the volume of traffic negligible. As a result, large distances can be covered at speed, provided one is constantly on the lookout for wandering goats or camels, as well as police road-blocks.

Few large towns straddle the route. I hasten through Goulimine because on an earlier trip I was conned there by a youth who asked me to go to his home and write a letter in English for his father. This was simply a ploy to get me into the house. Once there, and the letter written, a large chest was opened. Sitting on the floor I was soon surrounded by artefacts and jewellery allegedly of great antiquity and brought by caravan from the Tuaregs in Mauretania. Even to my inexpert eye the whole thing looked suspicious. Only after insistence bordering on rudeness was I able to escape and get back on the road, an hour of valuable time squandered.

The Anti-Atlas are quite different from their neighbours further north, being lower and drier. In fact their rounded silhouette is attractive, but the absence of any significant vegetation makes them more an extension of the desert than anything else. As a result of the lack of water, few villages exist like those perched in the High Atlas, and therefore fewer people are in evidence.

As I drive up a long valley between rolling hills, a caravan of camels comes into view. Nose to tail, they plod slowly south about a kilometre from the road. I stop the car and walk towards them with the intention of taking a photo. It is only as I get near that I notice two youths on donkeys. I could simply use the zoom to take a picture from some distance, but, conscious of local sensibilities, walk all the way over to the youths to seek their permission. The leading one is a typical Berber – thick black hair over a fine young face with rather serious expression. His friend sits behind on his donkey.

'Do you speak French?'

'A little.'

'Do you mind if I take a picture of you and your camels? I will give you ten dirhams.'

'That's OK.'

I give him ten dirhams and raise the camera to get a picture of the two of them before turning to the camels.

'Ten dirhams for me too,' says the other rather rudely.

'No, we agreed ten dirhams for the picture,' say I.

'In that case I will not be in it.' With that he jumps off the animal and walks out of the frame. Extraordinary really, but I suppose he has been spoiled by other tourists. Out of sheer bloody-mindedness I do not pay him but take a picture of the first boy on his own.

This one is obliging. After the picture he pulls a dead snake from a pocket in his djellaba and holds it out for my inspection. I recognise it straight away as a hooded viper, a highly poisonous variety that frequents the UN camps in the desert. The creature must have been hibernating and can only recently have been killed as its body is still limp in his hand. I have never held a snake before and am impressed by its feel, the skin having a soft, dry silkiness quite at odds with the idea of danger lurking in its fangs. I thank him for the opportunity to buy it but decline. It is impossible to think of anything I need less as a companion for the rest of my journey.

The camps used by the UN in the desert are prefabricated out of thick rubberised fabric over metal frames. They were placed in situ by the biggest helicopter in the world, flown down from Russia specially for the job. Two places in the camps are favoured by snakes; one is beneath the flooring of the accommodation huts. Here they are relatively harmless except at night, when they come out and patrol the gravelled pathway to the latrines – not of course searching for humans, but it is a foolish man indeed who takes a midnight walk without a torch. The other place they like is amongst aviation-fuel barrels. Most camps keep a stockpile of several thousand litres to supply helicopters used for patrolling. When empties have to be moved, boots and gloves become essential.

On my first encounter with a horned viper I was told the story, possibly embellished, of one of the Russian majors who had served there with the UN just before my arrival. Late one night he had disturbed a viper on his way to the loo and had ended its patrol with a smack on the head with a shovel. Hoping to skin it in the morning, he had carried it along to the kitchen and hung it in the deep-freeze room. Next morning when he went to deal with the unfortunate thing he found it had frozen solid and now resembled a two foot rod. To the casual observer it looked like a live, if uncharacteristically straight, snake.

Whenever visitors came, they would be sat in front of a map. Prior to the briefing our friend would draw the snake from the freezer and casually use it as a pointer, causing dismay and alarm among the guests. The briefing over, the wretched creature would be returned to its appointed hook in the deep-freeze room.

One day, so the story goes, the briefing ended and the Russian was called away on urgent business. The pointer was abandoned on the table, but when he returned an hour later, it had gone. After a quick search the snake was discovered alive and angry and coiled in a corner ready to strike. It seems it had only been stunned that night on the path and its hibernation mechanism had adjusted to the temperature of the deep-freeze. In the heat of the briefing room it had thawed out and was now bent on revenge!

One thing that has always mystified me about the surface of the desert is the amazing effect caused by water. Practically all desert regions are crossed by wadis (*oueds* in the Maghreb), the definition being quite simply a dried-up river-bed. Flying over a desert so dry that literally no vegetation exists, one still looks down onto sometimes vast old watercourses joined by thousands of smaller ones. To me it is impossible to imagine a situation when such barren country could ever carry water, but it obviously does, otherwise these features would never have come about.

On this occasion, as I near the Sahara just north of Tan Tan under a clear blue sky, I suddenly notice in the mirage along the horizon, a line of lorries parked on the road. I can hardly believe my eyes when I find that the cause of their halt is a torrent of water gushing out of the desert and across the road. Further progress is impossible. Sand and scrub pour past, coming from nowhere and disappearing towards the coast 2 kilometres away. I can do nothing except join the drivers paddling in the edge, laughing and joking at what to them must seem like a gift from Allah. No one speaks French, but as far as I can gather it rained last night in the Anti-Atlas, causing the flash flood which I now see before me.

I would have expected the water to be instantly absorbed, but conclude that the depth of sand must be very shallow over non-porous rock. Even so, I am more than a little amazed by such an unexpected phenomenon. I can at last believe what I have previously thought of as apocryphal stories about people in the Western Desert sleeping in wadis and being washed away in the night. In the mountains, possibly, but surely not, I used to think, in the desert. The pity of this one is that there is no means of harnessing the water, so its beneficial effect is lost to those struggling to husband crops and animals in such a wilderness.

I wait for perhaps two hours until the water subsides enough to allow us to pass. On arrival in Tan Tan I find the whole village watching a similar flood overspilling the banks of the *oued*, submerging the road and placing the main bridge in some danger. I believe there has been a drought here for three years and now suddenly this!

In the summer of 1995 there were severe storms around Fez and Marrakech with a death toll of over a hundred caused by flash floods in the mountains.

After Tan Tan the road follows the coast for over 300 kilometres to Laayoune, my destination and place of work. Apart from Tarfaya and a few beaches where *oueds* run into the sea, it is a desolate stretch affording no possibility of swimming. The sea is perpetually restless, beating against cliffs peopled only by gulls and cormorants and the occasional tent of solitary fishermen whose lifestyle is hard to contemplate.

As I drive the last few kilometres, the air becomes thick with swallows wheeling and diving above the road as they pause on their migration from southern Africa to Europe. I probably see more swallows here than I have done in England in the last 20 years. At home I have always loved swallows as the harbingers of summer. Soon I am to go with them on their journey north. But I will not, like them, be a transitory visitor; will not, like them, return to the exotic warmth of Africa when autumn stirs in the byways of England.

Nearing Laayoune for the last time, a feeling of sadness overtakes

234

me as I realise my days in the desert are coming to an end. Over the last ten months I have discovered an entirely new part of the world and fallen in love with it. Soon I must change this solitude and simplicity for a life altogether more complicated.

My visits to Morocco have been for rest and recuperation from work in the Sahara. Technically they are holidays. But backpacking with no fixed itinerary, sleeping on floors in peasant shacks, eating strange food and communicating in an unfamiliar language, all require conscious effort. In fact, by opting to avoid the resorts and smart hotels, I have chosen a far from restful lifestyle. I prefer to look upon these trips as adventures, the physical and mental demands of which are more than balanced by the knowledge that for many people of my age, the days of such adventures are over.

Laayoune sits on its own in the desert. The outline of buildings appears on the horizon just before last light. To the west in the direction of the sea a mackerel sky is making an unusually beautiful sunset. Palms skirting the *oued* stand out against bands of cloud merging gently from orange to pink to deep violet. By the time I come to my journey's end, darkness is stealing swiftly out of the desert and securing the streets.

When I step from the car the evening prayer-call is drifting over the rooftops from minarets across the town. As a result of my happiness in Morocco that haunting cry will forever thrill me with an uplifting sense of excitement.

L'ENVOI

I am standing at a smart cocktail party in London. I arrived late because it is raining and the traffic is heavy tonight. I have left my umbrella inside the front door. Rainwater has penetrated the soles of my shoes. The room is full of people and noise, but despite the crush I have already looked quickly around to see who is here. Friends, mostly – a good crowd. Middle-aged couples whose lifestyles conform to a certain pattern. They were here last year. They will be here again next year. Comfortable, affable, predictable. I do not see anyone to quicken my pulse.

Inside, the room is cramped and the noise becomes louder. Outside in grey September twilight the rain continues. Sodden leaves hang dank and dying. I am making small talk to an old friend who was never a lover. We both know she is not receiving my full attention.

Suddenly in my mind I hear a crack. Quite unmistakable. The sound of a big Atlantic roller breaking far out after a lull in the waves. It is certain that if I look up I will see the first tell-tale strip of foam showing white against deep green sea. The sun is burning into my back. I do not need to turn to know that along the foothills of the Atlas argan trees are standing motionless and deserted on rock that shimmers in heat. I am on my own with all the world to myself.

If I wait long enough I can watch the sun slide into the sea; hear the crickets' night-time call; see the heavens tremble with stars; feel on my face the dry wind that has touched both desert and mountain.

I am not sick, but I feel a restlessness and longing which some would call the symptoms of an affair.

APPENDIX

Morocco that is – the Historical Context

Some of the oldest human remains in the world have been found in North Africa. Rock paintings and frescoes from prehistoric times have been discovered in caves in the Sahara and further north near Casablanca. From these it can be deduced that abundant rainfall sustained forests well down into what is now desert, providing food and shelter for elephant, rhinoceros and crocodile, as well, of course, as Homo Erectus.

Received wisdom is that about 10,000 years ago, at the end of the last ice age, a general heating of the continent saw forests disappear, and savanna give way to desert right up to the foothills of the Atlas. The paler-skinned stone-age hunters and gatherers drifted north to the mountains while their darker brethren headed south. In the following millennia trade routes developed from east to west between Upper Egypt and the Atlantic, and north to south between Europe and the Niger river, caravans bringing slaves and gold in exchange for salt, dyes, herbs and artifacts of civilisation.

The coastline of Morocco was settled by Phoenician traders from the second millennium BC, their influence giving way later to Carthage and subsequently the Romans who named the north-west portion of Africa 'Mauritanea'. Although Paulinus crossed the Atlas, Roman cities were built only in the north, their remains being easily seen nowadays, in Rabat and Volubilis.

By the fifth century AD, vandals who had invaded Italy, supplanted the Romans in North Africa. By then both Christians and Jews were flourishing in what is now Morocco, living peacefully, as far as can be gathered, beside their pagan Berber neighbours.

However the vandal influence was not long-lived, due to events at the other end of the Mediterranean. In AD 632 the Prophet Mohammed died, and fifteen years later an Arab army under the banner of Islam was fighting Berber tribes in what is now Libya and Algeria. By the end of the seventh century the Arabs had reached the Atlantic and

239

got as far south as the Souss valley of Agadir. Ten years later they were settled in large numbers in the north of the country alongside the indigenous Berbers. The conversion of the remainder to Islam was undoubtedly the most significant event in the history of the Maghreb. Only in the Atlas Mountains and way down in the desert did Arab influence and the seeds of Islam take longer to germinate.

Fired with religious fervour and encouraged, no doubt, by the prospect of material gain, Moors under Tarik assembled an army in Tangier and crossed the straits via the Djebel el Tarik (Gibraltar), into Spain, subsequently defeating the Visigoths and proclaiming at Toledo the sovereignty of an Islamic Caliphate (AD 713).

A Moslem army then entered France, fighting for half a century with the Christians and getting at one stage to within 200 miles of Paris. Although finally pushed out by Charlemagne (AD 732), the Moslems defeated him at Roncesvalles (778), closing the door on the Pyrenées, and ensuring eight centuries of Moorish civilisation in Spain.

The history of the Moorish Empire during this period is one of constant friction between the Christian kingdoms to the north of Spain, and Berber tribes in the south of Morocco whose wish for independence was well served by the hostile terrain in which they lived. Keeping on top of both threats proved increasingly difficult and brought about a gradual acceptance that the government in Morocco would be independent from that in Spain. However the eleventh century saw a Christian resurgence in Spain under Charlton Heston (El Cid), and a call for help to a Saharan leader, Youssef ben Tachfin. By moving to Spain, Tachfin and his Almoravid followers founded a new Islamic empire stretching from Granada to Timbuktu; from the Atlantic Ocean to the Libyan border.

Although dynasties changed and Christian kingdoms gradually became re-established in Leon, Castille and Navarre, the next three hundred years marked the zenith of Moorish civilisation in Spain. Art, architecture, philosophy and science flourished.

In the second half of the fifteenth century the Moors faced two serious challenges. In 1453 the Turks took Constantinople, the Turkish empire under Suleiman the Magnificent expanding rapidly along the shores of North Africa. The Moors were the first nation to halt the Turks, defeating them at what is now the Algerian border and denying them access to the Atlantic.

Soon afterwards the Moors were challenged once more by their traditional Christian enemies. Granada fell in 1492, finally bringing Moslem rule in Spain to an end. What had become a trickle of Moors and Jews returning to Morocco, became a deluge, refugees bringing with them Spanish culture and civilisation whose influence

240

can be detected in Morocco today. This shift of population took place at the same time as the discovery of America.

Without tabulating a series of dynasties and sultans, suffice it to say that the next four centuries saw a repeating pattern in the history of Morocco. Successive warlords from the Arab east or desert south would detect a weakness in the Sultan and sweep in to seize power and establish a dynasty. This lasted until their successors became soft, easy prey to those still hard and hungry. Certain factors precipitated this pattern.

The virility of the Moroccan male appears to have remained constant throughout history. In early recognition of this, gentlemen were entitled to several wives in the form of a harem. The result was an almost unbelievable number of children being born to most sultans – five or six hundred being not uncommon. Coupled with that was an absence of any tradition of primogeniture, a sultan's choice of heir being influenced as much by his liking for the mother as to the son's suitability to rule. With such capricious rules of succession, dissatisfied customers inevitably abounded.

Each sultan had a retinue of courtiers and advisors among whom were representatives of many different sects and brotherhoods. Each would have his own ideas about the succession, encouraging 'palace politics' on a grand scale with a vicious power struggle following the death of every sultan. It is not hard to see why successive dynasties were quickly weakened.

One of the inevitable outcomes of the various changes of dynasty, was the wish of each new sultan to perpetuate his memory in stone. At the same time the memory of earlier dynasties had to be obliterated unless the building was dedicated to Allah. As a result, most of the early palaces and grand buildings were constructed out of stone from Roman remains, later ones being built from the materials of their predecessors. This spoiling of the old to provide material for the new accounts for the scarcity of historic secular buildings in a country with such a long history.

The advanced civilisation enjoyed by the Moors in Spain was mirrored in Morocco. The cities of Roman origin, notably Tangier, expanded while others, such as Fez (ninth century) and Marrakech (eleventh century), developed into regional centres of government. Mosques and Koranic schools sprang up in many towns. New palaces were built on a grand scale, marble for one in Marrakech for example, coming even in the sixteenth century all the way from Italy.

The status and wealth of the Sultans was not lost on Europe. While Portugal took by arms various enclaves on the Moroccan coast, Queen Elizabeth of England, acutely aware of the value of

Moroccan ports during her quarrel with their mutual enemy Spain, accredited a Mr Edward Hogan as envoy to the 'King of Marucos and Fesse'. Indeed she signed a letter to Sultan El Mansour 'Your sister and relative according to the law of crown and sceptre'. One wonders if the Sultan summoned Mr Hogan to his palace to celebrate the defeat by his sister of the Spanish Armada!

Morocco therefore has the distinction of being the first African country to receive diplomatic representation from England. Some one hundred and fifty years later the connection was to be renewed in a different way when King Charles II's wife, Catherine of Braganza, brought in her dowry the Portuguese town of Tangier. One cannot help speculating on the pleasure it must have given her father to rid himself of this particular chattel! The British army raised two regiments to garrison the town, but the old British fort was reduced to rubble when they left twenty years later.

Another first for Morocco occurred during the American War of Independence. In 1810, Sultan Mohamed Bin Abdulla was the first foreign Head of State to recognize the newly created United States of America. The ambassador was given a palace in Tangier, the first recorded US State property on foreign soil.

The nineteenth century saw the European scramble for Africa, assisted by the terminal decline of the Ottoman Empire. In 1832 France grabbed Algeria, but a rebellion by local tribes broke out almost immediately, supported by the Moroccan Sultan. This brought Morocco into the sights of the French government, where it remained ever after. The Algerian problem solved, the French started propping up the Sultan with aid and money until by the end of the century their financial stranglehold made independent rule impossible.

The European powers had anyway been looking askance at the absence of law in Morocco, one of the few African countries to have avoided colonisation. Corsairs from the Rif Mountains had been active in the Mediterranean for centuries, as indeed had pirates from a stronghold at Sale across the estuary from Rabat. In 1904 the Rif bandit Raisuni had kidnapped and ransomed an American citizen.

Internal law was also less than civilised. When the sultan's forces caught up with transgressors justice was summary and primitive. Less than one hundred years ago the gates of cities were still decorated with the heads of enemies. Other captives (if Walter Harris is to be believed) were fed live to lions.

When, in 1911, a new sultan was besieged by Berbers in Fez, he requested assistance from the French, giving the Quai d'Orsay the chance to negotiate a protectorate treaty. This deprived the Sultan of power, effective control going to Spain in the north and France in the south. At the same time Tangier became an International Free Trade Zone, bringing about its unique status outside the law of any state. It was re-integrated into the Kingdom in 1956.

The French found the Berbers of the High Atlas no less a problem than had Sultans over preceding centuries. The French commander, General Lyautey, a fascinating man worth a separate study by anyone who can read French, waged unceasing war with them while never losing his respect for their qualities as warriors. The French occupation was set up in such a way that traditional lifestyles could continue. An example was the building of 'New Towns' outside city walls in such places as Fez and Marrakech. There French administrators could live in relative comfort and safety while within the medina the Moroccan way of life went on unaltered.

Despite inevitable shortages of garrisons during the First World War, the French retained their hold on the country to the extent that the 1923 'Rif Rebellion' by Abdul El Karim against the Spanish was finally put down by a French army. Not, however, before the Spanish had been soundly defeated by the Berbers. This event confirmed the predominance of France rather than Spain and precipitated a considerable influx of French settlers and farmers into the country.

Although Morocco never was a French colony, the French 'Protectorate' administration permeated most aspects of Moroccan life and, to a third party like myself, appears to have been beneficial. *Rogerson* tells us that during the Second World War over one hundred thousand Moroccan troops fought with considerable distinction with the Free French, earning particular praise for their tenacity at the capture of Monte Cassino and crossing the Rhine into Germany.

Even so most Moroccans objected to French control. In the 1940s the underground Istaqlal party was founded to seek independence. In 1953 Sultan Mohammed V, who openly championed the cause, was exiled but such an uproar ensued that in 1955 he was allowed to return and in 1956 declared the first King of an independent Morocco. In 1961 he was followed by King Hassan II who was succeeded in 1999 by his son Mohammed 6th.

Their dynasty, the Alouites, dates from the middle of the seventeenth century, the first Sultan ruling when Charles II was King of England and Louis XIV of France. In addition to being an older dynasty than our own, the present king is also descended from the Prophet Mohammed, giving him a position and status in the Islamic world which is perhaps hard for Europeans to fully comprehend.

243